PUBLICATIONS OF

THE COLONIAL SOCIETY
OF MASSACHUSETTS

VOLUME LXXXII

NEW VIEWS OF NEW ENGLAND

STUDIES IN MATEIAL AND VISUAL CULTURE, 1680–1830

NEW VIEWS OF NEW ENGLAND

Studies in Material and Visual Culture, 1680–1830

MARTHA J. McNAMARA

GEORGIA B. BARNHILL

EDITORS

BOSTON · 2012

The Colonial Society of Massachusetts

Distributed by the University of Virginia Press

FRONTISPIECE:
Jonathan Fisher, *A Morning View of Bluehill Village September 1824*,
oil on canvas, 25⅛″ x 52¼″, 1824–25, (detail). Farnsworth Art Museum, Rockland, Me.
Museum purchase, 1965.1465.134.

Printed from the income of the Sarah Louise Edes Fund

Table of Contents

List of Illustrations

KEVIN MULLER, Navigation, Vision, and Empire: Eighteenth-Century Engraved Views of Boston in a British Atlantic Context

·

KEVIN D. MURPHY, Buildings, Landscapes, and the Representation of Authority on the Eastern Frontier

•

MARTIN BRÜCKNER, The "New England" Cartouche: Tablets, Tableaux, and Theatricality in Eighteenth-Century Cartography

·

Foreword

GEORGIA B. BARNHILL

VOLUMES SUCH AS the one before you often have a long history. This one is no exception. When Martha J. McNamara arrived at the American Antiquarian Society (AAS) to begin a long-term fellowship in December of 2004, neither of us would have guessed that we would end up organizing a major conference or that the conference would be the inauguration of the Center for Historic American Visual Culture (CHAViC) at AAS. At the time, Martha was an associate professor of history at the University of Maine. Her research at AAS on the representation of New England's landscape in history and art from 1790 to 1850 was a topic of interest to me as well and I enjoyed peering over her shoulder in Antiquarian Hall as she examined hundreds of prints. She returned to Worcester for the New England American Studies Association conference held at Worcester Polytechnic Institute in September 2005, *Sightlines: The Culture and Science of Vision.* As a result of that conference and our shared interests, we began a conversation in Worcester about collaborating on a conference about New England imagery. Shortly after *Sightlines,* Martha mentioned this idea to the Colonial Society of Massachusetts's editor of publications, John W. Tyler, who quickly encouraged her to undertake such a project under the auspices of the Colonial Society.

At precisely the same time, the Council of the American Antiquarian Society was poised to establish the Center for Historic American Visual Culture, an idea that came into being in April of 2005 during the annual conference of the Organization of American Historians. By the time of the October meeting of the Council's committee on programs and collections, the broad outlines of what CHAViC might accomplish over time were approved. Again by chance, John Tyler was a member of the programs and collections committee and very generously proposed that the Colonial Society of Massachusetts would sponsor the inaugural conference based on the very preliminary ideas that Martha had shared with him. We scheduled it for November 2007. In preparation for the call for papers and the selection of speakers, Martha and I assembled a steering committee that included Joanna L. Frang, then a graduate student at

Brandeis, David Jaffee, then of the Graduate Center at the City University of New York and now at the Bard Graduate Center, Jane Kamensky of Brandeis University, Jennifer L. Roberts of Harvard University, Eric Slauter of the University of Chicago, Caroline F. Sloat of the American Antiquarian Society, and John Tyler. We selected speakers and invited Leora Auslander of the University of Chicago to offer the keynote address on "American Exceptionalism? Material Culture in Colonial and Revolutionary America." Those present at the conference heard fifteen papers over the day and a half of the symposium, including several that are not presented in this volume.

Again, by chance, 2007 marked the twenty-fifth anniversary of the Museum of Fine Arts, Boston's, extraordinary exhibition, *New England Begins,* which thoroughly examined the material and visual culture of seventeenth-century New England through the lens of history. Now out of print, the three-volume catalog of artifacts gathered from all over the United States and scholarly essays remains a model for exhibition teams. We decided that the conference would celebrate that pathbreaking exhibition by inviting several of the people involved in its creation to speak after a festive conference dinner at the John Woodman Higgins Armory. David D. Hall, Jonathan L. Fairbanks, Robert B. St. George, Wendy Kaplan, Abbott Lowell Cummings, and Robert F. Trent spoke in a session moderated by Jane Kamensky about their roles in that endeavor and how *New England Begins* changed scholarship on early New England material culture. I am convinced that this gathering encouraged some of the most senior scholars and curators in the field to attend the full conference. We were stunned when 185 people registered for it. To be sure that members of the next generation of scholars shared in the experience, a generous donor made a gift to the Colonial Society to provide stipends for five graduate students.

The papers at the conference in some ways built upon the scholarship of the Museum of Fine Arts's 1982 exhibition. Some examined familiar items, but with an expanded context. Others focused on unfamiliar materials and presented new visual and material resources to scholars. In contrast to *New England Begins,* we brought the time period forward into the era of the New Republic so that presentations covered the time period from settlement through 1830. The papers fell into interesting thematic groups: "Geography: Envisioning an Expanding World," "Economy, Authority and Material Life," "Vision, Memory, and Remembrance," "Animate Objects," and "Object, Text, and Context." Margaretta M. Lovell of the University of California at Berkeley and Wendy A. Bellion of the University of Delaware provided summations. Jennifer Roberts, Kevin M. Sweeney of Amherst College, David Jaffee, Edward S. Cooke, Jr. of Yale University, and Marcy J. Dinius of the University of Delaware (now at DePaul University) moderated the sessions.

On behalf of the American Antiquarian Society, I would like to express our gratitude to the Colonial Society of Massachusetts for its generous sponsorship of the conference. Even though the Center for Historic American Visual Culture did not yet have a budget line and registration fees did not begin to cover the expenses incurred by the speakers, this conference was a brilliant inauguration for the Center. One of the Center's goals is to encourage research and the conference was a perfect illustration of how this might work. We are also grateful to the Colonial Society for publishing this collection of essays that makes this new scholarship available to an expanded audience. The scholars whose work is represented in this volume are deserving of this fine publication and they join me in expressing thanks to the Colonial Society. The American Antiquarian Society is also grateful to the Department of Humanities and Arts at Worcester Polytechnic Institute for hosting the sessions on the Saturday of the conference.

Martha McNamara has brought her knowledge of New England history and material culture to bear on the essays as she shaped them into this volume. I have so enjoyed working with her that we are collaborating on programming for an exhibition at the Wellesley College's Davis Museum on French and American lithography. We thank our authors for their patience and the many institutions that granted permission to reproduce materials from their collections. We appreciate John Tyler's constant support, Jane Ward's excellent editorial skill, and Paul Hoffmann of Hoffmann Design for his role in this elegant publication.

Introduction: The Materiality of Experience in Early New England

MARTHA J. MCNAMARA

NEW ENGLAND'S regional identity is more closely associated with artifacts from its colonial past than perhaps any other area of North America. For many, the term "New England" conjures images of eighteenth-century farmhouses, spinning wheels, and women in colonial-era dress. In one sense, this fascination with the *things* of early New England is surprising given the equally powerful view of early New Englanders as grim-faced ascetics whose legacy, for better or worse, lay in their zealotry and their devotion to the printed word. But, the late nineteenth-century burst of enthusiasm for early New England, fueled by the writers, artists, designers, collectors, and antiquarians associated with the Colonial Revival movement, ensured that the region's artifacts would take primacy over print in the popular imagination.[1]

The study of New England's past, then, has been tightly bound with a desire to understand the material dimensions of life in the region. Beginning at the turn of the twentieth century with publications and museum exhibits on "everyday life" by influential antiquarians like Alice Morse Earle and George Francis Dow and extending to the academic institutionalization of the field of "material culture studies" in the 1960s and 70s, academic and public historians of early New England have turned to the study and interpretation of a wide variety of artifacts from the landscape of towns and villages, to domestic architecture, mass-produced clocks peddled by itinerant merchants, and the work of schoolgirls bent over embroidery frames.[2] But what can all this attention to

1. I would like to thank Rebecca Bedell, Alice Friedman, Alison Isenberg, Jane Kamensky, and Liam Riordan for their thoughtful comments on this essay. I would also like to thank my co-editor Georgia Barnhill for her wonderful insights, patience, and good humor as we worked together on this volume. The creation of "Old New England" through images and artifacts in the late nineteenth century and its relationship to national interest in the American past is discussed extensively in William H. Truettner and Roger B. Stein, eds. *Picturing Old New England: Image and Memory* (New Haven, Conn.: Yale University Press, 1999).

2. For an overview of the history of "material culture" as an academic field of study, see Helen Sheumaker and Shirley Teresa Wajda, eds., *Material Culture in America: Understanding Everyday Life* (Santa Barbara, Calif.: ABC-CLIO, 2008). Scholars of early New England have nota-

the material dimension of past experience tell us about a specific region? How can it help us to understand the particularities of life in early New England? How can it illuminate the effect of overlapping local, regional, and international influences on the people who lived there? Last, how can objects and images explain the dramatic changes taking place in New England during the period stretching from 1680 to 1830?

The essays in this volume take up these questions with the tools provided by two allied fields: material culture studies and the more recent field of visual culture studies. Neither of these modes of scholarly inquiry sits comfortably in any single academic discipline, but, rather, they both draw practitioners from a wide variety of disciplines and emphasize interdisciplinary methods.[3] Material culture studies can most succinctly be described as an analysis of the artifacts of human endeavor with the goal of understanding their expressive function in a particular society at a particular time. As art historian Jules Prown points out, the term "material culture" can also refer to the artifacts themselves, but, material culture studies is less a category of objects than a method for understanding past experience through its physical manifestations.[4] Emerging in the early 1990s, the definitions, methods, and theoretical underpinnings of

---

bly worked with artifacts on a wide variety of scales from landscapes and buildings to textiles and decorative arts. See, for example, Joseph Wood, *The New England Village* (Baltimore: Johns Hopkins University Press, 1997); Abbott Lowell Cummings, *The Framed Houses of Massachusetts Bay* (Cambridge, Mass.: Harvard University Press, 1979); Laurel Thatcher Ulrich, *The Age of Homespun: Objects and Stories in the Creation of an American Myth* (New York: Alfred Knopf, 2001) and David Jaffee, *A New Nation of Goods: The Material Culture of Early America* (Philadelphia: University of Pennsylvania Press, 2010). For an insightful and beautifully illustrated exploration of New Englanders' objects as seen through the collections of the nation's first historic preservation organization (founded in 1910) see Nancy Carlisle, *Cherished Possessions: A New England Legacy* (Boston: Society for the Preservation of New England Antiquities, 2003).

3. For some visual culture scholars, the field's location "betwixt and between" disciplines is precisely the point: they argue that the radical nature of the field requires it to resist institutionalization as a discipline. For a classic statement of this position, see W.J.T. Mitchell, "Interdisciplinarity and Visual Culture," *Art Bulletin* 77 (1995): 540–44.

4. Jules David Prown, "Mind in Matter: An Introduction to Material Culture Theory and Method," *Winterthur Portfolio* 17 (no. 1), 1982; Sheumaker and Wajda, "Introduction," in *Material Culture in America*, xi–xii. For a sample of the diversity of approaches to material culture studies, see Robert Blair St. George, "Introduction" and the essays by Prown, Rhys Isaac, and Henry Glassie in St. George, ed., *Material Life in America, 1600–1860* (Boston: Northeastern University Press, 1988).

"visual culture studies" are currently the subject of rigorous debate.[5] It does share with its sibling field of material culture studies an interest in broadening the scope of objects under scrutiny by essentially casting aside the hierarchical categories that define some images as "art." And, like "material culture," the term "visual culture" is often invoked to describe the objects under study—from easel paintings to greeting cards. For some scholars, though, visual culture studies is also the analysis of historically contingent ways of seeing; they focus particularly on the social construction of vision and its implication with structures of power and knowledge.[6] Last, visual culture studies has also been articulated as a method for understanding the thorough penetration of images and visual technology into everyday life and the global circulation of visual "events" in contemporary Western society.[7] Because of this preoccupation with new visual technologies—from photography to pixelation—scholarship in visual culture studies has been heavily weighted toward the twentieth and twenty-first centuries. But the methods of visual culture studies can also quite usefully be applied to earlier periods and many of the essays in this volume profitably take up that challenge.[8]

While material and visual culture studies share fluid disciplinary boundaries and have somewhat divergent methods and goals, drawing these two fields together provides scholars with a powerful set of analytic tools. As the essays in this volume show, close attention paid to the physical attributes of an object or image (a method practiced so well by material culture scholars) combined

5. For a cogent overview of debates about "visual culture" and "visual culture studies" see Deborah Cherry, "Art History Visual Culture," *Art History* 27 (September 2004): 479–93. For a discussion of the impact of "visual culture studies" on scholarship in American art, see John Davis, "The End of the American Century: Current Scholarship on the Art of the United States," *Art Bulletin* 85 (2003): 540–80.

6. See Jonathan Crary, *Techniques of the Observer: On Vision and Modernity in the Nineteenth Century* (Cambridge, Mass.: MIT Press, 1990).

7. Nicholas Mirzoeff, "The Subject of Visual Culture," in Mirzoeff, ed., *The Visual Culture Reader*, 2d edition (London: Routledge, 2002), 5–6.

8. Vanessa R. Schwartz and Jeannene M. Przyblyski, "Visual Culture's History: Twenty-First Century Interdisicplinarity and its Nineteenth-Century Objects," in Schwartz and Przyblyski, *The Nineteenth-Century Visual Culture Reader* (London: Routledge, 2004), 1–14; Deborah Cherry, ed., *Art: History: Culture* (Malden, Mass.: Blackwell Publishing, 2005). For a study of the relationship between late nineteenth-century visuality and the rise of mass culture see Vanessa R. Schwartz, *Spectacular Realities: Early Mass Culture in* Fin-de-Siècle *Paris* (Berkeley, Calif.: University of California Press, 1998).

with visual culture studies' emphasis on the social construction and historic contingency of human interaction with the physical world, gives us a compelling understanding of the materiality of past experience. That understanding encompasses both the expressive nature of objects and the network of ideas, assumptions, strategies, techniques, and hierarchies that physically structure human endeavors. All of these essays situate objects and images within various overlapping networks of political, economic, and cultural exchange. Ultimately, they elucidate the local experience of a broadly-cast net of associations that gave life in early New England a specific valence.[9] In short, these essays give us a new way to think about early New England by tracing the movement of images, objects, and texts across networks of exchange that may have only vaguely been perceived by their creators, transmitters, conductors, and receivers.

The orientation of the authors in *New Views of New England* toward scholarship that embraces the goals and methods of both material and visual culture studies is, of course, not mere happenstance. These essays were first presented at a conference co-sponsored by the Colonial Society of Massachusetts and the American Antiquarian Society: two institutions with long histories of supporting the study of early New England. Founded in 1892, the Colonial Society publishes documents—both primary sources and conference proceedings—related to the history of colonial New England and these publications have included landmark volumes exploring the region's material and visual culture including *Boston Prints and Printmakers* (1973); *Boston Furniture of the Eighteenth Century* (1974); *Architecture in Colonial Massachusetts* (1979); *Seventeenth-Century New England* (1984) and, most recently, *New England Silver and Silversmithing* (2001).[10] The American Antiquarian Society, founded in 1812 to

9. For a groundbreaking study that analyzes the densely associative nature of early New England culture as a "poetics of implication," see Robert Blair St. George, *Conversing by Signs: Poetics of Implication in Colonial New England Culture* (Chapel Hill, N.C.: The University of North Carolina Press, 1998).

10. *Boston Prints And Printmakers, 1670–1775*, edited by Walter Whitehill and Sinclair Hitchings (Boston: Colonial Society of Massachusetts, 1973); *Boston Furniture of the Eighteenth Century*, edited by Walter M. Whitehill, Brock Jobe, and Jonathan Fairbanks (Boston: Colonial Society of Massachusetts, 1974); *Architecture in Colonial Massachusetts*, edited by Abbott Lowell Cummings (Boston: Colonial Society of Massachusetts, 1979); *Seventeenth-Century New England*, edited by David D. Hall, David G. Allen, and Philip C. F. Smith (Boston: Colonial Society of Massachusetts, 2001); *New England Silver & Silversmithing, 1620–1815*, edited by Jeannine Falino and Gerald W. R. Ward (Boston: Colonial Society of Massachusetts, 2001).

collect and preserve documents relating to the history of North America, similarly has a distinguished record of publication in the field and a commitment to visual culture studies that has been underscored with the founding of the Society's "Center for Historic American Visual Culture" in 2005.

New Views of New England also continues a scholarly tradition embodied in the close relationship between the region's academic and public historians. By the 1980s these collaborations produced thoroughly researched and beautifully presented museum exhibitions that explored the region's history through objects and images. *New England Begins*, the 1982 Museum of Fine Arts, Boston exhibition and three-volume catalog, kicked off this scholarship by examining a wide range of seventeenth-century artifacts—from Anglo-American ironwork and maps to Native American ceramics and beadwork.[11] *The Great River* exhibition and catalog followed in 1985 by surveying the seventeenth- and eighteenth-century Connecticut River Valley from New London to Deerfield.[12] Last, *Agreeable Situations: Society, Commerce, and Art in Southern Maine, 1780–1830*, focused on the material culture of Maine in the decades following the Revolution.[13]

But, the vision of New England in these evocative volumes offered a somewhat restricted view. Coming as it did out of the new "material culture studies" scholarship of the 1960s and 1970s, a tight focus on objects often meant an attention to detail that came at the detriment of the bigger picture. This scholarship pays limited attention, for instance, to concerns about race, gender, or class and, with the exception of *New England Begins*' focus on English antecedents, most of this work depicts New England as a region somewhat isolated from broader cultural, economic, and political exchange networks.[14]

---

11. *New England Begins: The Seventeenth Century*, 3 vols. (Boston : Museum of Fine Arts, 1982).

12. *The Great River: Art & Society of the Connecticut Valley, 1635–1820* (Hartford, Conn.: Wadsworth Atheneum, 1985).

13. *Agreeable Situations: Society, Commerce, and Art In Southern Maine, 1780–1830*, edited by Laura Fecych Sprague ; essays by Joyce Butler, et al. (Kennebunk, Me.: Brick Store Museum ; Boston: Distributed by Northeastern University Press, 1987).

14. The absence in this volume of scholarship on Native American culture reflects the content of the proposals submitted for the conference from which these essays were drawn. For recent work on early New England Native communities that addresses material and visual culture, see Lisa Brooks, *The Common Pot: The Recovery of Native Space in the Northeast* (Minneapolis, Minn.: University of Minnesota Press, 2008); Amy Den Ouden, *Beyond Conquest: Native Peoples and the Struggle for History in New England* (Lincoln, Neb.: University of Nebraska Press,

New Views of New England builds upon this earlier literature but also participates in the recent transformations taking place in scholarship on early America. In particular, the volume's authors embrace an understanding of New England as a place of overlapping identities and, importantly, a place where the conflicts of empire were played out in a cultural as well as a political, commercial, and military context.[15] On one level, these essays operate within a new framework for the concept of regionalism. While still primarily concerned with pinpointing characteristic material and visual expressions, the authors provocatively link local concerns with those of interregional and transatlantic significance. Early New England, as much recent scholarship has underscored, participated in the broader exchanges of the "Atlantic World" and the complexities of those relationships are brought to bear in this volume on the region's material and visual culture.

If regionalism constitutes one important interpretive strand emerging from these essays, it is closely linked to another overarching, but more intangible theme—the formation of identity. Fundamentally, objects define our place in the world. Maps, clothing, portraits, houses (to name just a few objects under consideration here) all shape and reshape intersecting identities tied to kinship, community, and geography. Seventeenth-, eighteenth-, and early nineteenth-century New Englanders inhabited a world defined by the connections they forged and maintained with people around the Atlantic and, ultimately, around the world. The essays in this volume foreground these connections but they do not merely add to our list of places that New Englanders encountered. Going further, these scholars recast our understanding of how New England's material and visual expressions constituted local, regional, and transatlantic networks of cultural exchange that defined both individual and community. Tracing the networks that stretched between places as disparate as Maine, Mexico, London, and Manila leads to a powerful reenvisioning of New England's wider world: the material expressions of those networks defined, conditioned, and communicated regional identity.

2005), and Colin G. Calloway and Neal Salisbury, eds., *Reinterpreting New England Indians and the Colonial Experience* (Boston: Colonial Society of Massachusetts, 2003).

15. For a recent synthesis of early New England history see Joseph Conforti, *Saints and Strangers: New England in British North America* (Baltimore: Johns Hopkins University Press, 2006).

In order to structure the interpretive threads running through this volume, the essays are grouped into three thematic sections: "Early New England's Oceanic Context," "Domestic Exchange and Regional Identity," and "Envisioning New England." None of these sections are mutually exclusive and, surely, the essays could profitably be organized in many different ways. Nevertheless, the volume begins with scholarship placing New England in its broadest context. Emerson Baker, Patricia Johnston, Kevin Muller, and Kevin Murphy all explore how the exchange of images, objects, ideas, and people across oceans shaped the experience of those living in early New England. The second section includes essays by Katherine Rieder, Catherine Kelly, Katherine Stebbins McCaffrey, and Steven Bullock that center on the exchange of gifts, tokens, and legacies among kinship and local community networks. Last, Martin Brückner and Wendy Bellion focus specifically on the role of vision in structuring ideas and posing questions about the region.

The creation and maintenance of New England's connections with the wider world—both circum-Atlantic in the seventeenth and eighteenth centuries and extending eastward to Asia after the Revolution—are directly explored in the opening group of four essays. Emerson Baker's essay on the hardscrabble Maine frontier in the late seventeenth century fundamentally alters our vision of these towns as places on the edge of empire. Baker analyzes artifacts from a range of Maine sites: the Humphrey Chadbourne complex in Berwick; a fishing station on Sagadahoc Island; and a coastal farmstead owned by the yeoman farmer Richard Hitchcock at Biddeford Pool. Each of these sites reveals the rapid spread of consumer goods and status objects in the region and poses questions about the nature of social hierarchies in early Maine. What do we mean by "frontier," Baker asks, when Maine's elites set their tables with ceramics from Portugal and Mexico City? How do we reconcile their seemingly contradictory choice to build foundation-less houses that would rot away in a generation, but then to adorn those houses with expensive hardware, brick, and plaster? Silver spoons, brass spurs (and the "fine gray stallion" they pricked), fancy door hardware, and European ceramics marked elites in Maine as participants in oceanic trade as much as their earthfast houses grounded them in their local communities.

The eighteenth century's vast expansion of the production and consumption of material goods both accelerated the pace and scale of Atlantic trade and extended New England's reach to the Pacific. By the 1790s, the merchant elite of Salem, Massachusetts, sent their ships around the Capes of Good Hope and Horn to engage in the East Indian and China trades. Along these routes traveled geographical and cultural knowledge that was as vital to Salem's merchants as the goods they bought and sold. Patricia Johnston's essay argues that visual culture, manifest in print, in manuscript, and in everyday practice, formed the basis of these knowledge networks. Images effectively communicated knowledge of the unfamiliar world through the familiar representational forms of prints and sketches made by fellow townsmen of foreign ports and harbors. Equally important, the collecting and archiving of these materials in newly established libraries and museums created a shared sense of identity for Salem's merchants. Their active cultivation of global knowledge powerfully constituted them both as local elites and as members of the international mercantile community.

Kevin Muller's close examination of William Burgis's *A South East view of . . . Boston in New England*, published first in 1725, similarly considers the impact of images on the formation of identity within Boston's early eighteenth-century merchant community. Muller argues that the Burgis view's perspective from an elevated position east of Boston was particularly meaningful to the town's merchants because it allied them with transatlantic trade. In addition, by adopting the visual language of sea charts—in particular by incorporating both plan and elevation into one image—Burgis was responding to the merchants' inclination to see Boston as one point in a larger network of transatlantic trade. However, while this vision of Boston placed merchants as active creators of empire, it also put the town under an imperial gaze. Burgis's representation of Boston, then, inscribed both local and imperial identities—a Janus-faced view that New England merchants were required to negotiate as citizens of a maritime empire.

The juxtaposition of global knowledge and local practice so usefully enacted by New England's merchants could also readily be deployed through the built environment. In his study of architecture and landscape on Maine's late eighteenth- and early nineteenth-century frontier, Kevin Murphy explores the power relations at play in the construction of new communities. Drawing on the work of theorists Michel Foucault and Henri Lefebvre, he explores local elites' attempts to spatialize their claims to political, economic, and cultural

authority through the construction of ambitious houses carefully sited in relation to local villages. From Thomas Ruggles's mansion house constructed in
the far downeastern village of Columbia Falls, to Coventry Hall, built by Judge
David Sewall in the prosperous southern Maine town of York, local elites drew
simultaneously on local building practices, academic designs, and a regional
discourse of gentility in attempts to establish a social order that positioned
them at the top. Material expressions of elite status were not always completely
successful, but understanding them as mechanisms for constituting local hierarchies enables us to see the power relations embedded in the landscapes of
daily life.

While large-scale global networks—from merchant shipping to the influence
of transatlantic aesthetic codes on elite-designed landscapes—clearly shaped
life in early New England, they also overlapped with local exchange. The essays
in the second section, "Domestic Exchange and Regional Identity," have a
more restricted, often an intimate focus. They address the circulation of objects
among family members or local communities while keeping in mind the effect
that transatlantic exchange brought to bear on local hierarchies. Katherine
Rieder's study of Loyalists and their possessions, for instance, explores the psy-
chic role played by the transatlantic exchange of people, images, and household
objects. In this context, object exchange had personal as well as political consequences and the movement of furniture, silver, paintings, and other "effects"
across space and through time helped Loyalists cope with the upheaval and
trauma of their refugee experience. Risking his safety and freedom to retrieve
some of his family's belongings before fleeing into exile, Loyalist Peter Oliver
clearly saw these objects as more than just markers of elite status. For instance,
the family's silver sugar box made by Boston silversmith Edward Winslow in
1702, had the advantage of portability and easy conversion to currency, but it
also represented the Oliver family's long and prosperous New England tenure.
Transporting the artifacts that defined them as a New England family was
important enough to cause Oliver to risk missing the boat that would carry
him into exile.

Rieder's Loyalists hoped to cement personal ties through the transfer of
objects. Their actions, though engendered by political and military struggle,
remind us that artifacts also circulated outside of market entanglements. The
giving of gifts, legacies, or tokens was rarely evaluated in terms of profit or loss,

but it was still embedded in networks of obligation, reciprocity, and dependency. Catherine Kelly's essay on early nineteenth-century portrait miniatures examines how race and gender shaped these small, intensely personal artifacts. Kelly focuses on two revealing portraits: an image of Elizabeth "Mumbet" Freeman, a freed slave who worked as a servant for the prominent western Massachusetts Sedgwick family, and an unfinished self-portrait by New London miniaturist Elizabeth Way Chapman. Juxtaposing Chapman and Freeman's portraits, Kelly explores the way that race and gender shaped the depiction of each woman. The goal of painting on ivory was to layer tints thinly enough to let the natural material shine through and give white skin a luminosity that was associated with depth of feeling—an association created as much through ideas about race as by eighteenth-century color theory. Freeman's dark skin is striking precisely because it breaks these aesthetic rules. The artist, Susan Ridley Sedgwick, used layers of color and thick lines to define Freeman's features, resulting in "a catalogue of racial signifiers." Gender also conditioned the creation and exchange of each portrait because the objects are as much about dependency as about bonds of affection. Chapman's self-portrait is unfinished precisely because she depended upon her own labor for her family's livelihood. Freeman's portrait, by contrast, circulated within the Sedgwick family and therefore also constituted an act of repossessing a formerly enslaved person and reinforcing the idea of racialized dependency long after slavery's abolition in Massachusetts.

Kelly's portrait miniatures connected family members separated by distance, but they were also legacies that moved through time to link generations. For Katherine Stebbins McCaffrey, the legacy of a pair of spectacles and their elaborate case carries intellectual and spiritual freight along with the memory of deceased family members. Viewing the world through the spectacles passed to Bostonian Samuel Dexter by his father in 1810, we see a tug between materialism and piety. McCaffrey describes the multivalent nature of reading and its accoutrements for eighteenth- and early nineteenth-century elites. At once a path to intellectual, moral, and spiritual improvement, reading was also implicated in the rapidly expanding consumer culture of the eighteenth century. Expensive and fashionable spectacles like Dexter's could easily signal enslavement to the vice of luxury rather than devotion to the virtue of reading. After inheriting his father's London-made "temple spectacles" (fashioned in gold rather than cheaper silver or steel), Dexter's son purchased a gold-plated case inscribed with a classical passage lifted from an issue of the eighteenth-century literary magazine *The Spectator*. Published almost a century earlier, the inscription connected both Dexters to a transatlantic public sphere, but it also hints at their struggles to reconcile the lure of the material world with the promise of salvation. The spectacles and their case, then, memorialize the inheritance of material goods and intangible philosophical conflicts. Moreover, like many of the objects discussed in this volume, the Dexter spectacles drew their meaning precisely from their place in exchange networks that linked New England and its people across space and through the generations.

Steven Bullock's study of New England's somewhat mystifying mortuary rituals, the "large funerals" of the late seventeenth and early eighteenth centuries, extends our attention to the local circulation of goods beyond the family and into the local community. He reveals that the basic elements of New England funerals would have been recognizable to any Englishman, but the ceremonies' vast elaboration of traditional ritual forms—the expensive distribution of gloves, sashes, rings, and coats of arms among community members—marked these events as a peculiarly New England practice of the eighteenth century. Despite legislative attempts to squelch the often ruinous expenditure of family resources on staging a large funeral, they continued unabated until the 1780s when funerary practices shifted in light of changing material and political circumstances. In a culture awash in objects and growing more visually rich with each passing decade, the large funeral, with its extensive distribution of material goods, no longer possessed the expressive power it had commanded at the start of the century. Rather than inscribing mourning into civic space and using funerals to cement local social, political, and economic relationships, new mourning rituals privatized and sentimentalized grief. Paying close attention to ordinary landscapes and to the specificity of local practice helps us to identify New England's unique cultural expressions while keeping in mind the shaping power of extra-local forces and the inevitability of change over time.

The volume's closing section, "Envisioning New England," contains two essays that problematize how we interpret visual representations of and in the region. Martin Brückner probes questions of regional identity by exploring early New England's cartography. He points out that maps exclusively depicting New England were a new phenomenon in 1700 and that their increasing uniformity over the course of the eighteenth century represented a broader trend in cartography to "strip" maps of their decorative flourishes and fantastical creatures. The survival of pictorial elements in the form of a map's cartouche complicates our understanding of a "New England map." Brückner unpacks the "spatial work" performed by the cartouche in Thomas Jefferys's *Map of the most Inhabited part of NEW ENGLAND* (1755) that includes a substantial and detailed image of Puritans being welcomed to New England's shores and making contact with Native Americans. Comparing this "New England" cartouche with others, Brückner finds the deployment of aesthetic codes drawn from architecture, decorative arts, and the theater more significant than any attempt at communicating a fixed or static representation of "New England." What the cartouche signals, then, is not a particular regional identification—the words "New England" serve that function—but, rather, the position of maps as material objects and consumer goods circulating in an intensifying, transatlantic marketplace.

Wendy Bellion's essay also explores the complexities and contradictions of interpreting regional expression. Understanding the contour of New England's physical and intellectual geography, she argues, requires us to pay attention to the "interdependent systems of knowledge production" that shaped the region's cultural expressions. As an example, she points to the appearance of the "Invisible Lady," a kind of sideshow exhibition that traveled up and down the eastern seaboard in the early nineteenth century. Visitors to the "Invisible Lady" exhibition seemed to encounter a spectral presence with whom they could converse though they could not see her. This was both a material object—a contraption of speaking tubes and a closet in which the performer could be hidden from view—and an exercise in vision and illusion. Early nineteenth-century viewers loved the puzzle of trying to determine the "lady's" materiality. But, as Bellion points out, the "Invisible Lady" only survives through its representations in print. The broadsides, advertisements, pamphlets, and newspaper articles describing her appearances are the "Invisible Lady's" only surviving material evidence and they circulated well beyond the region's geographic boundaries. In fact, most early nineteenth-century New Englanders themselves only encountered her on the printed page. Bellion's discussion reminds us that although the material conditions that produce images, objects, and text vary considerably, none of these artifact categories circulate independently.

Instead, they overlap, inform, and modify one another in ways that demand closer scholarly scrutiny and in ways that cause us to rethink the boundaries of regional expression.

So, if the objects and images of early New England are highly variable, enmeshed in broad, protean economic and social networks, and shifting in response to extra-local pressures, can we really identify a coherent set of cultural expressions that represent "New England?" It would seem that each time we narrow in on a specific practice, a peculiarly local expression, it very quickly spins out its broader web of associations and leaves us to wonder what, if anything, defines "New England?" Ultimately, these are the kinds of questions posed by the ever-evolving methods, theories, strategies, and inquiries of the fields of material and visual culture studies. With their openness to understanding the fluidity of past experience while also being rooted in physical expressions of culture, this type of scholarship, exemplified by the essays in this volume, brings us closer to understanding the materiality of past experience and, ultimately, our relationship to that past.

Early New England's Oceanic Context

The Archaeology of 1690:
Status and Material Life on
New England's Northern Frontier

EMERSON W. BAKER

IN THE EARLY 1680s two of the leading merchants of southern Maine engaged in a gentlemanly negotiation. Major John Davis of York, the Deputy President of the Province of Maine, desperately wanted Lt. Humphrey Chadbourne Jr.'s fine gray riding horse. Chadbourne, a wealthy sawmill owner in Berwick, at first refused Davis, claiming the stallion was his wife's, and she enjoyed riding him. Davis insisted that "he must have the horse" so the major gave Chadbourne his case of pistols in return for the steed. Furthermore, the elderly Davis promised that upon his death, the stallion would be returned to the lieutenant. Less than a month after Davis's death in October 1691, Chadbourne went to court to reclaim his prize mount. By this time, the horse had become one of his few remaining assets. In the spring of 1690 Humphrey's extensive complex including a mansion house, a large farm, and a sawmill were all destroyed by a combined French and Native force in the Salmon Falls raid, one of the early encounters of King William's War. Chadbourne had been virtually wiped out. The court took the matter under advisement. Unfortunately, before Chadbourne could get his stallion back, York also fell victim to a raid. In the Candlemas attack in January 1692 Wabanaki raiders killed or took captive about 120 residents, slaughtered livestock, and burned most of the town. It is likely that Chadbourne's fine gray stallion was one of the victims of Candlemas. The once wealthy merchant died insolvent three years later.[1]

The fate of Humphrey Chadbourne Jr. and his horse exemplifies the opportunities and dangers of life on New England's northern frontier. It was a place where people had the chance to better themselves, but there were substan-

1. *York Deeds* (Portland, Maine: Brown, Thurston and Co., 1889), 5, pt .1: 82; Sybil Noyes, Charles T. Libby, and Walter G. Davis, eds., *Genealogical Dictionary of Maine and New Hampshire* (Baltimore: Genealogical Publishing Company, 1979), 134, 184–85.

tial risks and few would ultimately achieve wealth and position. Most of the residents of the region were poor farmers, fishermen, and lumbermen who struggled to survive. They labored to harvest the resources that merchants would grow wealthy upon through their participation in the Atlantic trade. Davis, Chadbourne, and their colleagues would in turn draw upon this wealth to acquire their large tracts of land, build mansions, and purchase stallions, pistols, and other fine objects that were important visible reminders of the gulf between this rising would-be gentry class and their less prosperous neighbors. Such markers were clearly important in the newly established and fluid society of the colonial frontier.

The huge losses of the Chadbournes and others in King William's War (1688–1697) were an utter disaster for them, but a bonanza for present-day archaeologists. The rapid destruction of the northern frontier of English settlements by the Wabanaki and their French allies has left a series of archaeological "time capsules"—sites that were rapidly destroyed and abandoned. Archaeological work at several sites of this era provides a unique opportunity to examine the range of society and economy in coastal New England in the late seventeenth century, and to see just how important material possessions were in differentiating social rank in English settlements.

The primary site under consideration is Chadbourne's substantial homestead and merchant complex in Berwick (present-day South Berwick, Maine). The author directed thirteen seasons of excavation at the site (1995–2007). During the Salmon Falls raid the Chadbournes were forced to leave almost all of their possessions behind them, and it is a substantial array of finds—over 40,000 artifacts. From fancy door hardware to silver spoons and brass spurs, the assemblage is a conspicuous display that amazes archaeologists today just as it was meant to impress neighbors and servants 300 years ago.[2]

The Chadbournes belonged to the rising merchant elite of early New England. Humphrey Chadbourne Sr. migrated from Tamworth, Warwickshire, to the Piscataqua in 1634. He initially worked with his father to build and operate a sawmill for Captain John Mason on the present-day Great Works River. Ironically, while Mason was the leading investor in the new colony of

2. Emerson Baker, "The Chadbourne Site (1643–1690): Gentrification on the Early Maine Frontier," paper presented at the Society for Historical Archaeology Annual Meeting, Williamsburg, Va., January 2007.

New Hampshire, the sawmill was actually located just outside the bounds of his colony, in what would become the Province of Maine. The mill soon ceased operations but Humphrey remained in the area and in 1643 he purchased a large tract of land at the confluence of the Great Works and Salmon Falls River from the local Wabanaki sachem, Mr. Rowls. Here Chadbourne established himself as a merchant and fur trader. The construction of his sawmill in 1652 greatly expanded his operations and wealth.[3]

Humphrey's growing prosperity was also aided by a very favorable marriage. About the time he constructed his mill, Humphrey married Lucy Treworgy, a member of one of the leading merchant families of Devon, England, as well as the Piscataqua. Indeed, the town of Kittery, Maine, is named after the home, wharf, and warehouses of Lucy's grandfather, Alexander Shapleigh, which were located on Kittery Quay, in Kingsweare, Devon. Kittery Quay lies across the River Dart from the busy West Country port of Dartmouth. Lucy's uncle Nicholas Shapleigh, a prominent royalist, controlled the family merchant and sawmill interests in the Piscataqua. Living a few miles downriver from the Chadbournes on a large estate in present-day Eliot, Maine, Nicholas was a sometime business partner of Humphrey Chadbourne. Numerous artifacts from the West Country are found on the Chadbourne site, suggesting the family maintained these important trade ties to home. Pottery finds include North Devon gravel tempered wares and sgraffittos, as well as Totnes ware—a rare find on early New England sites. Its presence at the Chadbourne site is explained by its manufacture in Totnes, just a few miles up the Dart from Kittery Quay.[4]

Archaeological work on the Chadbourne site has focused on the mansion house compound, and several nearby outbuildings. The core of the house was raised in 1664. This date is known from dated window leads, a brick marked "64" and a 1662 oak tree twopence discovered in close proximity to the location of the threshold of the front door. Humphrey Chadbourne died in 1667, leaving an estate of over £1,700, making him one of the wealthiest men in northern

3. Emerson Baker, "The Great Works River and Humphrey Chadbourne," in Jeffrey Bolster, ed., *Cross-Grained and Wily Waters: A Guide to the Piscataqua Maritime Region* (Portsmouth, N.H.: Peter Randall Publisher, 2002), 176–77; Elaine Chadbourne Bacon, comp., *The Chadbourne Family in America: A Genealogy* (Camden, Maine: Penobscot Press, 1994), xxxiii-17.

4. Noyes et al., eds., *Genealogical Dictionary*, 133–34, 623–24; Emerson Baker, *The Devil of Great Island: Witchcraft and Conflict in Early New England* (New York: Palgrave, 2007), 52–53, 117–18. The Shapleigh trading network extended northward in 1652 when Oliver Cromwell appointed Lucy's brother as governor of Newfoundland.

Fig. 1. Coastal Northern New England in the late seventeenth century.

New England. His probate inventory confirms the archaeological evidence of a two-story hall and parlor house with rear lean-to. Sometime later, another room was added off the parlor, making for a dwelling measuring 42´ x 60´. This mansion house was connected to another domestic unit by a palisade and fencing, creating an enclosed compound, with central courtyard. A barn and dairy were located to the north of the compound, and the sawmill stood to the south, along the banks of the Salmon Falls River. After Humphrey's death, the house and 400 surrounding acres passed to his wife, Lucy, and his eldest son, Lieutenant Humphrey Chadbourne Jr. The Wabanaki burned the entire complex in March of 1690 during the Salmon Falls raid.[5]

Humphrey and Lucy Chadbourne were people on the make. They came to America with the goal of bettering themselves—of becoming members of the gentry. Virtually all of their actions were geared toward this objective. They constructed a manor house on a huge landed estate that was worked by numerous servants. Family members held high political office, and inter-married into prominent families. They employed high status markers in their dress and many expensive possessions. In all of these ways, the Chadbournes sought to distance themselves from their servants and neighbors. Perhaps their location on the untamed New England frontier, far from the estates of England, made it particularly important to visibly demonstrate their wealth for the Chadbournes. As such, their possessions offer an impressive study of the significance of status in objects in early Maine.

Anyone aspiring to become members of the landed gentry needs an estate, and the Chadbournes did indeed build an impressive stand of buildings. The homestead, barn, and outbuildings sat on 400 acres and was valued at £350. The family sawmill, which was appraised at £300, stood nearby. The mansion had a commanding presence, sitting high on a hill, overlooking the conflu-ence of two rivers. It was meant to be seen. It was big and showy—complete with a very rare plastered parlor. Expensive imported hardware went into the house, including cock's head hinges, fancy locks, and many glass windows. The house was part of a courtyarded compound, a formal space—no artifact scatter has been found here, not even outside the front door, or windows. In addi-tion, the compound included a second domestic unit, perhaps occupied by the

---

5. Baker, "The Great Works River and Humphrey Chadbourne," 176–77; *York Deeds*, 2:30–31; Noyes et al., eds., *Genealogical Dictionary*, 133–34.

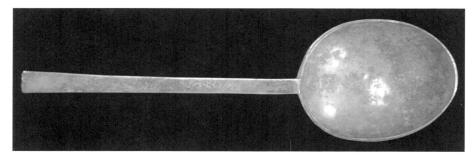

Fig. 2. Silver spoon from the Chadbourne site, made by John Hull and Robert Sanderson. 7½ inches in length. Old Berwick Historical Society Collection, South Berwick, Me.

Chadbourne servants, for when Humphrey died in 1667 his probate inventory includes five indentured servants. A barn was located out behind the house, as well as what appears to be a dairy. This large, impressive stand of buildings is a fairly unique discovery for early New England, but it is just one of many signs of the Chadbournes' wealth.[6]

Objects made out of precious metals have always served as important status markers, and the Chadbournes were no exception. Silver was incredibly rare in seventeenth-century Maine, yet excavations at the Chadbourne site recovered one complete silver spoon as well as a silver spoon handle. The complete specimen was made by the first American silversmiths, John Hull and Robert Sanderson. The Boston silversmiths engraved the spoon with the monogram "HLC" so there would be no mistaking that it belonged to Humphrey and Lucy Chadbourne. Humphrey's 1667 probate inventory included £16 in silver, including his "great silver beaker" that he specifically bequeathed to his young daughter Alice and was to be "quietly delivered unto her at the day of her marriage." Silver objects show up in only a handful of Maine estates of the era, including two of Humphrey's kinsmen. Brother-in-law Thomas Spencer's 1681 inventory lists a silver cup and spoon, and Nicholas Shapleigh's 1682 inventory included £21 of silver.[7]

6. *York Deeds*, 2: 30–31.
7. For a discussion on the rarity and symbolic importance of silver in early Maine see Edwin A. Churchill, "Glistening Reflections of Stability: The Roles of Silver in Early Maine," in Jeannine Falino and Gerald Ward, eds., *New England Silver and Silversmithing, 1620–1815* (Boston: Colonial Society of Massachusetts, 2001), 213–45; *York Deeds*, 2: 30–31; 5:13, 16. The quote is from *York Deeds*, 2: 30.

A considerable quantity of fine imported ceramics complimented the silver on the Chadbournes' table. Excavations recovered fragments of a minimum of twenty tin-enameled vessels, as well as combed-wares, and several nice German stonewares. Tin-enameled wares were the finest European ceramics of the day. Hand-painted earthenware in a variety of colors and finished with a shiny white glaze, these wares were meant to imitate expensive and hard to find Chinese porcelain. They were manufactured across Europe, and called delft, faience, or majolica. Although most New Englanders of moderate wealth owned at least a piece or two of English delft, as wealthy merchants the Chadbournes had access to the best and latest ceramics, and the means to afford them. Consider their fancy lobed plate, or their Bleu Persan (or Persian Blue) plate, an English imitation of a ware made in Nevers, France, which in turn imitates a Persian ceramic. Striking and quite rare in its day, Bleu Persan was also the height of fashion in the 1690. Equally in fashion would have been their English delft plate decorated in the Chinese Scholar pattern, an early expression of chinoiserie that was first made in the 1680s. While most families reserved their tin-enameled wares for use at the table, a polychrome tin-enameled pitcher was recovered in what is believed to have been the Chadbourne barn.[8]

As merchants who sold lumber in the Caribbean and participated in the wider Altantic trade, the Chadbournes owned many non-English tablewares. They owned at least three different patterns of Portuguese majolica, or Lisbonware. When Humphrey's sister and next-door neighbor Patience Chadbourne Spencer died in 1683, her "lisborne dishes" are specifically mentioned three times in her probate inventory. While other residents of Maine owned an occasional piece of Lisbonware, no one could match the Chadbournes' set of at least four hand-painted platas (or plates) made of Aucilla polychrome ware, manufactured in Mexico City. These are the first confirmed seventeenth-century Spanish colonial tablewares found north of the Chesapeake—a truly unique adornment for the Chadbourne table that would have impressed all dinner guests. Presumably acquired through their Caribbean lumber trade, the

8 Amanda Lange, *Delftware at Historic Deerfield, 1600–1800* (Deerfield, Mass.: Historic Deerfield, 2001), 108. For the Chinese Scholar pattern, see Sarah Fayen, "The Chinese Scholar Pattern: Style, Merchant Identity, and the English Imagination in the Late Seventeenth-Century Tin-Glazed Earthenware," paper presented at the annual meeting of the World History Association, Salem, Massachusetts, June 2009.

platas must have been purchased clandestinely, for it was illegal for the English to trade with the Spanish.[9]

The Chadbournes showed their rank in their dress and adornment as well, in such objects as a hand mirror with an ivory handle. Few clothing related artifacts survive, though excavations found three passmenterie buttons—two made with silver wound thread. Other striking status markers are the Chadbournes' horse furniture. Two spurs have been found; one is iron with a brass rowell, while the second is a highly decorated brass spur. The harness of Humphrey Chadbourne Jr.'s fine stallion was decorated with a large brass Tudor rose boss. In the late seventeenth century this was a badge of loyalty to the royalist cause of the Stuart monarchy. At a time when streets were rare in Maine and oxen pulled plows, horses were a true luxury item. Riding a fine stallion with elaborate brass spurs and a decorated harness across the rugged Maine countryside, Humphrey Jr. would have been a mobile statement of authority and wealth. In his 1667 will Humphrey Sr. bequeathed "to my son Humfrey Chadbourne my now riding horse with all the furniture to him belonging, and my intent is that the said horse with ye furniture bee at his owne dispose, immediately after my decease." Clearly father and son recognized the power of this symbol of authority and status, and the importance of its maintenance and immediate transfer from one generation to the next.[10]

The symbolism certainly would not have been missed by Humphrey Jr.'s wife, Sarah Bolles Chadbourne, who was a descendant of King Edward I (1239–1307; king 1272–1307). Sarah's father, Joseph, was a gentleman, born at his parent's estate of Oberton Manor, in Nottinghamshire. Joseph had been an early immigrant to the Province of Maine, a high officeholder and a leading citizen of Wells. Today the term gentleman has little true meaning but in the seventeenth century it was reserved for people of wealth and position. Joseph Bolles was one of the few gentlemen to take up residence in Maine. Bolles's daughters were probably the only young ladies in Maine of known royal descent. Possessing wealth and status, but lacking noble blood, it should come as no surprise that young Humphrey Jr. married one of the Bolles girls, thus bolstering the claim of gentleman status for himself and his descendants.

9. *York Deeds*, 5, pt. 1: 23–24: Kathleen Deagan, *Artifacts of the Spanish Colonies of Florida and the Caribbean, 1500–1800* (Washington, D.C.: Smithsonian Institution Press, 1987), 1: 76–77.
10. *York Deeds*, 2: 30.

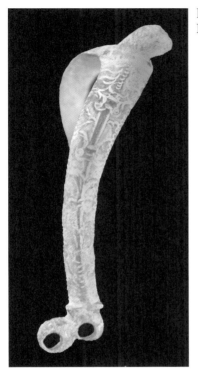

Fig. 3. Brass spur from the Chadbourne site. Old Berwick Historical Society Collection.

Fig. 4. Brass harness boss with Tudor Rose medallion from the Chadbourne site. 1½ inches in diameter. Old Berwick Historical Society Collection.

The marriage also allied him with another prominent merchant family, for Sarah's oldest sister was married to Major Charles Frost, another of the leading magistrates and merchants in southern Maine.[11]

The Chadbournes, their possessions, and their quest for status demonstrate the process Richard Bushman has called "the refinement of America." This evolution of polite society was reflected in changes in everything from speech and manners to houses, clothing, and ceramics. Bushman suggests this push for gentility began in America around 1690, yet the evidence from the Chadbournes suggests the process was well underway by that date for them, their fellow elites, and at least some of the middling sort of the region.[12]

Archaeological data from contemporary sites as well as probate inventories provides supporting evidence for the beginnings of this process of refine-

11. Noyes et al., eds., *Genealogical Dictionary*, 101, 246–47.

12. Richard Bushman, *The Refinement of America: Persons, Houses and Cities* (New York: Vintage, 1993), i–ii.

ment. The author has directed excavations at two other Maine sites that were destroyed at the outbreak of King William's War: the fortified fishing station on Sagadahoc Island at the mouth of the Kennebec River and a coastal farmstead owned by the Hitchcock family at Biddeford Pool. When considered along with the Chadbourne excavations, the sites are distributed from one end of early Maine to the other, and range from poor fishermen to yeoman farmers and merchant elites. In addition to these domestic sites, the excavation of the wreck of the *Elizabeth and Mary* adds another perspective. This ship, full of Dorchester, Massachusetts, militiamen, lost on Sir William Phips's ill-fated 1690 invasion of Quebec, was recently excavated by Parks Canada and the Province of Quebec. Together these sites provide a view of material life in late seventeenth-century New England.

The artifacts from the Chadbourne site are closest to those from the *Elizabeth and Mary*. This is not surprising, given that the officers of the Dorchester militia were prosperous merchants who had many similar high status artifacts. They wore silver brooches and shoe buckles and silk ribbons and passmenterie buttons. Such luxury items as an exotic wassail cup made of lignum vitae and a brass, tin-covered three-tined fork would have been noteworthy in Dorchester, and must have truly stood out onboard a troop ship. No sword hardware was recovered at the Chadbourne site, but one suspects that Lieutenant Humphrey would have owned a fancy sword, similar to the ones found on the *Elizabeth and Mary*, that included a sword grip with elaborate silver wire wrap, and brass counterguards with classical or floral decoration.[13]

The Hitchcocks were yeoman farmers, not wealthy merchants from Dorchester or the Piscataqua. Richard Hitchcock arrived in Saco by 1636, starting with a very modest estate. He rose to become a civic leader and a man of moderate wealth, leaving an estate valued at £278 at the time of his death in 1671. His heirs left behind an assortment of fine possessions when they abandoned the home during a Native American raid in the spring of 1690. Although the Hitchcocks owned earthenware that was much smaller in number and value than the Chadbournes, they owned a minimum of eight pieces of English delft

13. Charles Bradley, Phil Dunning and Gerard Gusset, "Material Culture from the *Elizabeth and Mary* (1690): Individuality and Social Status in a Late 17th Century New England Assemblage," in Christian Roy, Jean Belisle, Marc-Andre Bernier, and Brad Loewen (eds.), *ArcheoLogiques*; Collection Hors-Serie 1. Mer et Monde: Questions d'archeologie maritime, 2003, 152–55, 160–67.

Fig. 5. English lobed delft plate with chinoiserie decoration, burned and broken in the destruction of the Hitchcock homestead in 1690. Saco Museum Collection, Saco, Me.

tableware that were found, including three fancy lobed plates, two bowls, and a porringer. Two plates have early Chinoserie decoration—very fashionable in the 1680s. The finds also include parts of at least three combed yellow cups, a Westerwald mug, three Bartmann jugs, and a North Devon Sgraffitto plate. That is a minimum of sixteen pieces of tableware, most of it in use at the time the house burned down.[14]

Richard Hitchcock's family possessed quite a few articles of clothing and personal possessions, a fact supported by the inclusion of four chests in his 1671 probate inventory and in the excavation of five chest or trunk locks. In a time before houses had closets, chests and trunks held textiles and other valuable possessions. A part of the face of a brass sundial was also excavated, presumably a rare and cherished possession. And, as befitting a militia officer, his inventory included a gun, a sword, and even a mare. However, the excavation of a pair undecorated iron stirrups suggests Lieutenant Hitchcock would have commanded a much less impressive presence than Lieutenant Humphrey Chadbourne Jr. The same can be said overall for the Hitchcocks. They were a yeoman farming family who had prospered in Maine, and owned a few fine possessions to reaffirm their status, which certainly was higher than their fisherman neighbors at Biddeford Pool. However, they would definitely take a back seat to the Chadbournes and other merchant elites. Still, the growing prosperity and number of status objects enjoyed by yeomen such as the

14. Emerson W. Baker, "The 1991 Excavations at the Richard Hitchcock Site (ME 041–12)," report on file at the Maine Historic Preservation Commission, Augusta, Maine, 1991.

Hitchcocks meant that elites had to go to extra lengths to reaffirm their own economic, political, and social leadership. The Hitchcocks' pewter plates would be no match for Chadbourne silver.[15]

About thirty miles northeast of the Hitchcock homestead lay Sagadahoc Island, a fishing station at the mouth of the Kennebec River, near the eastern edge of English settlement in early Maine. Occupied as early as the 1640s, it saw its most intensive use from 1680 to 1689 when it was reoccupied and fortified by the poor fishermen of the Kennebec who had been forced out of the region during King Philip's War. Artifact density is very high, reflecting intense occupation of a small site. The objects themselves tend to be relatively pedestrian—numerous tobacco pipe fragments and pieces of redware. Still, pieces of tin-enameled wares, combed-yellow slipwares, North Devon sgraffito, and even German stoneware were present in very small quantities. The Chadbournes had far more extensive and expensive high status objects than the fishermen of Sagadahoc Island. Yet even these poor men possessed an occasional nice item. Once shipments arrived in Massachusetts ports, new fashionable goods quickly spread into all New England households. Take the example of combed-yellow slipware. This ware was first manufactured in England in 1670, but there is no evidence of its arrival in Maine until after King Philip's War. So, in the 1680s it was a stylish new tableware for New Englanders. Combed-yellow slipware was in active use on all three Maine sites and on board the *Elizabeth and Mary* in 1689–1690.[16]

Combed-yellow slipware is just one of many objects common to these sites. Most of the artifacts from the *Elizabeth and Mary* look like they could have walked right off the Maine sites. The type, quality, and range of goods available to people in Dorchester, within the urban core, were apparently just as accessible to people on the Maine frontier. All you needed was the credit to purchase them. This similarity is not surprising, considering that all the sites in Maine are located on navigable water, which is at most a two-day sail from

15. Emerson W. Baker, "The 1995 York County Archaeology Survey: A Report on ME 041–12, the Richard Hitchcock Site," report on file at the Maine Historic Preservation Commission, Augusta, Maine, 1995; Noyes et al., eds., *Genealogical Dictionary*, 339; Charles T. Libby, ed., *Province and Court Records of Maine* (Portland, Maine: Maine Historical Society, 1931), 2:453–55.

16. Emerson W. Baker, "The 1995 Survey of the Lower Kennebec River: A Report on ME 168–3, Sagadahoc Island," report on file at the Maine Historic Preservation Commission, Augusta, Maine, 1995.

Boston—areas regularly visited by the Essex County fishing fleet. Also, many Massachusetts merchants had operations and trading partners in Maine, so the same goods they marketed to residents of Dorchester were also shipped to Maine for sale. For example, Samuel Sewall, one of the wealthiest Boston merchants of the day, owned a sawmill roughly a mile up the Salmon Falls River from the Chadbourne site. The artifacts suggest that by 1690 Boston has clearly established its regional economic hegemony, creating a fairly uniform access to and distribution of most goods throughout the region. As early as 1672, Scarborough resident John Josselyn complained that "shopkeepers there are none, being supplied by the Massachusetts with all things they stand in need of . . . but they set excessive prices on them."[17]

There is one noticeable difference in artifacts between the Maine sites and the *Elizabeth and Mary*. The Maine sites all have the presence of West Country artifacts, while the shipwreck does not. North Devon gravel tempered wares and sgraffito wares were recovered at all three Maine sites. All of these sites also have a very strong presence of Bristol-made tobacco pipes, particularly those made by the Evans family. Maine had significant ties to the West Country in the seventeenth century. The Shapleighs were among many early settlers who came from Cornwall, Devon, and Somerset. Even the Proprietor of Maine, Sir Ferdinando Gorges, lived in Plymouth, Devon, and had an estate in Bristol. West Country ships traded directly with Maine, and indirectly through Newfoundland. Although West Country ceramics and Bristol pipes are found in excavations throughout the English colonies, their strong presence in these Maine sites suggests the region may have maintained some of these trade ties into the late seventeenth century. They did so despite the growing dominance of Massachusetts merchants who tended to have strong connections to London rather than Bristol.[18]

17. Paul J. Lindholdt, ed., *John Josselyn, Colonial Traveler: A Critical Edition of Two Voyages to New England* (Hanover, N.H.: University Press of New England, 1988), 142; for Sewall's mill see Samuel Sewall, *The Diary of Samuel Sewall, 1674–1729*, ed. M. Halsey Thomas, 2 vols. (New York: Farrar, Straus, and Giroux, 1973), 1:148–50; Bernard Bailyn, *The New England Merchants in the Seventeenth Century* (Cambridge, Mass.: Harvard University Press, 1955), 94–103.

18. Emerson Baker, "The World of Thomas Gorges: Life in the Province of Maine in the 1640s," in Emerson Baker et al., eds., *American Beginnings: Exploration, Culture and Cartography in the Land of Norumbega* (Lincoln: University of Nebraska Press, 1994), 267–71; Peter Pope, *Fish into Wine: The Newfoundland Plantation in the Seventeenth Century* (Chapel Hill, N.C.: University of North Carolina Press, 2004), 151–55, 240–42.

Fig. 6. Broken cocks head door hinge from the Chadbourne site. 8¼ inches in length. Old Berwick Historical Society Collection.

The residents of Maine had common sources for their material goods, even if the wealthy elites could distance themselves by purchasing more fancy objects. Yet, when you scratch their veneer of gentility, people like the Chadbournes had more in common with their neighbors than first appears. The Chadbourne mansion is a study in opposites. It is large and impressive, adorned with many windows, and fancy imported hardware, such as cocks head hinges. Great expense went into the windows the thousands of nails, as well as the hundreds of bricks used to make two substantial chimneys. The plastered parlor must have been one of the earliest in New England, a real rarity on the Maine frontier. Yet, the mansion was largely of earth-fast construction. Only the front wall of the cellar was stoned, with the remaining three sides being wood-lined. Parts of the building employ earth-fast posts, buried sill construction, and sill on grade. Aside from the mansion, the rest of the Chadbournes' stand of buildings was entirely earth-fast. Here the Chadbournes had much in common with the Hitchcocks and the fishermen of Sagadahoc Island, for all the structures at these sites were completely earth-fast. Even the two cellars under the Hitchcock home were wood-lined and held in place with earth-fast posts.

Earth-fast, or "post-in-ground" construction has been defined as buildings with framing members "standing or lying directly on the ground or erected in post holes."[19] Essentially it is construction that does not use a stone or brick

19. Cary Carson, Norman F. Barka, William M. Kelso, Garry Wheeler Stone, and Dell Upton, "Impermanent Architecture in the Southern America Colonies," *Winterthur Portfolio* 16:2/3 (1981):136.

foundation. First recognized as the prevailing form of construction in the Chesapeake in the seventeenth century, more recently it has been seen as a common form of architecture in early northern New England. Indeed every seventeenth-century Maine site found in the past twenty-five years is least partially earth-fast. This was a traditional English practice that required relatively minimal work by trained carpenters, and needed no stone mason. This technique remained popular because it was quick, cheap, and minimized the need for skilled labor in a land where such talents were in great demand. John Josselyn complained that "handcraftsmen there are but few, the tumelor or cooper, smiths and carpenters are best welcome."[20]

Why did the Chadbournes employ earth-fast architecture? Rather than distancing themselves from their less well-off neighbors, it gave them the common ground they sought to avoid. Not only was Humphrey Sr. a carpenter, but he also kept indentured servants. For example, five are included in his 1667 probate inventory. Furthermore, the site is littered with lumbering and carpentry tools, ranging from hammers and saws to axes and draw knives. Humphrey Chadbourne probably chose earth-fast construction for several reasons. First, there were probably limits to even his available supply of labor, especially when the entire 30´ x 42´. core of the house was raised at one time. Running a sawmill and lumbering operation required extensive labor, and only so much could be spared. And, given the fact that Chadbourne owned a sawmill, it would be easy to get lumber to repair the rot that eventually resulted from earth-fast construction. Furthermore, given its practicality and widespread use among all ranks of society, it seems doubtful that it would have the negative connotations associated with it today, when it is called "impermanent architecture." Anyone visiting the Chadbourne estate would have been impressed by the enormous sums of money and labor expended on the construction and embellishment of the mansion house and outbuildings. Nor could anyone doubt that the Chadbournes intended for themselves and their would-be manor to be permanent fixtures on the Maine landscape. The necessities of life on the frontier meant

20. Emerson Baker, Robert Bradley, Leon Cranmer, and Neill DePaoli, "Earthfast Architecture in Early Maine," paper presented at the Vernacular Architecture Forum annual meeting, Portsmouth, New Hampshire, 1993; Carson et al., "Impermanent Architecture in the Southern America Colonies," 135–96; for the quote see Lindholdt, ed., *John Josselyn, Colonial Traveler*, 142; Daniel Vickers, *Farmers and Fishermen: Two Centuries of Work in Essex County, Massachusetts* (Chapel Hill, N.C.: University of North Carolina Press, 1994), 52–53.

they may have cut some corners in the construction of the home, but these tended to be well hidden and thus easily missed by the casual observers.[21]

In some ways, the Chadbourne house is symbolic of the young society that was evolving in Maine during the seventeenth century. Large and striking, the Chadbourne residence was hastily constructed using the minimal standards of the day. Well appointed with expensive hardware and brick and plaster, it was designed to impress the Chadbournes' workers and neighbors, and to reinforce their leading position in the evolving frontier society of northern New England. It was a house and a culture built upon the rapidly acquired wealth of the frontier, with a promise of more to come, along with growing status and power. Yet, not enough care had gone into the construction of this society. In the late seventeenth century the rotten foundation quickly gave way under the weight of war, leading to the collapse of the entire edifice. By early 1692, almost all the English settlements of Maine had been abandoned with just a few hundred settlers clinging to hope in the southernmost settlements. Not until a generation of warfare ended in 1713 would people be able to return to Maine and build society anew.

21. Carson et al., "Impermanent Architecture in the Southern America Colonies."

Depicting Geographic Knowledge: Mariners' Drawings from Salem, Massachusetts

PATRICIA JOHNSTON

THE ATLAS of the French Pacific explorer La Pérouse was one of the most popular books in Salem at the turn of the nineteenth century. Its title page illustrates contemporary ideas about the vital role that words, images, and objects played in conveying knowledge about the far reaches of the globe (fig. 1). In the 1797 image a winged figure holding an armillary sphere, likely a personification of the wind that drove La Pérouse's sails, leads the classically draped figure of Navigation toward a large, unscrolled map. Navigation holds a paddle adorned with the image of a dolphin, as it was commonly portrayed on eighteenth-century decorative arts, with a flat rounded bill and split tail. The sea mammal, which in Greek mythology helped sailors by guiding their boats, symbolizes marine power. Circling around the map is a series of putti, some of whom hold the tools of navigation. Counterclockwise from the top, these include a sextant, telescope, hourglass, anchor, and a telltale compass. A large quadrant, a precursor of the sextant, is partially obscured by the map.

Though the map is clearly labeled at the top as the route of La Pérouse, it is somewhat difficult to read because the south is oriented toward the incoming figure on the right rather than toward the viewer. In contrast, the map's labels are oriented toward the readers; thus the land and sea names are upside down when the map is studied to trace the explorer's route. In a process perhaps analogous to the experience of Salem's Federal-period citizens, the resulting initial confusion forces the reader to stop and study before new information can be integrated into existing conceptions of the charted world (fig. 2).

While the figure on the right introduces readers to the world, two on the left record it. At the bottom left, a figure with brushes and palette on the ground to her left sketches the peoples that La Pérouse encountered on his mission; the figure above her looks toward these same subjects with her pen poised to write about them (fig. 3). On his departure from France in 1785 La Pérouse was instructed to "observe the genius, character, manners, customs,

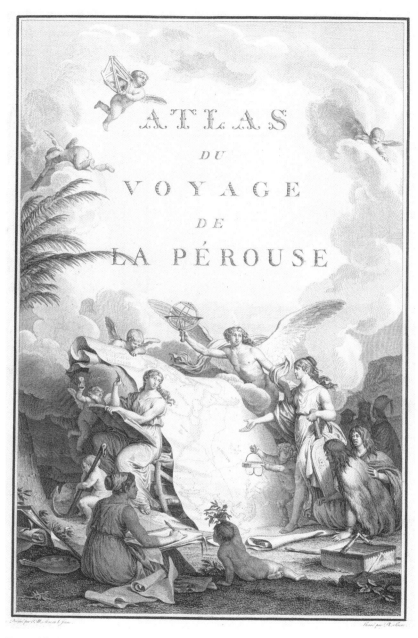

Fig. 1. Title Page to *Atlas du Voyage de La Pérouse*. Paris: L'Imprimerie de la Republique, 1797. Designed by J. M. Moreau le Jeune; engraved by Ph. Triere and L. Aubert. Courtesy of David Rumsey Map Collection.

Fig. 2. Detail of Title Page to *Atlas du Voyage de La Pérouse*.

Fig. 3. Detail of Title Page to *Atlas du Voyage de La Pérouse*.

Fig. 4. Detail of Title Page to *Atlas du Voyage de La Pérouse*.

bodily constitution, language, government and number of inhabitants." These directions specified an interest in anthropological observation more intensive than comparable instructions to earlier European expeditions. La Pérouse was also directed to follow Captain Cook's lead and continue to make botanical and zoological discoveries, to collect "natural curiosities, both of land and sea" that were "to be arranged in order; and a descriptive catalogue of each kind to be drawn up."[1]

The indigenous peoples that La Pérouse encountered are represented in striking contrast to the idealized Grecian beauties, perhaps arguing for the superiority of Europe and thus justification of exploitation (fig. 4). In the case

1. Jean-François de Galaup, comte de La Pérouse, *Voyage of La Pérouse Around the World*, 4 vols, ed. M. L. A. Milet-Mureau (London, 1798), I: 37–38. For discussion of the directions given to La Pérouse see Bernard Smith, *European Vision and the South Pacific* (2nd ed. New Haven: Yale University Press, 1985), 137–40.

of the two fur-clothed figures, who wear clothing similar to those of Alaskan natives pictured in later parts of the book, there is an obvious attempt to represent them as crude and animalistic; the illustrator emphasizes unique cultural practices, such as the labret implanted in the lips, that would be shocking to European readers. The three native figures in the background have more distinctive costuming, with headdresses that suggest Aleutian and Asian identities. At the bottom center, another putto holds up a botanical specimen. The native peoples and plants refer to the research goals of La Pérouse's expedition. In essence, the title page of the atlas is an allegory of the acts of gathering and studying botanical and ethnographic information via text and image.

La Pérouse's atlas was read by the intellectual and maritime elite in Salem, likely because it reinforced their belief in the value of studying the wider world. The atlas illustrated the importance of recording geographical and cultural information, just as Salem's merchants and mariners were developing new American trade routes. British colonial regulations had limited American ships to the Atlantic Basin. Building new legal global trade after the Revolution required geographical information, such as the location and depth of harbors, channels, and shoals, and cultural knowledge, such as indigenous customs and currencies.

By 1800 Salem was a thriving seaport of 9400 people nestled along a shallow, protected harbor halfway between the bustling state capital of Boston and the small fishing village of Gloucester at the tip of Cape Ann. Vessels preparing for, or returning from, international voyages lined Salem's nearly thirty wharfs. Tea, coffee, spices, wines, textiles, shoes, and ceramics packed its harbor stores. The Salem fleet traded from the Baltic to the Mediterranean, and from the Indian Ocean to the Pacific—truly a global reach. By 1800 international trade had transformed Salem into the sixth largest city in the new United States, after Boston, New York, Philadelphia, Baltimore, and Charleston.[2]

2. There are few modern histories of Salem; a good summary is National Park Service, *Maritime Salem in the Age of Sail* (Washington, D.C.: U.S. Department of the Interior, 1987). For recent cultural analysis of the city see *Salem: Place, Myth, Memory,* Dane Anthony Morrison and Nancy Lusignan Schultz, eds. (Boston: Northeastern University Press, 2004). There is a significant body of literature on the city's infamous witch trails and its colonial and federal architecture. Most histories of the city, however, date to the colonial revival period, particularly the work of James Duncan Phillips, *Salem in the Eighteenth Century* (Boston: Houghton Mifflin Co, 1937); and *Salem and the Indies: The Story of the Great Commercial Era of the City* (Boston: Houghton Mifflin Co., 1947). An excellent study of the career paths of mariners is Daniel Vick-

Salem's merchants and mariners shared a remarkable visual culture of prints and drawings that provided specific knowledge of distant parts of the world at a level of detail that made them more competitive in the emerging Asian and Pacific trade. Part of this visual culture consisted of printed images—often expensive, luxurious illustrations for voyage narratives, such as those engraved for the La Pérouse atlas, which were typically imported from London or printed in the larger American cities.[3] Another part of this visual culture was made up of unique images; these maps and sketches were drawn by mariners and incorporated into ships' logs and other navigational documents. Both print and manuscript representations were significant in building the rich archive available in the town. Many Salem sea captains and traders felt an obligation to contribute to the archive, using the language of drawing to share information they gathered on their voyages.

Modes and venues for sharing geographic knowledge have existed for many centuries; for instance, manuscript maps circulated in the middle ages. In the colonial period, Americans shared knowledge primarily through kinship networks, fraternal organizations, and fledgling libraries. During the Early Republic, these venues for the circulation of information and ideas became more formalized. By 1800 Salem had flourishing networks for sharing information. Subscription libraries such as Salem's Social Library acquired and circulated published materials to members, while fraternal organizations such as the East India Marine Society promoted exchanges of personal seafaring and trading experiences. These institutions strengthened ties among the community's elite and provided them with a competitive edge in trade. Access to global geographic information—combined with navigational skill, business sense, and

ers with Vince Walsh, *Young Men and the Sea: Yankee Seafarers in the Age of Sail* (New Haven: Yale University Press, 2005). For a study of how international trade influenced the early American economy see James R. Fichter, *So Great a Proffit: How the East Indies Trade Transformed Anglo-American Capitalism* (Cambridge, Mass.: Harvard University Press, 2010).

3. There is an extensive bibliography on eighteenth-century voyage narratives. Some key works that connect art and science include Barbara Maria Stafford, *Voyage into Substance: Art, Science, Nature, and the Illustrated Travel Account, 1760–1840* (Cambridge, Mass.: MIT Press, 1984); Bernard Smith, *European Vision and the South Pacific,* 2nd ed. (New Haven: Yale University Press, 1985); and Rudiger Joppien and Bernard Smith, *The Art of Captain Cook's Voyages,* 3 vols. (New Haven: Yale University Press, 1985). More recent literature in this area has focused on exploring the colonizing or imperial eye, such as Beth Fowkes Tobin, *Picturing Imperial Power: Colonial Subjects in Eighteenth-Century British Painting* (Durham, N.C.: Duke University Press, 1999).

a measure of good luck—could lead to great wealth and prestige. This commercial success, built on international trade, reinforced a change in American identity from colonial subjects on the margin of empire to international trading partners in a thriving global marketplace.

The Social Library

Following patterns established in other American seaports, Salem quickly built institutions to provide the knowledge necessary for success in the expanded international economy.[4] Founded in 1761, Salem's Social Library grew out of an earlier intellectual men's gathering called the Monday Night Club. The Social Library counted among its members many of Salem's merchants and sea captains, along with doctors, lawyers, and ministers—and sometimes their widows and daughters, who could inherit shares. The original collection of the Social Library conformed to typical American eighteenth-century reading patterns: doses of Greek and Roman history, philosophical and theological treatises, and the new literary form of the novel. However, as might be expected in a seaport, the holdings also had a strong international focus with a large selection of published chronicles of sea voyages.[5] The prominent physi-

4. For a discussion of the movement to found comparable subscription libraries, on Charleston and other cities, see James Raven, "Social Libraries and Library Societies in Eighteenth-Century North America," and James Green, "Subscription Libraries and Commercial Circulating Libraries in Colonial Philadelphia and New York," both in *Institutions of Reading: The Social Life of Libraries in the United States,* Thomas Augst and Kenneth Carpenter, eds. (Amherst, Mass. and Boston: University of Massachusetts Press, 2007), 1–23; 24–52. Like the Salem Social Library, libraries in other seaports functioned as elite social institutions collecting a wide range of books; like the East India Marine Society, they collected unusual objects for their cabinet of curiosities. See also Martha McNamara, "Defining the Profession: Books, Libraries, and Architects," in *American Architects and Their Books to 1848*, Kenneth Hafertepe and James O'Gorman, eds. (Amherst, Mass. and Boston: University of Massachusetts Press, 2001). For extensive study of American imprints and their circulation see the series *A History of the Book in America,* particularly Volume 1, *The Colonial Book in the Atlantic World,* Hugh Amory and David D. Hall, eds. (Cambridge, Eng.: Cambridge University Press, 2000), and Volume 2, *An Extensive Republic: Print, Culture and Society in the New Nation, 1790–1840,* Robert A. Gross and Mary Kelley, eds. (Chapel Hill, N.C.: American Antiquarian Society and University of North Carolina Press, 2010).

5. My account of the holdings and charge records of the Social Library is derived from its archives held at the Phillips Library of the Peabody Essex Museum, Salem, Mass., collection MSS 56. The Social Library published its holdings several times. See for example, *Bylaws and Regulations of the Incorporated Proprietors of the Social Library in Salem* (Salem, Mass.: Printed by Thomas C. Cushing?, c. 1797); Evans 32800 in *Early American Imprints* digital database. The

cian Edward Augustus Holyoke donated a *Book of Mapps*. The original library also held the *Koran Tales,* the *Life of Mahomet, Piratical States of Barbary,* and the *Life of Czar*.[6]

In the Early Republic the continuing Social Library was a significant resource for global information in town, though as a private library access was restricted to the families of those who could afford to purchase a share. The library closed during the Revolution, and its archives show little activity through the 1780s, a period of economic depression in Salem. The phenomenal growth of shipping and disposable income in the 1790s, when Salem traders opened new paths to the East Indies, was matched by lively interest in the library. After a long lull, the library admitted eleven new members in 1796. Each year afterward, several members joined until 1810, when the Social Library merged with the Philosophical Library (whose members were largely ministers and its collections comprised primarily of science, philosophy, and theology texts) to form the present Salem Athenaeum.[7] New members of the Social Library circa 1800 included physicians, lawyers, shopkeepers and pharmacists, as well as some of the town's leading shipowners and sea captains.

The Salem Athenaeum archives hold extraordinary resources in the form of two charge books that record the books that Social Library members took home. The first one begins with the library's establishment in 1761. The second begins with the influx of new members in 1796. Arranged by shareholder, these charge books allow study of both the popularity of specific books and the taste of individual readers.[8] The acquisitions and circulation patterns reveal how widely read were Salem's citizens and how wide-ranging their knowledge of the world.

The most in-demand books were voyage narratives. The publication of Cook's *Voyages* set off a publishing trend on both sides of the Atlantic that

---

Social Library's books are held by the Salem Athenaeum, which was formed in 1810 when the Social Library and Philosophical Library merged. Secondary sources on the Salem Athenaeum include Cynthia B. Wiggin, *The Salem Athenaeum* (Salem, Mass.: Forest River Press, 1971) and the Athenaeum's website at www.salemathenaeum.net.

6. See for example, *Bylaws and Regulations*; Evans 32800 in *Early American Imprints*.

7. The records of the Philosophical Library are at the Phillips Library of the Peabody Essex Museum, MSS 56. They include financial, catalogue, and charge records.

8. The charge books are presently held for the Salem Athenaeum in the Phillips Library of the Peabody Essex Museum, MSS 56.

was reflected in Salem's libraries. It seemed that readers could not get enough illustrated natural history and travel adventure literature; tales by Anson, Volney, Park, Coxe, La Pérouse, Bruce, Shaw, Anacharsis, Ulloa, and Niebuhr were always checked out.

Two examples of members' reading lists, one a merchant and one a sea captain, suggest the reading patterns of the elite. William Gray—shipowner, merchant, and one of the wealthiest men in Salem—preferred travels, histories, and nature studies. Much of his reading focused on the Middle East: Shaw's travels to the Barbary Coast, Cyrus's travels to Persia, Dallaway's *Constantinople*, and the *Life of Mahomet*. Gray was equally interested in Europe; he checked out Nugent's *Grand Tour* and Robertson's *History of Scotland,* as well as compilations of comedies and tragedies. Like most other members of the Social Library, Gray did not seem concerned that information might be outdated. With equal regard, members checked out the new books and the original 1761 collection (which included books such as the *Life of Mohamet,* written decades before the library was founded).

Benjamin Hodges, who sailed to China in 1788–90 as captain of Gray's ship, the *William and Henry,* had a reading list heavy on history, literature, and aesthetics. Typical of most library patrons, he examined Park's travels to Africa, Moore's travels to Italy and France, Bourgoanne's travels in Spain, and Wilson's account of the Pelew Islands. Though Hodges might be intrigued by such firsthand narratives, the books he took out had little to do with the destinations to which he actually sailed: China, Russia, India, the Caribbean, and others. Of these he had firsthand experience, and his charge records show no evidence of research or reading about these places. It might be however, that the Social Library was not Hodges's key repository for research for his own travels. He was a founding member of the East India Marine Society, and thus had access to their more specialized library and owned a number of books himself, although it is impossible to say which, because the titles of his personal library were not listed in his estate inventory.

Other libraries in Salem followed much the same pattern. The Library of Arts and Sciences, another private subscription institution founded in 1802, was heavy on expedition narratives, with holdings such as the twenty-volume collection of Mavor's *Voyages,* as well as history, theology, philosophy, and aesthetics. While some selections, such as *Roman History* or the *Encyclopedia*

Britannica might have been found anywhere in the United States, some, such as *Gentoo [Hindu] Laws,* were unusual holdings but appropriate for an international seaport.[9] Libraries continued to be founded in Salem; by 1830 there were seventeen specialized libraries in the city.

One of the most popular reading emporiums was run by John Dabney, a newspaper publisher who in 1786 started the *Salem Mercury,* then published the *Salem Gazette.* In his newspapers, Dabney advertised the great variety of holdings for sale or rent: "divinity, history, biography, travels, voyages, memoirs, miscellanies, novels and poetry." While some holdings overlapped those of the other libraries in town, the titles here tilted more toward entertainment. Visitors could chose selections such as Henry Fielding's *Amelia, or the Distressed Wife,* the *Arabian Nights Entertainments,* or other popular literature.[10]

Private collections augmented Salem's libraries. In a town that had both money and culture, some personal libraries became quite extensive. Ministers, of course, collected books. Reverend Thomas Barnard had 600 volumes, which he frequently lent out.[11] Reverend Bentley collected over 4000 books during his thirty years in Salem. Wealthy merchants also bought books; Elias Hasket Derby, for example, bought a London collection of 700 books that came on the market, practically sight unseen. Books from these personal libraries circulated among friends and family.

East India Marine Society: Books and Charts

The East India Marine Society, founded in 1799, was the most significant organization in Salem for sharing global knowledge. Marine societies, common in seaports, typically emphasized charitable activities. The EIMS was a more select marine society, with an elite membership limited to sea captains and supercargoes (that is, the head traders) who had rounded either the Cape of Good Hope or Cape Horn to engage in Asian commerce.[12] Global knowl-

---

9. *Rules and Regulations of the Library of Arts and Sciences* (Salem, Mass.: Printed by Thomas C. Cushing, 1802); Shaw & Shoemaker 2532.

10. John Dabney, *Catalogue of Books, for Sale or Circulation in Town or Country, by John Dabney, at His Book and Stationary Store, and Circulating Library, in Salem* (Salem, Mass.: J. Dabney, 1801).

11. Harold L. Burstyn, "The Salem Philosophical Library: Its History and Importance for American Science," *Essex Institute Historical Collections* 96 (1960): 169–206.

12. The most synthetic history of the EIMS is Walter Muir Whitehill, *The East India Marine Society and the Peabody Museum of Salem: A Sesquicentennial History* (Salem, Mass.: Peabody Museum, 1949).

edge was traded at its regular meetings and dinners, and also through its map, book, and object collections. Unique among such organizations, members were required to collect objects for its museum and to keep voyage logs for its library.[13] The EIMS collection of books and voyage logs provided the members with information, and thus a competitive edge, not available otherwise. Members could view visual records of the wider world in the illustrations of published voyage narratives, or in images drawn by their brother mariners for their own voyage logs.

Though large selections of published sea chronicles also filled other Salem libraries, the East India Marine Society library was designed to do more: it targeted acquisitions tightly rather than comprehensively. The book committee, authorized to use the dues to buy any published "Books of History of Voyages and Travels and of Navigation" that might be useful to members, focused on very expensive volumes that even their well-off members chose not to purchase for their personal collections. While no early catalogue of the books has survived, the minutes of the meetings mention some specific acquisitions, and the number of volumes seems to have reached about 250 by 1830. As would be expected, the library held an elaborate multi-volume edition of Cook's *Voyages*, which was checked out by Captains Gardner, Pickman, and others. Most members, however, probably owned their own editions, even if they were less elegantly illustrated.[14]

One of the first purchases for the EIMS library was the large 1799 London edition of La Pérouse's voyages, with deluxe engravings copied after the earlier French edition. The EIMS's *luxe* edition of La Pérouse was continually checked out—to mathematician Nathaniel Bowditch, then Captains Devereux, Lambert, and Prince.[15] La Pérouse was one of the most popular authors in Salem, perhaps because he traveled to less well-known parts of the Pacific, such as the

---

13. Daniel Finamore, "Displaying the Sea and Defining America: Early Exhibitions at the Salem East India Marine Society," *Journal for Maritime Research* (May 2002) [On-line edition: http://www.jmr.nmm.ac.uk]; and James M. Lindgren, "'That Every Mariner May Possess a History of the World': A Cabinet for the East India Marine Society of Salem," *The New England Quarterly* 68 (June 1995): 179–205.

14. Papers of the East India Marine Society, Phillips Library of the Peabody Essex Museum. MS 88, Box 1, Folder 1. The EIMS Library charge records are intermingled with the Society minutes each month.

15. Ibid.

northwest coast and south sea islands, which Salem mariners targeted as the next areas of opportunity.[16]

In 1801 the East India Marine Society decided to purchase the heavily illustrated volume of Vancouver's voyages. Vancouver also traveled to Pacific territories unknown to Salem voyagers. They paid book dealer John West the enormous sum of $39.12 for the three quarto volumes of text and a fourth folio of maps and engravings, then incurred the further expense of $8.25 for West to bind the volumes.[17] No doubt Salem mariners were so eager to study La Pérouse and Vancouver because they planned to initiate trans-Pacific routes to replace the traditional Salem route to India and China by way of the Cape of Good Hope.

The EIMS also purchased fifteen of John Churchman's variation charts for $52.50.[18] Churchman's variations were a series of sea charts of the Mid-Atlantic coast that were very useful for the frequent runs that distributed imported Asian goods to the American cities to the south. Churchman's variations were among the library's most valued items; individual charts were continually checked out by Captains Taylor, Sage, Orne, George Hodges, and Benjamin Crowninshield in preparation for their journeys.[19]

Voyage Logs and the Topographical

Perhaps most importantly, the EIMS library collected unique information valuable for international navigation and trade. The bylaws required that all members returning from voyages present their journals to the library committee, and beginning in 1801, the Society even provided blank printed jour-

16. Jean-François de Galaup, comte de La Pérouse, a highly experienced French naval officer and explorer, left Brest in 1785 on an expedition funded by Louis XVI. Over the next three years, La Pérouse crossed the Atlantic and rounded Cape Horn; stopped at Easter Island and the Hawaiian archipelago, then sailed to the west coast of North America, exploring from Alaska to California. He crossed the Pacific to Macao and Hong Kong, then headed north to Taiwan, the Phillipines, Korea, Japan, and Siberian Kamchatka, then turned south to Tonga, Samoa, Australia, and eventually the 1788 wreck of his ship on the coral reefs of Vanikoro in the Solomon Islands. Fortunately for his legacy, La Pérouse had the foresight to send back to Europe from Australia via a British ship, his journals to date and some works by the three ship illustrators. This was the basis of the sumptuously illustrated atlas published in French in 1797.

17. Papers of the East India Marine Society, Phillips Library of the Peabody Essex Museum. MS 88, Box 4, Folder 2.

18. Papers of the East India Marine Society, Phillips Library of the Peabody Essex Museum. MS 88, Box 4, Folder 2.

19. Papers of the East India Marine Society, Phillips Library of the Peabody Essex Museum. MS 88, Box 1, Vol. 1.

nals for seafarers. As Inspector of Journals, Nathaniel Bowditch, author of the pathbreaking *New American Practical Navigator,* arranged and wrote a table of contents for the voyage logs, then had them bound. The blank logs provided form fields to systemize the requested information, yet left blank pages for flexibility in individual contributions. Following established maritime traditions of voyage logs, the book was labeled with the name of the ship's master and the person keeping the journal (who might be the master, supercargo, or first mate), and the destination. The writer recorded each day's longitude and latitude, and the "general state of the weather, winds, currents, bearings of capes, islands, &c. with their estimated distances and, any other remarks that may be useful to navigators."

These journals were sometimes illustrated. Salem mariners' drawings reflect the conventions of European naval illustration and charting, popular drawing manuals, and engraved voyage illustrations. They were following a long history of drawing as a language for communicating knowledge about the world. Mapping and some landscape representations were practiced in the ancient world. As early as the fourteenth century, meticulous botanical studies were drawn for Italian textbooks. Global exploration in the sixteenth century encouraged the development of images of panoramic views.[20]

In the eighteenth century, topographical studies provided both informational and aesthetic value.[21] Artistic representation was an integral part of eighteenth-century expeditionary voyages; Captain Cook, for example, brought artists on each of his three voyages. Military officers in training at the Royal Naval College and men preparing to join the British East India Company received artistic training, particularly in drawing and watercolor, before they were deployed abroad.[22] Drawing coastal outlines and perspec-

20. "Landscape," in *Oxford Art Online.*

21. For a study of ideological aspects of mapping see Matthew H. Edney, *Mapping an Empire: The Geographical Construction of British India, 1765–1843* (Chicago: University of Chicago Press, 1997). See also Martin Brückner, *The Geographic Revolution in Early America: Maps, Literacy, and National Identity* (Chapel Hill, N.C.: University of North Carolina Press, 2006).

22. For example, John Thomas Serres was a drawing instructor at the Chelsea Naval School in London and published *Liber Nauticus, and Instructor in the Art of Marine Drawings* in 1805–06. See David Cordingly, *Marine Painting in England, 1700–1900* (London: Littlehampton Book Services Ltd, 1974). A catalogue of East India Company drawings is published in Mildred Archer, *Company Drawings in the India Office Library* (London: Her Majesty's Stationery Office, 1972).

tive views for future ventures was perhaps an even more important visual task than recording scientific and cultural information, and voyage narratives such as Cook and La Pérouse often had an equal or greater number of charts than illustrations. Although much of the literature on the history of drawing in the eighteenth century has emphasized its role as a polite art, practiced by women, it was also a very practical and valuable masculine art, with military, scientific, and commercial applications.[23]

Salem mariners recognized the limits of published information and the dangers that could befall them in unfamiliar waters and ports. They also recognized the value of their experience for others. Luther Dana displayed such self-awareness when he served as the ship's master and journal keeper of the *Recovery* on its voyage from Salem to Mocha, a port city on the coast of the Red Sea in Yemen, which was renowned for its chocolate flavored coffee. Referring to a compass that consistently gave him erroneous readings, Dana wrote that he, "The Journalist," omitted the readings to avoid misleading others. Dana commented throughout the log that the charts he had were incorrect. He recorded no information about people or customs, rather his prose attempted to capture his views of the coast so that others could replicate his journey with greater ease. Passing "Cape Guardufoi" [Cape Guardafui] on the horn of Africa in present-day Somalia, Dana noted "This land is remarkable for appearing like two white Peaks, one with a block Top." It reminded him of "a large rigged vessel." He observed that at first it appears as five islands, but as one gets closer he can see they are joined as one. Perhaps Dana simply described landmarks rather than comment on them because he saw little charm in the landscape: a place "without the least appearance of verdure."[24]

Dana's drawing style parallels his prose style: it is informational. In his drawing of Cape Babel Mandel, his concern is to provide enough detail that future mariners can recognize they have reached the landmark, and know what to do to get from there to Mocha. In a sketch that he titled *Appearance of Cape*

23. On drawing as a polite art for men and women see Ann Bermingham, *Learning to Draw: Studies in the Cultural History of a Polite and Useful Art* (New Haven and London: Yale University Press and the Paul Mellon Centre for Studies in British Art, 2000).

24. Luther Dana, Log of the *Recovery*, Salem to Mocha, December 1800 to October 1801, in the East India Marine Society logs, Volume 1, 568–621, Phillips Library of the Peabody Essex Museum. There are approximately 3000 ships' logs in the Phillips Library of the Peabody Essex Museum; references to logs below are drawn from this repository.

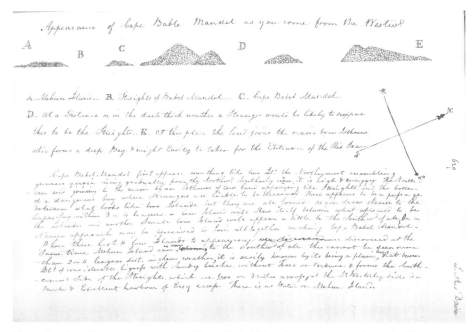

Fig. 5. Luther Dana, *Appearance of Cape Babel Mandel as you come from the West[d]*. Log of the *Recovery*, Salem to Mocha, 1800–1801. East India Marine Society papers MH-88, Volume 1, p. 620. Courtesy of the Phillips Library at the Peabody Essex Museum, Salem, Massachusetts.

Babel Mandel as you come from the West[d], Dana labels five distinct landmarks with the letters A through E (fig. 5), and places a compass underneath. Dana's drawing of the coastline spreads across the full length of the page. The sea is simply suggested: it is the void between bases of the horizontally aligned land-masses. Yet the implied sea passages between the land are as much the point of the drawing as the land forms. The key beneath the first land form on the left labels A as an island, but it is the empty area B that is more significant—the famous "Streights of Babel Mandel," which voyagers must enter to reach their destination of Mocha. C labels Cape Babel Mandel itself, and D demonstrates the primary point of the drawing. This empty area to the left of the Cape could be treacherous: "At a Distance or in the dark thick weather a Stranger would likely to suppose this to be the Streights." The sea at the letter E, where a land-mass seeming to be an island is connected to the mainland by an isthmus, is another possible deception that "might Easily be taken for the Entrance."

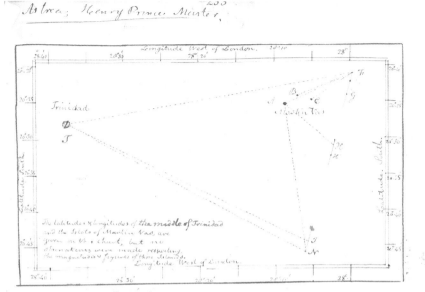

Fig. 6. Nathaniel Bowditch. *Longitude and Latitude of Trinidad.* Log of the *Astrea,* Salem to Lisbon, Madeira, and Manilla, 1796–1797. East India Marine Society papers, MH-88, Volume 1, p. 255. Courtesy of the Phillips Library at the Peabody Essex Museum.

Dana's drawing and its labeling warn his fellow seamen to be on the look-out for this critical juncture since they might easily be confused and drawn off course here. Since the sea is suggested rather than represented, it projects a calm presence between solid landmasses. But Dana's words belie the idyllic scene: "Cape Babel Mandel first appears something like two Isl^d the North-ernmost resembling gunners quoin rising gradually from the Northwrd. South-erly where it is high and craggy," it has a "dangerous bay where Strangers are likely to be deceived."

Despite this geographic focus in Dana's drawing, his visual vocabulary bor-rows from the fine arts. He uses delicate hatches that are arranged into lines that curve and change direction to suggest volumes and shifting planes on the hilly coast. This drawing style, and the convention of alphabetic labeling, are drawn from the long history of engraving, an art he was familiar with from illustrated voyage narratives.

Indeed, many of the illustrations in voyage logs were even more mathemati-cal and less artistic in character. Nathaniel Bowditch, as journal keeper of the ship *Astrea* commanded by Henry Prince included a chart he made to plot the longitude and latitude of Trinidad (fig. 6).[25] Bowditch's visual language is comprised of numbers and triangles; his goal safer, more efficient navigation. It is based on standard conventions for sea charts, which he sought to make more reliable.

Drawings of harbors were very much tied to print traditions. William Haswell's drawings of the port of Manila illustrate the standard conventions of how mariners used different types of topographical charts and views to synthesize crucial information. In one example, Haswell presents a *Plan of the Bay of Manila in the Isle of Lucona,* a sea chart of the harbor that echoes the standard conventions (fig. 7). In a decorative cartouche, he clearly labels it a copy, even as he signs it. The image is based on a survey of the harbor by Señor Don Malaspina. It includes the symbols necessary for decoding it: a scale, a compass, numbers indicating harbor depths, and the names of notable features. In both Bowditch's visual computation and Haswell's more accessible chart, the sea is enlivened with both visual description and data; the land is a void, terra incognita to the seafarer.

25. Nathaniel Bowditch, Log of the *Astrea,* Salem to Lisbon, Madeira, and Manilla, March 1796 to May 1797, in the East India Marine Society logs, Volume 1.

Fig. 7. William Haswell. *Plan of the Bay of Manilla in the Isle of Lucona*. Logs of the *Elizabeth*, *Charlotta*, and *Pallas*, 1801–1803. Courtesy of the Phillips Library at the Peabody Essex Museum.

Fig. 8. William Haswell. *Appearance of the Entrance of Manilla Bay*. Logs of the *Elizabeth*, *Charlotta*, and *Pallas*, 1801–1803. Courtesy of the Phillips Library at the Peabody Essex Museum.

Mariners sometimes used this information in conjunction with their own personal observations as the basis of landscape drawings to depict harbors as they were perceived during arrival by sea. In another image, Haswell provides an experiential image of the more informational hydrographic survey, an acknowledgement that mariners needed both, and perhaps referencing the long tradition of drawing coastal profiles (fig. 8). Haswell neatly labeled the *Appearance of the Entrance of Manilla Bay* in both its title and the names of the mountains and islands, the key landscape features seen on entering the bay. In images such as this, documentary goals combine with artistic landscape ambitions. Haswell's pencil traces the light hitting the front of mountains and the islands rising out of the sea. Shadows emphasize their three-dimensionality. A single line separates the sea from the sky and the landforms are aligned on a single horizontal axis. A simple unlabeled compass placed in the center orients the viewer. The result is a drawing that captures the distinctive topography of Manila harbor. Only essential information is represented and a complex view is reduced to easily understandable information.

Like most mariners, Haswell came from a seafaring family. His father and grandfather had served in the Royal Navy; his brother Robert Haswell was a mate on the *Columbia,* which left from Boston to become the first American ship to circumnavigate the world, and his half-sister Susannah (Haswell) Rowson was the author of *Charlotte Temple* and founder of a school for girls in Boston.[26] Both William and his brother Robert were talented draftsmen, but it is not clear where they acquired their training. They received an early education in Boston, but the Tory family was forced to move to England during the American Revolution.

Like his brother, William Haswell shipped out of Boston. He sailed to Batavia on the barque *Lydia,* keeping the voyage logs as first mate. In Batavia he became master of the snow *Elizabeth,* sailing to Manila and Guam and back to Manila. There he joined the *Charlotta* to Calcutta, and returned to Salem on the *Pallas* under its master John Dallings. Haswell's career path was unusual for a Salem mariner of the period. Unlike most seamen, Haswell apparently looked for new employment at each major destination. He kept his logs with him, for despite the different ship's owners and masters that he worked for, his four logs were bound together in Salem, his final destination. Dallings was a member of the East India Marine Society, and thus under obligation to donate his voyage records. Haswell might have been pleased to see his work of the past two and one-half years enter a library and museum, for the three earlier logs are bound with the required one.

Haswell, with his long family ties to the sea, was undoubtedly steeped in the conventions of maritime representation. Like other mariners in the Atlantic basin, Salem seafarers were intimately familiar with the *English Pilot,* a series of books that were continually in print from the first editions in 1671 until the early nineteenth century.[27] This series disseminated visual conventions for geographic representation. Each of the five parts of the *English Pilot* was devoted to a different region. Originally compiled by John Seller, royal hydrographer, the first book focused on Europe and was illustrated with 29 double-page

26. Frederic W. Howay, *Voyages of the 'Columbia' to the Northwest Coast 1787–1790 and 1790–1793* (Boston: Massachusetts Historical Society, 1941).

27. These books, as well as maps and atlases were easily available. For an overview of the market, see David Bosse, "The Boston Map Trade of the Eighteenth Century" in *Mapping Boston,* Alex Krieger and David Cobb with Amy Turner, eds. (Cambridge, Mass.: MIT Press, 2001), 36–55.

plates. In words echoed on the first page of the Salem voyage logs, the title page of the *English Pilot* explained its goals: "Describing the sea-coasts, capes, head-lands, bays, roads, harbours, rivers and ports together with the soundings, sands, rocks and dangers in the southern navigation upon the coasts of England, Holland, France, Ireland, Spain, Portugal, to the straits-mouth, and so off to the Western Islands. Shewing the courses and distances from one place to another: the setting of the tydes and currents: the ebbing and flowing of the sea." The title page of the second book, on the Mediterranean, emphasized the *Pilot's* visual resources and its eyewitness authority: "furnished with new and exact charts, draughts, and descriptions, gathered from the experience and information of divers able and judicious navigators." The third book was intended to ease "oriental navigation"; the fourth book, exploration of the Americas; and the fifth book, Africa.[28] Like the later founders of the EIMS, the compilers of the *English Pilot* recognized the value of their enterprise to their nation: "Published for the benefit of our country-men."

The maps and drawings in the many volumes and editions of the *English Pilot* standardized conventions of geographic representation that had been developing for over a century and presented the most current state of knowledge. But they were not perfect guides. Salem mariners carried their *Pilots* with them, using them for reference, and correcting them where they fell short.

The need for this was clear; despite expert sailing skills and centuries of charting the seas and coasts, geographic knowledge was still incomplete and this hindered trade. Salem mariners were continually frustrated. Dudley Pickman, the journal keeper of the ship *Anna*, frequently corrected a latitude or longitude on a published map, and warned that maps of Tappanooley on Sumatra could not be taken at face value: "The English E. I. [East India] Pilot shews a plan of this Bay, which however is totally inaccurate & affords no Idea of the Place."[29] On his voyage to Sumatra, George Nichols complained that "my Port of Destination Mucat not being describ'd in any of my Books, and its Latitude given by Several Persons not corresponding nearer than 12 miles embarras'd me very much & was oblig'd to proceed with great Caution." This was despite his

28. See the British Library Integrated Catalogue online for many of the editions of the *English Pilot*, http://catalogue.bl.uk.

29. Dudley Pickman, Log of the *Anna*, Salem to Sumatra to Boston, January 1801 to November 1801, in the East India Marine Society logs, Volume 1.

access to the most current knowledge: "The Charts which I have are English and the latest extant State the Coast about Mucat is very badly laid down & the winds & Weather not better described in the E. I. [East India] Directory. After several days of anxiety and Fatigue, came to anchor at Mucat May 14th 1802."[30] Lack of information could be distressing, and even dangerous. By sharing their newfound information, American mariners gained a safer, more competitive edge over the British.

And information was currency. The directions in the blank logbooks handed out to ship's masters requested specific information in the directions printed on the first page: "an account of the coin, weights and measures . . . with the imports, exports, and manner of transacting business . . . Whatever is singular in the manners, customs, dress, ornaments, &c. of any people." A number of the EIMS members followed these suggestions and wrote detailed discussions of local currency and valuations. James Deveraux, who commanded the ship *Franklin* from Salem to Batavia and Japan and back to Salem, provided fascinating directions on how to negotiate the complex Japanese requirements for trade, including impersonating Dutch traders by flying a Dutch flag.[31] George Nichols shared his disappointment in market conditions in Manila, noting the great quantity of European goods depressed prices for American goods.[32] On sailing to India, Nichols advised it was not worth trying to trade at Columbo or Pondicherry where he had little luck because of recent political changes, but to continue on to Madras, a more lucrative port.[33] Luther Dana warned of the dangers of trading in Sumatra, where one should seek permission of the local rajah. Dana observed, "I should not feel Safe in a vessel doing Business at any of the out ports without a Sufficient number of hands & arms on board to defend her in case of any difficulty or attempt to surprise. A strong and vigilant watch is at all times required."[34] It is clear that these journals were not

30. George Nichols, Log of the *Active*, Salem to Sumatra to Manila, December 1801 to March 1803, in the East India Marine Society logs, Volume 2, 122.

31. James Deveraux, Log of the *Franklin*, Salem to Batavia and Japan, December 1798 to May 1800, in the East India Marine Society logs, Volume 1.

32. George Nichols, Log of the *Active*, Salem to Sumatra to Manila, December 1801 to March 1803, in the East India Marine Society logs, Volume 2, 129.

33. George Nichols, Log of the *Active*, Salem to East Indies, September 1800 to September 1801, in the East India Marine Society logs, Volume 1, 558–64.

34. Luther Dana, Log of the *Recovery*, Salem to Sumatra, in the East India Marine Society logs, Volume 2, 200–1.

simply private memoirs; journal keepers expected their fellow ships' masters to read their words. When captains were venturing to new ports, they provided detailed descriptions. When they were following well-worn paths, they barely mentioned their experiences. About his stop on the way to India, Nichols was concise: "the manner of doing business in Madeira is so generally known, it is unnecessary to say any thing respecting it."[35]

Manners and Customs

Following eighteenth century practice of observing "the genius, character, manners, customs, bodily constitution, language, government and number of inhabitants," as the instructions to La Pérouse put it, some Salem captains recorded keen observations of their trading partners. Nichols described the physical aspects of people he met as he tried to locate new ports to open up trade with Salem vessels. He found the population of Columbo large, and "the people are of Midling Stature and in general darker complexion than the Natives of any other place I have been at in India, but their features and dress are not Materially different from the Jentoos in Bombay."[36] Dudley Pickman noted in Madras, "The natives are of different castes or religions. The Gentoos do not shave the upper lip and wear a mark on the forehead resembling sealing wax generally a single perpendicular line. The Malabar caste shave the upper lip and daub over the forehead with something resembling blue paint. The Moormen cast have no mark."[37]

These descriptions were frequently mixed with commentary that shows that American traders perceived strong cultural differences between their own culture, which they saw as based on hard work and rational religion, and that of the people they encountered. In reading their words, however, it is important to keep in mind their comments referred to the class of working men in each port, not the elites with whom they did business. In Madras, Nichols found people "much like the other Natives of India in being indolent and Inofensive." Regarding the customs of the people, "I can only observe that they possess

35. George Nichols, Log of the *Active*, Salem to East Indies, September 1800 to September 1801, in the East India Marine Society logs, Volume 1, 556.

36. George Nichols, Log of the *Active*, Salem to East Indies, September 1800 to September 1801, in the East India Marine Society logs, Volume 1, 561, 563–64.

37. Dudley Pickman, Log of the *Belisarius*, 1799–1800; quoted in Susan Bean, *Yankee India* (Salem, Mass.: Peabody Essex Museum, 2001), 95.

a great Deal of Superstition with Regard to their Religion &c."[38] Nichols echoed this observation on his voyage to Sumatra the next year: "They are Naturally a very lazy Indolent people, dirty in their Persons & scarcely any uniformity in their dress; on their heads they wear a handkerchief, done up a little like a Turban, and about their loins several yards of cloth which reaches a little below their knees, which is their only dress."[39] Luther Dana reported on Sumatra, "There is no such thing as hiring the Malays or Accheenese to labour they are too lazy and Indolent to handle their own pepper unless obliged too."[40] On trading in Manila, Bowditch noted "The natives are about as honest as their neighbours the Chinese; they stole several things from us, but by the goodness of the police, we recovered most of them."[41] Nichols complained "it is not prudent to intrust any of them with business of importance, without looking much after them, as it is the natural dispositions of the Natives of India to defraud at all opportunities."[42]

Despite the pervasive impression, the mariners must have recognized that many people were required to work hard. They recognized, for example, that while they and their elite trading partners lived in relative luxury—as Dudley Pickman observed, "Every gentleman keeps his palanquin"—this must have been very difficult on those who served them.[43] The palanquin clearly fascinated American traders. Many journalists remarked on it in their voyage logs. Five sea captains acquired one in 1803, and donated it to the East India Marine Society Museum on their return to Salem to use in the parades preceding their annual meeting.[44] William Haswell provided a drawing of a *Palanquin and Bearers* to illustrate the intriguing sight of a palanquin in use in India. Four laborers, with a distinctive topknot hairstyle and dressed only in a piece of cloth wrapped around their loins, carry the handles of the elaborate conveyance on

38. George Nichols, Log of the *Active*, Salem to East Indies, September 1800 to September 1801, in the East India Marine Society logs, Volume 1, 561, 563–64.

39. George Nichols, Log of the *Active*, Salem to Sumatra to Manila, December 1801 to March 1803, in the East India Marine Society logs, Volume 2, 124.

40. Luther Dana, Log of the *Recovery*, Salem to Sumatra, in the East India Marine Society logs, Volume 2, 202.

41. Nathaniel Bowditch, Log of the *Astrea*, Salem to Lisbon, Madeira, and Manila, March 1796 to May 1797, in the East India Marine Society logs, Volume 1.

42. George Nichols, Log of the *Active*, Salem to East Indies, September 1800 to September 1801, in the East India Marine Society logs, Volume 1, 563.

43. Dudley Pickman, Log of the *Derby*, 1803–04; quoted in Bean, *Yankee India*, 113.

44. The EIMS palanquin is reproduced and discussed in Bean, *Yankee India*, 79–81.

PALANQUIN and BEARERS

Fig. 9. William Haswell. *Palanquin and Bearers.* Logs of the *Elizabeth, Charlotta,* and *Pallas*, 1801–1803. Courtesy of the Phillips Library at the Peabody Essex Museum, Salem, Massachusetts.

their shoulders (fig. 9). Surely such backbreaking labor by the very poor must have challenged their ideas of the natives' work ethic. In Haswell's drawing, we see that visual culture was used to convey cultural as well as geographic information to other mariners. Haswell chose as his subject one of the most unusual, and thus frequently described, sights of contact with India, and uses it to convey potentially useful information about customs, caste, and class.

Religion was perhaps the primary cultural characteristic the Salem voyagers saw as distancing themselves from the people they met. The Americans were fairly sophisticated about the distinctions between the religious practices of their various trading partners, even if ultimately they characterized all non-Protestant practices with the same pejorative adjectives. In India, they were aware of Hindu practices (which they called Jentoo or Gentoo). On Sumatra, Nichols observed "They are of the Mahometan Religion, but not very Super-stitious, excepting in the food of which they are very much."[45] William A. Rogers noted that just north of the Malabar Coast he "Passed Mangalore, seaport of some importance . . . Inhabited by Gentoos and Mahomeddans. The Gentoos on their festivals carry their idols in triumph in a wagon, to the

45. George Nichols, Log of the *Active,* Salem to Sumatra to Manila, December 1801 to March 1803, in the East India Marine Society logs, Volume 2, 124.

wheels of which are affixed crooked iron hooks, on these they throw themselves and are crushed to pieces."[46]

And there was always a good measure of anti-Catholicism. Bowditch observed, "There are great numbers of Chinese at Manilla, but they are all obliged to become catholics."[47] George Nichols thought that if Madeira were "Inhabited by any other People than Portuguese it would produce, exclusive of the Wine, every Necessary of Life, instead of which they are dependent upon other Nations for almost every thing they want. I think this might be remidied by banishing the greater part of the many Priests & Friars, who serve only to oppress the Inhabitants & encourage Indolence."[48]

In most instances, trade went smoothly. In Sumatra, Dana reported "in these excursions we always met with the utmost attention & civility from the Inhab," which he attributed to American manners and honesty: "Probably that if we had treated them as Europeans in general are disposed to treat the meaner Casts of the Inhabitants of India we should not have had these priviledges & many others."[49] Dana showed unusual sensitivity to his trading partners' perspectives: "Sometimes traders get into a quarrel with the natives by the frauds used in their dealings with them. The natives do not easily forget it but embrace the first opportunity of doing themselves justice."[50]

The illustrations and written descriptions in the otherwise prosaic ships' logs provided a way to share cultural as well as geographical information as Salem mariners developed Asian and Pacific trade. Personal global experience helped develop American commercial networks.

Language of the Picturesque

Describing landscape was an everyday activity for ships' journal keepers. On the open seas they were required to record the weather, the currents, and

46. William A. Rogers, Log of the *Tartar,* September 1817–18, quoted in Bean, *Yankee India,* 153. Log in Phillips Library of the Peabody Essex Museum.

47. Nathaniel Bowditch, Log of the *Astrea,* Salem to Lisbon, Madeira, and Manila, March 1796 to May 1797, in the East India Marine Society logs, Volume 1.

48. George Nichols, Log of the *Active,* Salem to East Indies, September 1800 to September 1801, in the East India Marine Society logs, Volume 1, 556.

49. Luther Dana, Log of the *Recovery,* Salem to Sumatra, in the East India Marine Society logs, Volume 2, 201.

50. Luther Dana, Log of the *Recovery,* Salem to Sumatra, in the East India Marine Society logs, Volume 2, 200.

the stars that helped them plot their location. As they approached land they described in words and images the coastal features. Most of the time, their images primarily reflected geographic and topographic traditions. But the late eighteenth century was also the time when picturesque traditions of landscape representation became widespread in the Anglo-American world. Salem mariners were well aware of representation in both topographic and picturesque traditions and incorporated aspects of both into their drawings.

A brief look at merchants' and mariners' reading on aesthetics, as revealed by their charge records at Salem's Social Library provides insights into their artistic knowledge and level of sophistication.[51] Many members read Edmund Burke's philosophical treatise on the fine arts in the *Sublime and the Beautiful,* or Robert Dossie's analysis of the commercial potential for applied arts in *Handmaid to the Arts.*[52] Fresnoy's *Art of Painting* circulated, as did Nugent's *Grand Tour.*[53] Both of these provided Salem readers with education in classical and Renaissance arts. However, the most popular book on the arts in Salem was William Hogarth's *Analysis of Beauty* with its companion folio of plates, which was checked out by sea captains Jacob Ashton, William Cabot, and James King among others.[54] Rather than a history of arts or compilation of significant architectural sites, *Analysis of Beauty* provided a method of understanding the formal qualities of art and appreciating visual experience. Books on aesthetics and applied arts were held at other Salem libraries as well. Thus Salem mariners had many opportunities to become familiar with modes of representing landscapes.

Sometimes the aesthetic sophistication of a voyage's log keeper can be seen in his writing. Captain Benjamin Hodges, for example, kept track of the weather on his voyage to China as master of the *William and Henry.* Most

---

51. For a comparison with holdings on aesthetics in other libraries, see Janice G. Schimmelman, *Books On Art In Early America: Books on Art, Aesthetics and Instruction Available in American Libraries and Bookstores Through 1815* (New Castle, Del.: Oak Knoll Press, 2007). On sailors' literary culture and reading on the high seas see Hester Blum, *The View from the Masthead: Maritime Imagination and Antebellum American Sea Narratives* (Chapel Hill, N.C.: University of North Carolina Press, 2008).

52. Edmund Burke, *Philosophical Enquiry into the Origin of our Ideas of the Sublime and Beautiful* (London 1757); Robert Dossie, *Handmaid to the Arts,* 2nd ed. (London: J Nourse, 1764).

53. Charles Alphonse du Fresnoy, *The Art of Painting,* trans. William Mason (York, Eng., 1783); Thomas Nugent, *The Grand Tour* (London, 1749).

54. William Hogarth, *The Analysis of Beauty* (London, 1753).

entries are routine: "fair," "pleasant," "hot." Some are more elaborate, but still primarily descriptive, as the day the ship was loaded and ready and stalled in Salem harbor waiting for an auspicious beginning:

> Coald & much snow the Wind Northe
> Lying at Anchor in Misery Harbour
> at 6 AM Weighed Anchor & came to Sea
> the Wind NNW a large swell from ENE
> & very Coald[55]

But rare entries described the weather in more curious and aesthetic terms. As he approached Sumatra, Hodges noted: "Light winds & squally weather the water much discolloured but no bottom--- Middle part light breezes & Calm Lay by the Night, the Sea covered with Luminary Particles which in Washing decks covered them in a Romantick maner, on examination we found them to be small pieces of (Gilly) round the size of small bird shot."[56]

Sometimes the men commented on the beauty of the landscape, including their native land. Leaving Salem harbor for a Boston departure to Bombay, William Rogers recorded: "I had an opportunity of witnessing the beauty of the scenery for which the entrance of the port is so justly celebrated. It was a most delightful morning and nothing could have interrupted the enjoyment of the view which would have enriched the imagination of a Vernet."[57] Later, appreciating the beauty of Ceylon and the coast of India, Rogers "took sketches as I passed along."[58] George Nichols was also impressed with Ceylon: "in sailing this Coast, the land had a beautiful appearance, being very level & quite covered with Coconut Trees."[59] Nichols was delighted by Madeira:

> The best Season for visiting the Island is in the Summer when the weather is always warm and pleasant & the Isl[d] under a State of Cultivation. I never was more pleased with any place although it was in the Winter Season all the Time

55. Benjamin Hodges, Log of the *William and Henry,* Salem to Canton, December 1788 to 1790, Phillips Library of the Peabody Essex Museum. Entry for December 18, 1788.

56. Benjamin Hodges, Log of the *William and Henry,* Salem to Canton, December 1788 to 1790, Phillips Library of the Peabody Essex Museum. Entry for July 25, 1789.

57. William A. Rogers, Log of the *Tartar,* 1817–18, quoted in Bean, *Yankee India,* 143. Log in Phillips Library of the Peabody Essex Museum.

58. William A. Rogers, Log of the *Tartar,* 1817–18, quoted in Bean, *Yankee India,* 149. Log in Phillips Library of the Peabody Essex Museum. The sketches are reproduced in Bean, 150.

59. George Nichols, Log of the *Active,* Salem to East Indies, September 1800 to September 1801, in the East India Marine Society logs, Volume 1, 559.

Fig. 10. Benjamin Carpenter, *A View of Gingeram on the Malabar Coast.* Log of the *Hercules*, Salem to Calcutta, 1792–1793. Courtesy of the Phillips Library at the Peabody Essex Museum, Salem, Massachusetts.

of my being there. from the Roads you have one of the finest prospects imaginable; the great number of handsome Seats rising one above another almost to the summit of the highest mountains (which are frequently lost in the clouds) together with the beautiful verdure which appeared upon every part.[60]

"One of the finest prospects." With this phrase Nichols reveals his familiarity with the language of landscape aesthetics and the picturesque.

The illustrations that Benjamin Carpenter drew in his journals demonstrate familiarity with picturesque conventions of landscape. A small drawing that he labeled *A View of Gingeram on the Malabar Coast* illustrates the journal Carpenter kept in 1792–93, when he went to Calcutta as commander of the ship *Hercules* (fig. 10). Born in 1751, Carpenter was a career merchant mariner who engaged in sea trade from before the Revolution. He was among the first captains to go to Asia after direct trade began in 1784; and, since he also served in the role of supercargo on other voyages, he had a sharp eye for commercial possibilities in addition to maritime skills.[61]

Carpenter's Gingeram is a phonetic transcription of Janjira. The island fortress Janjira was legendary for remaining unconquered—first repelling rival Asians, then later attempts by the Portuguese, Dutch, French, and English.

60. George Nichols, Log of the *Active,* Salem to East Indies, September 1800 to September 1801, in the East India Marine Society logs, Volume 1, 556.

61. For a discussion of Carpenter's career as well as extensive excerpts from his Journal of the *Ruby,* 1789–90, see Bean, *Yankee India,* 44–63.

Said to originate in the fourteenth century, it was fortified and shaped into its present form in the seventeenth century. The structure towers ninety feet above the sea, with thick stone walls rising more than forty feet directly out of the sea at high tide. There are nineteen rounded bastions heavily armed with cannon, connected by a rhythmic line of dark windows piercing a crenulated horizontal battlement. The fort's interior held a palace, mosque, and deep well for access to fresh water.

Though the island is sited about a mile out to sea, there is little in Carpenter's drawing to suggest that the fort is surrounded by water. The space is compressed and the fort reads as connected to the hilly shore rather than isolated by the sea. The landscape is constructed from a highly decorative series of lines; these hatchings change direction as needed to suggest sunlight and shadow on the planes of the architecture and landscape elements. Bursts of circles that make up the clouds animate the sky and lighten the ominous mood of the fort standing guard over the bay.

Carpenter's drawing style seems to embrace picturesque ideas of balance. He plays against each other the light and the dark, the organic and the geometric, the moving and the still. The stylistic approach of the drawing seems to echo the linear treatment Carpenter would have seen in the engravings that accompanied the many illustrated voyage narratives that circulated in Salem. While some fine engravings, such as the La Pérouse title page (fig. 1) are built from barely discernible lines and stipples that read as tonal areas, other engravings retain the prominence of their linear components. Though Carpenter seems not to have had the classical training nor belonged to subscription libraries as other sea captains did, he would have had exposure to aesthetic and classical ideas through his very active participation in the civic life of Salem. Along with Hodges and many other sea captains, he was a member of the Essex Freemasons, a member of the Salem Marine Society, and a founding member of the East India Marine Society to which he donated several significant items. His landscape drawings, executed in a style easily readable because its visual language derived from widely accessible engraved illustrations, made his first-person accounts more vivid for his brother mariners.

As the title page of La Pérouse's atlas illustrates, geographic and cultural representations in both words and images transmitted global knowledge—which was essential for trade and wealth in seaports such as Salem. Access to this knowledge became a bond that formed and united an elite class of merchants and mariners. Visual culture played a significant role in circulating this information, in both print and manuscript. Visual culture was essential to the transmission of information along personal networks, which were established various ways—through kinship, business relationships, membership in social or professional organizations, or other venues that were gradually becoming more institutionalized in the Early Republic. Salem's mariners both collected and created visual representations, and shared them along these dense and interconnected networks for their mutual benefit and that of American commerce.

* * * * *

I thank Martha McNamara, Georgia Barnhill, Jessica Lanier, Emily Murphy, Joanne Lukitsh, and Josilyn DeMarco for their comments on earlier versions of this essay. I am also very appreciative of the research librarians who suggested sources and located specific editions of books known to have circulated in Salem, particularly Jean Marie Procious and Gus Sousa of the Salem Athenaeum, and Barbara Kampus, Kathy Flynn, Irene Axelrod, Andrew French, and other librarians of the Phillips Library of the Peabody Essex Museum. I also thank members of the Salem State University Academic Writers Group: Peter Walker, Elizabeth Kenney, Avi Chomsky, Nancy Schultz, and Elizabeth Blood.

Fig. 1. Attributed to William Burgis, *A North East View of the Great Town of Boston.*
London, ca. 1723. Photograph Courtesy of the Peabody Essex Museum, Salem, Mass.
Object ID #1163.

Navigation, Vision, and Empire: Eighteenth-Century Engraved Views of Boston in a British Atlantic Context

KEVIN MULLER

IN THE WINTER and spring of 1722–23, an enticing series of advertisements appeared in the Boston-based *New England Courant*. Addressed to the gentlemen of the town, these notices informed readers of plans afoot to publish a view of Boston taken from the vantage point of Noddles Island, that is, from a position to the northeast looking back across the harbor towards the town.[1] The proposed engraving would be based on a drawing by William Burgis, a relative newcomer to Boston, who at various times in his life identified himself as a draftsman, painter, and innkeeper.[2] His drawing, the advertisements explained, was available for inspection at William Price's Map and Print Shop. Those who found it to their liking were directed to Thomas Selby's Crown Coffee House, located a few short blocks from Price's establishment, where subscriptions for its publication were being taken and, incidentally, where Burgis was then lodging. Upon completion, the print would be available for purchase at Price's shop. Soliciting subscriptions for a print was typical for the time, even in London where a much larger print market existed, because it helped those producing a print judge whether enough public interest existed to warrant the expense of publishing it.[3] In the case of the Boston view, the cost would have had to cover the expense of Burgis's handwork, and of sending Burgis's drawing to London to be engraved, as was noted in the advertisements.

1. *New-England Courant*, 8 October 1722; 12 November 1722; and 13–27 May, 1723, quoted in Henry H. Edes, "The Burgis-Price View of Boston," in Colonial Society of Massachusetts, *Transactions, 1906–07*, 11 (1910): 246–47. Edes suggests that this print was never produced, however, it was; see John W. Reps, "Boston by Bostonians: The Printed Plans and Views of the Colonial City by its Artists, Cartographers, Engravers, and Publishers," in *Boston Prints and Printmakers, 1670–1775* (Boston: The Colonial Society of Massachusetts, 1973), 33–35.

2. On Burgis and his works, see Richard B. Holman, "William Burgis" in *Boston Prints and Printmakers*, 57–81.

3. On subscriptions for prints, see Timothy Clayton, *The English Print 1688–1802* (London: Yale University Press for The Paul Mellon Centre for Studies in British Art, 1997), 52–57.

Evidently enough gentlemen did subscribe, because in December of 1723, an advertisement announced that the print was available for purchase at Price's shop (fig. 1).[4] The medium-sized engraving (measuring 9½ inches by 12¾ inches) offers a sweeping prospect of Boston from Fort Hill on the left to Charlestown on the right. The spires of the town's important buildings are silhouetted against the horizon, each numbered and identified in the print's legend, as are the masts of several sailing ships. These ships, along with other, smaller vessels, either ply the placid waters of the harbor or rest at anchor. Under a tree in the foreground, an artist, perhaps Burgis himself, sits sketching. Compositionally, Burgis organized the scene according to the familiar conventions of picturesque landscapes by seventeenth-century French painters such as Claude Lorrain and Gaspard Poussin, with a low horizon line, clear back-, middle- and foregrounds, the use of repoussoir (the tree to the right that helps establish a sense of spatial recession) and foreground staffage (the small figure sketching).

The team of Burgis, Price, and Selby must have had high hopes for this print, because it was among the first views of Boston ever engraved. However, they soon came to realize their subscribers wanted a decidedly different view. In the same notice advertising the sale of the completed northeast view, plans for a second print were announced.[5] This view would depict Boston from the southeast, perhaps from Governors, Bird, or Castle Island (although no specific location was noted). Once again Burgis made a drawing, it was displayed at Price's shop, Selby took subscriptions, and the print was engraved in London.[6] In August of 1725, Price advertised that this second Boston view was now available for purchase at his shop.[7]

Like its predecessor, this "New and Correct Prospect"—as it was identified in the advertisements—offered a view of Boston from across the waters of Boston Bay, taking in the broad sweep of the opposing shore. As per the printsellers' indication, however, the viewpoint is now shifted to the south so that Long Wharf is centered in the composition and Charlestown no longer pictured (fig. 2). Also like the first print, this second image includes specific

4. *New-England Courant,* 23 December–6 January, 1723–24, quoted in Edes, 247.

5. Ibid. See also Reps, 34.

6. John Harris is identified on the finished print as the engraver. On Harris, see Clayton, 21; and Edes, 253–54.

7. *New-England Courant,* 17 July–28 August, 1725, quoted in Edes, 247.

Fig. 2. John Harris after William Burgis, *A South East view of ye Great Town of Boston in New England in America*, London, 1725. I. N. Phelps Stokes Collection, Miriam and Ira D. Wallach Division of Art, Prints and Photographs, The New York Library, Astor, Lenox and Tilden Foundations, New York, N.Y.

architectural landmarks that are numbered and identified in a legend, although many more structures are now included. The second print is also much larger than the first, measuring an impressive 24½ by 52½ inches, so large that it needed to be printed with three separate plates. But where the second view diverges most noticeably from the first is in its composition. This scene is not organized according to the landscape conventions of the picturesque. Gone are the first print's low vantage point, framing foliage, orderly recession of space, and scale-establishing foreground figure. Instead, the second view is seen from an elevated position hovering somewhere out and above the waters of Boston harbor, an effect Burgis achieved by eliminating landmasses from the foreground, positioning the horizon nearer to the top of the frame, and dramatically foreshortening Long Wharf, so that it thrusts precipitously down and to the right. Also different from the first view are the second's inconsistencies in scale and perspective, which suggests it to be a composite scene, created from at least two distinct vantage points.

Of the two views produced by Burgis, Price, and Selby, the earlier version was neither reprinted nor repeated by later colonial artists. Moreover, its present-day rarity—only one copy is known to exist—suggests few were ever

Fig. 3. Headpiece engraved by James Turner from *The American Magazine and Historical Chronicle*, Boston, 1744. Courtesy, American Antiquarian Society, Worcester, Mass.

printed.[8] By contrast, the second, larger view was evidently more popular; it was reissued, with updates, in 1736 and 1743, and later colonial artists are known to have used Burgis's new compositional approach, depicting the town from a similarly elevated vantage point.[9] James Turner's simple engraving for the headpiece of *The American Magazine and Historical Chronicle* presents the town with Burgis's bird's-eye view (fig. 3), and Paul Revere, in his 1770 engraving (fig. 4), likewise places the viewer high in the air, looking out towards the town and down onto Long Wharf, where British troops can be seen disembarking. Only in the decades following the American Revolution did artists change their point of view and their aesthetic, returning to picturesque landscapes seen from eye level. However, these post-revolutionary artists now used an inland vantage point, planting their viewer firmly on American soil.[10] Thus

8. According to Reps, writing in the early 1970s, the only known copy exists at the Essex Institute (now the Peabody Essex Museum); see Reps, 33.

9. For a catalogue of these images, see Reps, 38–49.

10. On nationalism and landscape painting, see Angela Miller, *The Empire of the Eye: Landscape Representation and American Cultural Politics, 1825–75* (Ithaca, N.Y.: Cornell University Press, 1993), 1–20, 65–105.

Fig. 4. Paul Revere. *A View of Part of the Town of Boston in New-England and Brittish Ships of War Landing Their Troops!* Boston, 1770 Courtesy, American Antiquarian Society.

the elevated view from a point east of Boston was meaningful for Bostonians during those years they defined themselves in relationship to—and loyal to—lands in the east. In other words, Burgis's southeast view was meaningful to Bostonians when Bostonians were British.

To date, scholars have rightly interpreted this print as a document of early Boston's changing urban topography, as an expression of civic pride, and as a visual manifestation of a mercantilist ideology.[11] What has been left unanswered by these approaches, however, are questions surrounding the circumstances of the print's production, how those circumstances shed light on the print's intended audiences, and finally, how the print served to forge a sense of local and transatlantic identity. Based on where the print was advertised and sold, we can conclude its primary audience was Boston's merchants. How this fact affected Burgis as he shaped his southeast view has not been analyzed, to the detriment of our understanding of this print. I argue that, in targeting

11. For these interpretations, see Reps, 33–42; and John Hallam, "The Eighteenth-Century American Townscape and the Face of Colonialism," *Smithsonian Studies in American Art* 4: 3/4 (Summer/Fall 1990): 144–62.

merchants, Burgis designed his document to speak explicitly to them, first by fitting it to their particular skills of gleaning data from pictorial sources, and second by fitting it to a merchant's particular worldview. As to the first point, regarding the unique visual literacy of merchants, Burgis's composition actually mirrored the mechanics of a specific type of pictorial document, one familiar to merchants: sea charts. Early modern sea charts represented a visual culture of and for merchants (among others) and a close analysis of Burgis's composition reveals the logic of such charts underlie the southeast view's elevated viewpoint. As to the second point, regarding the merchants' worldview, I argue that the print's high, southeast perspective—that of a disembodied eye approaching Boston from a point east of its harbor—encoded a certain east-west duality that would have been evident to merchants. This dual subjectivity allowed merchants, more than others, to locate Boston, and by extension themselves, within the larger maritime geography of the British Atlantic. Even more, it allowed merchants to see themselves as both subjects and creators of the British Empire. Although this dual subjectivity was not originally available to all viewers, I argue that, eventually, the format of the southeast view came to stand for all of colonial-era Bostonians' collective view of themselves, because in the end, it could accommodate the subject positions of different viewers who, though perhaps not merchants themselves, shared a similar understanding of the mechanisms of empire.

The advertisements Burgis, Price, and Selby placed in the *New England Courant,* specifically solicited subscriptions from the town's "gentlemen." Where Burgis's drawing was put on display for examination, where subscriptions were taken, and where the print was sold, suggest that the category of "gentlemen" the publishing team sought consisted primarily of the town's merchants. The *New England Courant* was a Boston-based publication that included local and overseas news and listed vessels arriving into and departing from Boston Harbor.[12] Price's print shop, where Burgis's drawings were displayed, was located on King Street near the Townhouse, a focal point for merchant activities (the Townhouse is the structure above the lower case "a" in fig. 5).[13] Merchants met

---

12. See for example, the May 6–13, 1723 issue of the *New-England Courant.*

13. On the Townhouse, see Martha J. McNamara, " 'In the Face of the Court . . .': Law, Commerce, and the Transformation of Public Space in Boston, 1650–1770," *Winterthur Portfolio* 26:2/3 (Summer-Autumn 2001): 126–31, 134–35.

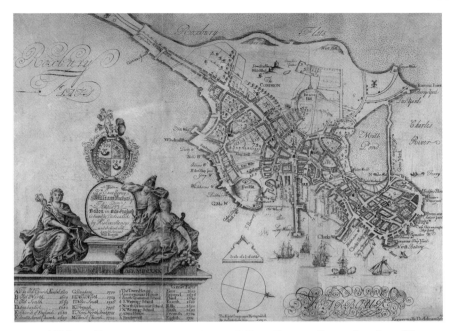

Fig. 5. William Burgis. *To His Excellency William Burnet, Esqr., this plan of Boston in New England.* [Boston: Sold at the Crown Coffee House, 1728]. Detail. Boston Athenaeum, Boston, Mass.

at the Townhouse daily to share the latest local, regional, and international news and negotiate financial instruments. Price's nearby shop was part of the merchants' information network, a place where they could purchase maps and sea charts, both of great importance to maritime commerce.[14] Thomas Selby's coffeehouse, where subscriptions were taken, was located further down King street, at the foot of Long Wharf, and was also a haunt of local merchants, where Selby's food and drink helped lubricate the agreements they struck with seacaptains, shipowners, and each other.[15] It was at Selby's that merchants could have spoken to Burgis directly when they subscribed to the first print, and it was there we can imagine they encouraged him to do a second view, one representing the town and its harbor from their own perspective.

14. For a short list of the items for sale at Price's shop, see *New England Courant,* 17 July–28 August, 1725 quoted in Edes, 247. For a brief biography of Price see Edes, 257–62.

15. On Selby's coffeehouse, see David W. Conroy, *In Public Houses: Drink and the Revolution of Authority in Colonial Massachusetts* (Williamsburg, Va.: University of North Carolina Press for The Institute for Early American History and Culture, 1995), 88–96. On Selby himself, see also Edes, 254–57.

Burgis, Price, and Selby were right to target Boston's merchants as their primary audience. Merchants possessed the capital needed to subscribe to the southeast view, and they possessed a desire for the information it presented. As historian Phyllis Hunter has shown, starting in the late seventeenth century merchants began to displace Puritans from positions of authority in New England port towns, and with them brought an ethos of capitalism.[16] While the success of individual merchants depended on a number of personal factors, the collective rise of merchants in the eighteenth century throughout the British Atlantic stemmed also from the very nature of the British Empire.[17] Today, the term "British Empire" invokes thoughts of colonial territories ruled by and subordinate to a central authority located in London, but this framework really only characterizes the British Empire of the nineteenth century. During the late seventeenth and for much of the eighteenth century, Britons living in North American colonies and elsewhere in British-controlled areas understood themselves as citizens of an empire defined more by commerce and trade than by the authority of the Crown or Parliament in London. Moreover, the empire in which they lived was primarily Atlantic in its geographic scope. Key figures in the creation and maintenance of this commercial empire were merchants. Essentially middlemen who organized trade between ports spread out across the Atlantic, merchants not only employed a range of producers, processors, and transporters, they more importantly satisfied consumers'—and their own—growing demand for the most recent and fashionable goods.

As Hunter also shows, starting in the late seventeenth century, New England merchants began to supplant Puritan values with a culture of gentility.[18] Given the growing consumption of objects that signified gentility, especially among Boston's elite, Burgis, Price, and Selby were right to create their first view of Boston according to picturesque conventions. In the 1720s, the pic-

16. On the rise of a capitalist ethos in New England, see Phyllis Whitman Hunter, *Purchasing Identity in the Atlantic World: Massachusetts Merchants, 1670–1780* (Ithaca, N.Y.: Cornell University Press, 2001), 3–12, 71–106.

17. The following discussion is drawn from P. J. Marshall, "Introduction" in *The Oxford History of the British Empire,* vol. 2 *The Eighteenth Century,* ed. P. J. Marshall (Oxford, Eng.: Oxford University Press, 1998) 1–22; Jacob M. Price, "The Imperial Economy, 1700–1776," in Ibid., 78–104; Patrick O'Brien, "Inseparable Connections: Trade, Economy, Fiscal State, and the Expansion of Empire," in Ibid., 59–63; and Jeremy Black, *The British Seaborne Empire* (New Haven: Yale University Press, 2004), 56–87.

18. On merchants and gentility, see Hunter, 71–146.

turesque aesthetic was coming into vogue as a signifier of a genteel sensibility, as elites in England began to appreciate and prefer landscapes rendered
according to the picturesque conventions found in the paintings of Lorrain
and Poussin.[19] Perhaps Burgis, Price, and Selby believed the time was right
for a picturesque view of Boston made to appeal to local gentlemen who took
their cultural cues from their Georgian counterparts in England. That Boston
merchants ultimately rejected the picturesque northeast view in favor of the
pictorially challenging view from the southeast, and that the latter had such
longevity up until the time of the American Revolution, suggests that even as
colonial merchants aspired to gentility, and surrounded themselves with the
markers of it, they also desired a visual culture that spoke their language—a
language associated with their own success in Boston—and one that, importantly, enabled them to claim their place within the local hierarchy, as well as
that of the burgeoning British Empire.

This unique visual language is the distinguishing feature of the southeast
view, and is that which most dramatically differentiates it from its predecessor.
How it spoke directly to merchants was in its reliance on the visual mechanics
of early modern sea charts. Like these sea charts, the southeast view represents
Boston from more than one vantage point. Indeed, whether the print is hung
on a wall like a painting or laid on a table like a map, the viewer cannot but
help find his or her focus pulled in two different directions: out towards the
town and down onto the vessels that fill the harbor below. These two viewing
positions roughly correspond to what we today commonly call plan view and
elevation view. In the former, an image functions like a map, representing the
contours of its subject from above, from a bird's-eye view looking downward.
In an elevation view, by contrast, an object is represented as if seen from ground
level so as to reveal its height, width, and profile. Plan and elevation views
are familiar to anyone who studies architectural renderings of buildings, for
buildings must be presented in both formats to be fully comprehended in two
dimensions. But plan and elevation views of buildings are presented separately,
while in early modern sea charts, the contours of coastlines seen from above,

19. On the introduction of the picturesque to early eighteenth-century English elites, see
Ellis Waterhouse, *Painting in Britain, 1530–1790*, 4th ed., (New York: Penguin Books, 1978),
154–56. On the rise of the picturesque, see Ann Bermingham, *Landscape and Ideology: The English Rustic Tradition, 1740–1860* (Berkeley, Calif.: University of California Press, 1986), 57–85.

and their elevations as seen from shipdeck, are often presented simultaneously. In the southeast view, Boston and its surrounding environs are represented more or less in elevation view, from a lowered position, allowing the unique features of both the townscape and the surrounding landscape, such as the church steeples and hills, to appear more or less in profile. Yet the shoreline and the wharves are represented from a much elevated vantage point, as in plan view. As a result, the distinct skyline profile of 1725 Boston is clearly visible, but so are the undulations of the shoreline and the position and relative sizes of the town's various wharves—features that could only be accurately discerned from above. All can be readily comprehended in Burgis's southeast view. Such is the logic of the sea chart, combining in a single document the world seen both by a ship's captain and by the gull hovering high above his head. Because the southeast view combines these two distinct viewing positions into a single image, however, we see neither a true elevation of the distant landscape nor a complete plan of the harbor, and as a result, the beholder's viewing position continually oscillates between looking out and looking down.

For modern viewers, this viewing experience may seem awkward, even illogical, but it was quite familiar to eighteenth-century merchants, because of their use of sea charts and their knowledge of the processes of navigation. While merchants were themselves mostly land-based, many had been taught the fundamentals of navigation by tutors, and many sailed aboard family-owned vessels as a form of apprenticeship.[20] Some even captained vessels themselves.[21] Thus they knew from firsthand experience that successful navigation at sea requires two distinct kinds of visual information: the plan and elevation views of the coasts to which they traveled.[22] By mentally combining overhead views of the contours of landmasses with eye-level views of what one should expect

20. Private schools in colonial Boston often taught commercial skills, including surveying, navigation, and bookkeeping, see Robert Francis Seybolt, *The Private Schools of Colonial Boston* (Cambridge, Mass.: Harvard University Press, 1935), 10, 14, 86–7. Obadiah Brown, a member of the Rhode Island family of successful merchants, served as supercargo on his brother James's ships. Obadiah subsequently became a merchant, owner of sloops, brigantines, and schooners see James B. Hedges, *The Browns of Providence Plantations: The Colonial Years* (Cambridge, Mass.: Harvard University Press, 1952), 5–8.

21. James Brown, founder of the Rhode Island merchant dynasty, began his career as a ship's captain see Ibid., 2.

22. On the basics of navigation, see Alfred Gell, "How to Read a Map: Remarks on the Practical Logic of Navigation," *Man*, n.s. 20:2 (June 1985): 271–86.

to see from the deck of one's vessel, a mariner could reasonably establish where at sea he was located.[23]

Early modern sea charts were a unique form of navigational visual culture that combined both plan and elevation views into a single image. Collections of sea charts, known as sea atlases, were first published in great number by the Dutch, starting in the sixteenth century.[24] However, as Englishmen took to the seas in ever greater numbers over the course of the seventeenth century, English publishers, most notably John Seller, began to provide such dual-focused charts for his seagoing countrymen in English language sea atlases.[25] For example, John Seller's 1675 *Atlas Maritimus* included a chart for the Cape of Good Hope that combines plan and elevation (fig. 6). The bottom two-thirds of the chart presents the coastline as seen from above, as in plan view, yet upon careful examination one sees the coast contours are actually outlined with hills and mountains as they would be seen from out at sea. The top third of the chart is a detailed view of the topographical features that surround Table Bay as seen on approach from the sea, thus in elevation view, yet the vantage point is elevated in order to show the viewer the shape of the harbor and important anchorage sites in relation to these topographical features. By combining plan and elevation views, Seller's chart thus enabled a mariner to know the specific land formations that would be visible as he sailed along this portion of the African coast and into Table Bay. Not all charts included multiple views; those that did usually represented coastlines the shape of which were not self-evident when viewed from sea level and thus were difficult to navigate. However, by combining both plan and elevation information together, sea charts could be used reliably for navigating such shores, allowing sea captains to situate their vessel in relation to particular bays and harbors. He could also understand

23. This procedure is the one typically used for coasting. Out of sight of land, mariners estimated the distance and direction sailed, measured the angle of the sun to determine latitude, and calculated longitude via mathematical equations in order to determine their ship's position. Until the invention of the chronometer, however, this procedure was prone to error, so landfall sightings—navigational elevations—were particularly important.

24. For an well-illustrated overview of early modern sea charts and sea atlases, see John Blake, *The Sea Chart: The Illustrated History of Nautical Maps and Navigational Charts* (London: Conway Maritime Press, 2004), 8–27

25. For Seller's reputation and other developments in maritime cartography in seventeenth- and eighteenth-century Britain, see A. H. W. Robinson, *Marine Cartography in Britain: A History of the Sea Chart to 1855* (Leicester, Eng.: Leicester University Press, 1962): 34–113.

Fig. 6. "Chart of Cape Esperanza" from John Seller's *Atlas Maritimus*. London, 1675. Courtesy of the John Carter Brown Library at Brown University, Providence, R.I.

his position within a larger geography, one either implied by the scope of an entire atlas that covered a specific region or, more practically, one implied by the context of the voyage. For example, upon viewing the chart of Table Bay, the mariner could position himself along the African coast and/or at a point in a longer voyage, perhaps one from England to India.

Although the images in early modern sea charts were functionally useful, they are no longer part of our visual culture. The charts and images published in Seller's atlases were plagued with inaccuracies, so much so that in the eighteenth century the English Admiralty took to sponsoring the creation of more accurate documents, which in turn required more precise surveys of coastal regions and a more accurate method of indicating coastal features.[26] As

26. On the development of more accurate survey methods, see Ibid., 47–70.

a result, by the late eighteenth century, Seller's type of sea chart more or less disappears, in large part because a regular system for rendering topographical features, most notably contour lines, had been developed. Mariners could now examine a chart that was executed entirely in plan view and create an accurate navigational elevation in his mind's eye from wherever his location offshore. However, for much of the seventeenth and eighteenth centuries, dual-focus sea charts were among the primary visual tools available for planning and sailing voyages to unknown coasts and harbors. Land-based scholars tend to overlook the substantial importance of sea charts, perhaps because the advent of radar and global positioning satellite systems have led us to forget their use. But they were the key tool of seventeenth- and eighteenth-century navigation, and therefore of commerce, and thus they were of real familiarity to Burgis's audience of merchants.

It would appear that when the merchants of Boston encouraged Burgis to create a second view of their town, they did so because they wanted an image that would allow them to see themselves and Boston from their own perspective, which is to say, from a navigational perspective. Indeed, the southeast view can be read in ways similar to Seller's chart of the Cape of Good Hope. In elevation, the hills and townscape identify a landfall in profile that is recognizable precisely because Boston was like none other. In plan, the anchorage spots and shoreline facilities are visible, especially Long Wharf. With its space organized like a sea chart, the southeast view encouraged its merchant-viewers to locate Boston within a larger set of transatlantic coordinates, one of a network of ports and harbors scattered around the Atlantic, a geography merchants knew well from studying maps and charts and directing sea captains in their employ to particular destinations.[27] In fact, the Burgis, Price, and Selby print explicitly reinforces a conceptualization of Boston within a broader imperial geography, as its text asserts by noting that the town is located "in the Latitude of 42 and 24 [degrees] North, and 71 Degrees West from London; the variation

27. As Martin Brückner has shown, map literacy increased dramatically among the general population of colonial British North America, but of course merchants had a vested interest in maps; see Martin Brückner, *The Geographic Revolution in Early America: Maps, Literacy, and National Identity* (Williamsburg, Va.,: Omohundro Institute of Early American History and Culture, 2006), 16–50. Incidentally, in the same advertisement published in the *New-England Courant* announcing the availability of the southeast view, William Price also announced a "new chart of the British Empire in North America," quoted in Edes, 247.

of the Needle about 9 degrees West." In other words, according to this print Boston existed only in relation to the fixed coordinates of London.

Burgis's use of a high, hovering, and disembodied eye gazing upon Boston town from a point east has another significance, however. Consider for a moment a merchant-viewer scrutinizing the print at Price's print shop. This merchant would have had the uncanny experience of looking back on himself, as his vision was directed along the receding Long Wharf and back to the Townhouse, the print's focal point and precisely where he was presently standing. At this moment, our merchant was simultaneously the observer and the observed. Like the print's double vantage points of looking out and looking down, this dualistic viewing position is also somewhat unstable, as this viewer could not help but oscillate between the two positions of watching and being watched. However, this duality and instability was important for the merchant-viewer, because it ultimately corresponded to his roles as simultaneously both subject and creator of the British Empire.

In seeing himself as observed, the merchant-viewer adopted the viewing position of the imperial administrators who oversaw the colonies from a distance and regulated the workings of the empire through laws and statutes that affected the merchant's everyday life. The most important of these were The Acts of Trade and Navigation.[28] These series of laws and statutes were implemented by Parliament in the second half of the seventeenth century and were designed to standardize transoceanic trade in lands under British sovereignty, as well as those simply under British control. They effectively made possible the maritime empire in which Boston's merchants operated because they put into place a relatively level playing field for all British citizens engaged in trade, regardless of where they lived, their religion, or their ethnic affiliation (although location, kin, and religious ties could be advantageous). The system known as mercantilism subsequently developed, whereby colonies shipped raw materials, in British-owned vessels, manned with mostly British crews, to Britain in exchange for manufactured commodities. Little direct trade was permitted with the foreign powers; instead, all raw materials and finished goods had to first pass through British ports. In addition to trade between Britain and her colonies, an extensive lateral trade developed, most notably between New England and the West Indies, but also between different ports located around

28. The following discussion draws on Marshall, 11–12; and Price, 81–91.

the Atlantic. Because handsome profits could also be made by smuggling—a vocation at which many Boston and New England merchants excelled—Parliament and the Crown placed customs officials and other officers in major ports to keep an unwavering eye on the activities of merchants.[29]

The merchant-viewer of Burgis's print would have been reminded of this administrative presence, this ever-gazing eye, by the clustering of British men-of-war in the print's foreground. These large ships can be identified by their three-masted rigs, flags, pennants, gun portals, and elaborate hull decorations.[30] The center ship, identified in the print's text as the "station ship," is a type of naval vessel commonly found anchored in colonial ports for defensive and administrative purposes.[31] But in addition to defense, this naval presence also served to deter smuggling, which, lucrative though it may have been for New England merchants, did not serve the good of the empire. Indeed, as a result of the viewer's elevated vantage point, the naval ships in the print's foreground show the intimidation meant by their placement, forming as they do a kind of gate to the harbor, regulating the passage of merchant ships as they sail to and from the town.

If the elevated viewing position of the print enabled merchants to see Boston, and themselves, as subject to an imperial administrative surveillance, this viewing position also, and perhaps more importantly, allowed merchants to see themselves as playing an important role in the creation of this empire. They could look upon the town as a product of their own creation and values, the result of hard work and prosperity that had enabled them to physically shape the town's urban topography.[32] While most of Boston's smaller domestic and commercial structures are rendered generically, some forty-seven specific structures associated with merchants are accurately delineated, numbered, and described in the legend below.[33] For example, amidst the jumble of houses

29. For an example of smuggling, see the activities of Thomas Hancock as discussed in W. T. Baxter, *The House of Hancock: Business in Boston, 1724–1775* (Cambridge, Mass.: Harvard University Press, 1945), 69–73, 114–18.

30. On eighteenth-century men-of-war, see E. H. H. Archibald, *The Fighting Ship in the Royal Navy, AD 897–1984,* rev. ed. (Poole, Eng.: Blandford Press, 1984), 33–50.

31. On station ships, see John W. Gordon, *South Carolina and the American Revolution: A Battlefield History* (Columbia, S.C.: University of South Carolina Press, 2003), 26–7.

32. On merchants and the changing urban fabric of New England, see Hunter, 84–88, 113–24.

33. By identifying specific structures in the print, Burgis, Price, and Selby might hope that individuals associated with these structures would purchase the print. Alternatively, they might have included the identifying numbers and labels only after subscriptions were paid.

hugging the distant hilltops, several well-to-do merchant's homes are pictured, including that of Andrew Faneuil.[34] Equally prominent along the town's
skyline are structures associated with a range of Christian faiths, including
the Quaker Meeting House, the Anabaptist Meeting House, and the Anglican King's Chapel. These too speak to the power of Boston's merchant's class,
whose ethos of capitalism transcended religious difference, thereby cultivating
religious diversity.[35] In fact, the construction of many of these houses of worship had been financed by local merchants.

The same is true of the many commercial structures made visible by Burgis's
lifted perspective. Many of these carefully rendered buildings had been funded,
directly and indirectly, by merchants, helping to make Boston a prosperous
port town. The shipyards, too, pictured along the shoreline, were essential for
the success of Boston's commercial life. Here local merchants commissioned
shipwrights to build vessels according to specifications based on needed cargo
carrying capacity and intended ports of call.[36] The print's text underscores the
success of Boston's shipbuilding industry, explaining that in the year 1723 over
700 ships had been built in the town's shipyards.[37] The most prominent and
unique commercial structure pictured is Long Wharf. Measuring an impressive 1800 feet long (nearly one-third of a mile), Long Wharf was used to dock
ships of great burden and draft so their cargos could be transferred directly to
and from their holds and into one of the over fifty warehouses built along the
wharf's length.[38] Completed in 1710, its construction had, perhaps predictably,
been financed by Boston's merchants, who also owned the warehouses located
on it and, we can imagine, many of the ships tied alongside. As the print's text
also notes, in the year 1723 an impressive 1000 ships annually cleared its harbor
(that's more than three each day) destined for England and the West Indies
laden with cargos of forest, sea, and agricultural products.[39] Returning vessels
brought desired manufactured goods and (hopefully) profit for the merchants

34. On Faneuil's house, see Hunter, 120–21.

35. On King's Chapel and Brattle Street Church, see Hunter, who notes that a diversity of
faith represented a shift away from Puritan control of Boston, 92–96.

36. On shipyards and shipbuilding, see Joseph A. Goldenberg, *Shipbuilding in Colonial America* (Newport News, Va.: The Mariners Museum, 1976), 68–76, 82–95.

37. The print's text is quoted in Edes, 248–49.

38. On Long Wharf, see "Long Wharf," *Bulletin of the Business Historical Society* 9:2 (March
1935): 17–22.

39. Quoted in Edes, 248–49.

who organized the voyage, which had enabled them to build the city in their image. Thus, Long Wharf, and the other wharves projecting from the shoreline, facilitated the prosperity of Boston.

Merchant-viewers of the southeast print would have also looked upon the many vessels pictured in the harbor with interest, which explains the care Burgis took in their rendering. Boston was home to a variety of sailing craft, because its merchants shuttled mixed cargoes to different ports around the Atlantic, each port possessing different harbor conditions and facilities.[40] Due to these challenges, a diverse fleet was necessary in order to knit the empire together through maritime trade. Boston merchants would have easily recognized the types of vessels depicted by Burgis, for example the small, single-masted sloops pictured throughout the harbor.[41] Because merchants often commissioned ships from local shipwrights according to requirements determined by intended cargo and potential ports of call, they were highly sensitive to their design, construction, and function.[42] They could easily have inferred the kind of voyages the vessels pictured in the harbor would be undertaking. They would have known that the sloops were ideally suited for coasting, that is, for navigating within the sight of land, because their fore-and-aft rigging, which has sails set in line with the keel of the boat, meant they could be confidently skippered along landmasses where the wind direction shifts regularly as a result of irregular landforms and offshore breezes.[43] As a result, sloops typically voyaged from Boston north to Maine and south to the West Indies.[44] They would have inferred similar information upon seeing the three-masted, square-sterned frigate to the right of the men-of-war (and elsewhere in the print). Frigates, unlike sloops, carried sails on spars, which are set perpendicular to the keel and thus sail best with a strong and consistent wind blowing from

40. On cargo carried by Boston-based vessels and the complexities of the transatlantic trade, see the career of Thomas Hancock as discussed in Baxter, 45–91.

41. On types and rigs of eighteenth-century sailing vessels, see Roger Morris, *Atlantic Seafaring: Ten Centuries of Exploration and Trade in the North Atlantic* (Camden, Maine: International Marine Publishers, 1992), 101–23.

42. On merchants commissioning ships, see Goldenberg, 82–86.

43. For a brief discussion of the sailing characteristics of a fore-and-aft rigged vessel, see Douglas Phillips-Birt, *A History of Seamanship* (London: George Allen and Unwin, 1971), 120, 128–29.

44. See William Armstrong Fairburn, *Merchant Sail* (Center Lovell, Maine: Fairburn Marine Educational Foundation, Inc., 1945), 1: 237. Depending on their size, sloops could also make transatlantic voyages, as did Thomas Hancock's *Sarah* in 1733; see Baxter, 57.

astern. For this reason they were typically sent on long-distance transatlantic routes, such as Boston to London or Bristol and back again.[45] As a result of knowing the kinds of voyages different vessels were designed to make, Boston's merchants looking at the southeast view could imaginatively connect the town to other ports in the Atlantic through the journey of specific ships, and thus see in the print the activities that ultimately created the British Empire.

If in the 1720s the primary audience for the southeast view was the town's merchants, within two decades this format came to stand in for a more inclusive, collective portrait of the city and its inhabitants. In 1743, James Turner engraved the headpiece of *The American Magazine and Historical Chronicle* (fig. 3), an image that depicts Boston from an elevated vantage similar to that found in the Burgis, Price, and Selby print. This locally published magazine included within its pages a range of essays and articles on literature, science, politics, and the arts, interspersed with verses of poetry, all intended to make the publication appealing to a diversity of readers other than merchants.[46] How was it possible that a view originally meant to encode the point of view of the town's merchants came to appeal to a greater percentage of its citizens? The answer lies in the fact that the activities of Boston's merchants brought together a range of producers and consumers who could share in their worldview and enjoy the nature of the empire they had helped create.[47] Acting as middlemen, merchants purchased raw materials—furs, grains, fish, and lumber—from local New England suppliers. These commodities were then shipped, perhaps in a locally-built vessel, manned with a New England crew, to distant ports where they would be sold. A new cargo, possibly including agricultural commodities (sugar or molasses from the West Indies) and/or manufactured goods (Irish linen, Chinese porcelain, or furniture from London), was loaded onboard and the ship returned to Boston. These items were then purchased by local individuals who either processed particular commodities (for example, molasses was distilled into rum) or who simply sold the manufactured items (such as a porcelain tea set) directly to New England consumers. Thus, from start to end, the merchants of Boston required the assistance of many others, includ-

45. On the sailing characteristics of a square-rigged vessel, see Phillips-Birt, 120–21.

46. *The American Magazine* was published for just over three years, from 1743 to 1746. On *The American Magazine,* see Moses Tyler, *A History of American Literature* (New York: G. P. Putnam's Sons, 1883), 305.

47. For an overview of the scope of trade and the individuals affected, see Price, 78–103.

ing producers, processors, handlers, and consumers of all kinds, who in turn stood to benefit from their activities. These minor, but in no way less significant players in the wheels of colonial commerce, could ultimately embrace an image that represented Boston as a prospering maritime empire because they too benefited as a result of merchant successes. As long as Bostonians saw themselves as citizens of a maritime empire, they could subscribe to this view of themselves and their town.

That the southeast view and its subsequent derivatives remained meaningful to Bostonians as long as they saw themselves as citizens of the British Empire suggests that this format was one that spoke to an imperial, rather than a national identity. Indeed, as we have seen, the format of these images drew on the visual culture and processes of early modern navigation, allowing merchants and then others to see Boston and themselves within large geographic and imperial frameworks that were ultimately maritime in nature. Given that merchants operated throughout the empire according to more or less the same procedures, and that maritime commerce structured the interaction between individuals and communities dispersed around the British Atlantic, it is perhaps not surprising that we find the same pictorial conventions used to depict other British port towns in the eighteenth century, for example, a 1712 engraving of Plymouth (fig. 7) and a 1719–21 print of New York (fig. 8), the latter also by William Burgis. These prints, and others like them, have generally been interpreted as part of a linear development of topographical views, a European landscape genre that has its origins in the fifteenth century and culminates with the nineteenth-century diorama.[48] However, when seen in the geographic context of the British Empire, we find a surge in the publication of such prints starting at the end of the seventeenth century, and then an abrupt end to that surge at the end of the 1700s, about the same time that Britain's empire shifts away from a maritime structure. While topographic in nature, I contend that these prints were meaningful for the inhabitants of these towns at this particular time in history for the same reasons that the Burgis, Price, and Selby southeast view was relevant to Bostonians for much of the eighteenth century. They allowed viewers to see themselves and their community

48. For example of this approach, see Ralph Hyde, *Gilded Scenes and Shining Prospects: Panoramic Views of British Towns, 1575–1900* (New Haven: Yale Center for British Art, 1985). Interestingly, Hyde omits views of towns in the colonies.

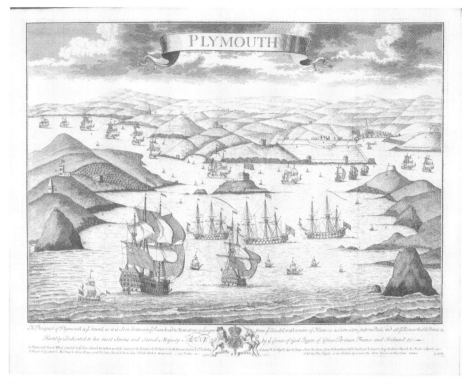

Fig. 7. Johannes Kip. "Plymouth," plate 57 from volume two, part one of *Nouveau Theatre de la Grande Bretagne*. London: David Mortier, 1716. Yale Center for British Art, Paul Mellon Collection, New Haven, Conn.

within a maritime, imperial framework and did so precisely because the imagery of these prints was also predicated on the common-shared visual culture associated with early modern navigation.

Atlantic navigation remained important for all these individuals and communities well into the nineteenth century; however this pictorial format could not convincingly encode a maritime imperial framework once London became the imperial center of the British Empire. For Bostonians, that process began in the late 1760s and included the event depicted by Paul Revere in his aforementioned engraving (fig. 4). In 1768, the royal governor of Massachusetts requested that royal navy ships and soldiers be sent from England to Boston in order to reestablish the rule of law among the town's citizens, who, as he

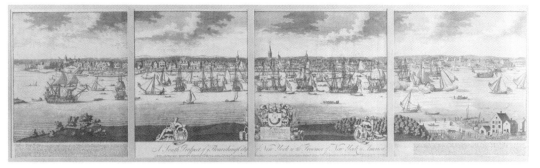

Fig. 8. John Harris after William Burgis, *A South Prospect of ye flourishing city of New York in the Province of New York in America.* London, ca. 1719. Print Collection, Miriam and Ira D. Wallach Division of Art, Prints and Photographs, The New York Public Library, Astor, Lenox and Tilden Foundations.

saw it, refused to follow the instructions and orders of royal customs officials charged with enforcing the laws of trade.[49] Two years later, Revere rendered the town and its harbor according to the familiar, dual-focused perspective established decades earlier in Burgis's southeast view. However, instead of filling the fore- and middle- grounds of his print with merchants vessels, Revere replaced them with men-of-war, troop transports, and soldiers disembarking. If the merchant vessels included in earlier prints had enabled the citizens of Boston to understand themselves as both creators and subjects of the British Empire, this overwhelming presence of royal authority signaled that Boston's place in the empire had changed. Bostonians now saw themselves as subjects, and as such could be punished like disobedient children for their transgressions by an imperial authority located across the Atlantic in London. When seen within the context of the pictorial tradition established by Burgis, representing merchants and the entire community of Boston as possessing agency and self-determination, the implications of this substitution must have been immediately clear to Bostonians, especially those who shared Revere's politics. The events of the American Revolution ultimately shattered the imperial framework for Britain's North American colonists, and in turn the pictorial paradigm established by the Burgis, Price, and Selby southeast view became

49. For a short account of this incident, see Edmund S. Morgan, *The Birth of the Republic, 1763–89*, rev. ed. (Chicago: University of Chicago Press, 1977), 35–46.

meaningless. In the following decades, a new nationalist discourse emerged, one that coincided with renewed interest in the picturesque and emerging ones of the sublime, all of which encouraged Americans to turn to other pictorial strategies by which to render their landscape, and by extension, their own identity.

*   *   *   *   *

I would like to thank Georgia Barnhill, Martha McNamara, Eric Kimball, and especially Diane Zuliani for their helpful and constructive advice. This essay is part of a book-length study tentatively entitled Envisioned Communities: Colonies, Empires, and Visual Culture in the British Atlantic, 1600–1776.

Buildings, Landscapes, and the Representation of Authority on the Eastern Frontier

KEVIN D. MURPHY

IN HIS SEMINAL CONTRIBUTION to the *New England Begins* catalogue from 1982, Robert Blair St. George starts his article, "'Set Thine House in Order': The Domestication of the Yeomanry in Seventeenth-Century New England," with the rumination that "Perhaps the historian's persistent lack of attention to space is rooted in an unhealthy positivism. Space, after all, implies to the modern mind a kind of phenomenological absence." St. George goes on to argue against such a conception of space and to suggest that indeed the very organization of the yeoman's property—comprising his house, farmyard, and outbuildings—was "crucial both to his economic livelihood and to his psychological stability."[1] At the time of St. George's writing, the extent and significance of the so-called "spatial turn" in cultural studies could scarcely have been imagined. Some of the texts that have been key to postmodern reconsiderations of the nature of space and its implications in social and political transformations had only just been published or had yet to appear, at least in English, and had yet to exert what would become their important influence on such fields as geography, social and political history, architectural history, and others.

Later in the 1980s, however, the writings of Henri Lefebvre, Michel Foucault and other North American and Continental theorists would profoundly alter the ways in which space was conceptualized.[2] Space went from being generally thought of as an empty stage on which meaningful action might take place to being considered as something at once produced by knowledge and mobilized

---

1. Robert Blair St. George, "'Set Thine House in Order': The Domestication of the Yeomanry in Seventeenth-Century New England," (1982) in Dell Upton and John Michael Vlach, eds., *Common Places: Readings in American Vernacular Architecture* (Athens, Ga. and London: University of Georgia Press, 1986), 336–37.

2. For instance, Henri Lafebvre's *La Production de l'Espace* (1974) appeared in English translation in 1991 (Oxford, Eng. and Cambridge, Mass.: Blackwell) and Michel Foucault's *Surveiller et Punir: Naissance de la Prison* (1975) appeared in translation as *Discipline and Punish: The Birth of the Prison* (New York: Pantheon, 1977). For an overview of the spatial turn, see: Denis Cosgrove, "Landscape and *Landschaft*," *GHI Bulletin* 35 (Fall 2004): 57–71.

in relation to social struggles and other contests. Correspondingly, the system of perspective, in use since the Renaissance, could no longer be thought of as a neutral technique for representing three-dimensional space on a flat surface, but instead had to be considered as historically and geographically contingent, and its implications for the construction of an ideal, immobilized viewer had to be taken into account. Moreover, the ways in which buildings and landscape elements positioned viewers in relation to the objects of their "gazes" were increasingly considered in light of a general skepticism about the politics of sight, that is to say, as a consequence of a new attentiveness to the power relations embedded in the act of looking itself.[3] These intellectual developments of the last twenty-five years make it possible to pursue St. George's suggestion, made in *New England Begins* (and as he himself has done subsequently), to consider how space, rather than acting as a neutral ground devoid of political importance, was instead constructed through social interactions and became a site for self-fashioning as well as for social and political positioning.

While St. George transformed our understanding of the landscape of seventeenth-century New England, his insights can apply to other places and times where the spatial turn offers some interpretative models that might be applied to familiar objects, in this case, the eastern frontier of northern New England during the Early Republic, and particularly the District of Maine prior to its separation from Massachusetts in 1820. Specifically, I would like to consider how the shaping of the natural and built environments, as well as some early representations of that process, were intended to fix social relations in a period of considerable struggle. Further, I would like to evaluate—to the extent possible given the character of the historical record—how efficacious such attempts to use landscape, architecture, and representation for political purposes truly were.

In Maine at the turn of the nineteenth century, two sites provided particularly rich opportunities for staging power relations in architecture and landscape designs: the settled towns of southern coastal Maine that were extensively rebuilt in the period to give them more definite centers, and the frontier settlements just then being established. In both contexts, elite men and women used their economic and cultural resources to give physical expression to their

3. This tendency is most incisively and comprehensively described and critiqued in Martin Jay, *Downcast Eyes: The Denigration of Vision in Twentieth-Century French Thought* (Berkeley, Calif. and Los Angeles: University of California Press, 1994).

Fig. 1. Jonathan Fisher, *A Morning View of Bluehill Village, September 1824*, oil on canvas, 25⅛″ x 52¼″, 1824–25. Farnsworth Art Museum, Rockland, Me. Museum purchase, 1965.1465.134.

self-perceptions as superior in their communities. In doing so, they brought to bear two architectural and landscape models: the townhouse and the country seat as both had been developed in more southern sections of New England. Personal and trade associations between Maine settlers and their Massachusetts counterparts provided one means for the transmission of design concepts to the frontier. Builders' guides—both American editions of English volumes of the 1760s and 1770s, as well as slightly later works by American authors— also contributed to the transfer of ideas from more established New England towns and cities to the District of Maine.[4]

The town of Blue Hill was one community on the eastern frontier that was built up in the Early National period along the lines of nucleated villages in Massachusetts, and it is depicted in Jonathan Fisher's large painting entitled "A Morning View of Bluehill Village, September 1824" (fig. 1). Fisher (1768– 1847) was originally from Dedham, Massachusetts, and was the son of a Revolutionary War widow who had funded his Harvard education largely through weaving and with the assistance of fairly wealthy relatives. Fisher's education at Harvard was fortuitous since the college was in the late eighteenth century

4. Richard M. Candee, "Maine Towns, Maine People: Architecture and the Community, 1783–1820," in Charles E. Clark, James S. Leamon, and Karen Bowden, eds., *Maine in the Early Republic: From Revolution to Statehood* (Hanover, N.H. and London: University Press of New England, 1988), 29.

Fig. 2. Jonathan Fisher House, Blue Hill, Maine, showing 1814 addition. Tad Goodale photo.

the primary center for the study of perspective,[5] a subject in which the budding minister excelled and of which he made use when he was settled in Blue Hill as the town's first permanent Congregational minister in 1796.[6] Early in his tenure at Blue Hill, Fisher produced elaborate drawings for his own house and other architectural projects and began to establish himself as a professional designer. His representational skills enabled him to position himself as a cultural and religious authority in the new town, where white settlers had only arrived in the mid-1760s. In 1814, Fisher added a massive two-story block to his earlier story-and-a-half house (fig. 2), again with the aid of elaborate drawings, and even a model (now lost). Although the new house took years to finish on

5. James F. O'Gorman, *The Perspective of Anglo-American Architecture: Notes on Some Graphic Attempts at Three-dimensional Representation in the Colonies and Early Republic* (Philadelphia: Athenaeum of Philadelphia, 1995).

6. Fisher received an invitation to become minister at Blue Hill on October 5, 1795, according to his diary entry for that day, although he had preached in Blue Hill during the summer months in previous years.

the interior, on the exterior it proclaimed its designer/builder's conversancy with the classical tradition through the detailing around the front door and with the wide frieze below the roof.[7]

A decade after its completion, Fisher would depict his enlarged house in one of the very few surviving landscape paintings in oil on canvas from Maine dating to before 1830. On September 15, 1824 Jonathan Fisher recorded in his diary that he had that day carried his camera obscura to a hill on the outskirts of Blue Hill, his home on Maine's Penobscot Bay, and "sketched the outlines of a view of the village." He spent the next evening enlarging the design, working from the original drawing, and in the following days stretched and primed the canvas. Meanwhile, getting down the view of the village in a drawing continued to occupy Fisher: in mid-October he was making a stiff paperboard surface "to lay paper on when sketching a landscape" and working and re-working the drawing itself.[8] At the very end of October (the 28th) he "went over the pencil marks with the pen." Transferring the image to canvas, however, had to wait until the following spring when on the nineteenth of May, 1825, Fisher announced to his diary: "Finished my view of Bluehill village."[9]

The result of this project, which stretched over some eight months, was Fisher's best-known work.[10] "A Morning View of Bluehill Village" is an image of the many transformations that had occurred in the town, and indeed throughout New England, in the years since 1796. The picture's perennial appeal may derive in part from its close correspondence to a romanticized image of the prototypical New England village, developed in the nineteenth century. That prevalent stereotype of neat white houses grouped around a meetinghouse and village green bears little resemblance to actual colonial settlements. Such images do, however, correspond to the nucleated villages that emerged in the

7. The chronology of drawings for the house is laid out in Abbott Lowell Cummings, "The House the Parson Built," *Old-Time New England*, Vol. 56, No. 204 (April-June 1966): 91–107.

8. Diary entries for October 13 and 15, 1824. Throughout the text, diary references are to the typescript translation now in the Blue Hill Library, Blue Hill, Me. This discussion of Fisher closely follows the text of my book, *Jonathan Fisher of Blue Hill, Maine: Commerce, Culture, and Community on the Eastern Frontier* (Amherst, Mass.: University of Massachusetts Press, 2010).

9. On April 19, 1825 Fisher wrote in his diary: "Began to sketch on canvas a view of Bluehill village."

10. The painting is in the collection of the William A. Farnsworth Museum and Library, Rockland, Maine (FM). In Fisher's time, his town's name was written as one word ("Bluehill") whereas today it is customarily written in two words ("Blue Hill"). Except when quoting directly from Fisher, or referring to a period title, the modern form is used here.

Early National period and were celebrated in literature and works of visual art, starting in the 1820s, the very moment that the social order the villages were supposed to make manifest was being challenged by historical change.[11] Fisher's painting serves just this ideological function of representing order and stability—indeed, almost timelessness—in the face of manifest challenges to the institutions and social groups in which he had participated since the 1790s. The artist's insistent rendering of boundaries—wood fences and stone walls—seems an ill-fated attempt to contain a community that was growing, changing, and increasingly questioning the authority of the Congregational church and its minister. The picture inscribes Fisher's conception of order onto the space of Blue Hill at the same time that it uses the system of perspective to create order in the representation itself.

During the decades leading up to the completion of Fisher's Blue Hill picture, the town had been settled and Fisher had played important roles in founding many of its cultural, religious, social, and educational institutions, from the library to the singing school, from the Academy to the Sabbath School association. The same quarter century had also witnessed the larger transformation of Maine from a "District" of Massachusetts to an independent state in 1820. The area's changed political status reflected its enormous population growth from 1760 when a variety of factors, including the exhaustion of land and timber further south in Massachusetts, had begun to push settlers into the Northern New England "hill country" south of the White Mountains and east of New Hampshire's Lake Winnepesaukee.[12]

At the turn of the nineteenth century, the eastern shores of Penobscot Bay, where Blue Hill is located, were at the northern edge of the thinly-settled hill country. The town of Bucksport, at the head of the Penobscot River, was the gateway from the west to a spit of land—the Blue Hill peninsula—that runs some thirty-five miles southeast to Eggemoggin Reach, which separates the mainland from Deer Isle which lies on the other side. Situated on the

11. Joseph S. Wood, *The New England Village* (Baltimore: The Johns Hopkins University Press, 1997).

12. David C. Smith has borrowed the definition of the hill country from Harold Wilson, *The Hill Country of Northern New England* (New York: Columbia University Press, 1936) in his *Studies in the Land: The Northeast Corner* (New York and London: Routledge, 2002). The first chapter ("The Changing Landscape of Maine to 1820") is a useful overview and originally appeared as chapter one in Clark, Leamon, and Bowden, eds., *Maine in the Early Republic*.

peninsula, southeast of Bucksport, the town of Blue Hill, like the rest of the Penobscot Bay region, was almost entirely uninhabited by whites until the 1760s. After that time settlers were drawn there and even further "downeast" by the possibility of procuring available land. In addition to the land itself, this eastern frontier also held out the prospect of valuable natural resources, like fish and timber, to be exploited for profit, which constituted another draw for people from further south in New England.[13]

In the post-revolutionary period up to the moment of statehood in 1820, the District of Maine gained nearly a quarter million inhabitants, many of whom were farmers and others who participated in shipbuilding and maritime trade, both of which prospered in Maine, although after 1800 political and economic instability caused periodic disruptions to industry and commerce. The Embargo Act of 1807, the Non-Intercourse Act of 1809, and the War of 1812 all imposed limitations on American international trade, with varying degrees of severity, and all interrupted Maine shipbuilding and shipping in different ways, creating hardships for many in the recent coastal settlements. Blue Hill was among the Maine towns whose shipbuilding industry was threatened by the national government's policies regarding international trade and that formally protested against the Embargo, with Jonathan Fisher sitting on the committee that drew up the resolution.[14]

Fisher, who commented rarely on political events in his diary, recorded salient information regarding the War of 1812 in a commonplace book, in which he copied a line from the Boston *Weekly Messenger* in 1813: "District of Maine, distressed for want of provisions," probably because it resonated with his own experience. At about the same time, he noted that "Hunger prevails in some sections of our District. A woman and two children have died of it in Frankfort [a nearby town on the Penobscot River]. Our own bread allowance

13. Charles E. Clark, *The Eastern Frontier: The Settlement of Northern New England, 1610–1763* (Hanover, N.H. and London: University Press of New England, 1983), 354–55; Jamie H. Eves, "The Acquisition of Wealth, or of a Comfortable Subsistence': The Census of 1800 and the Yankee Migration to Maine, 1760–1825," *Maine History* Vol. 35, No. 1–2 (1995): 6–25.

14. A useful overview of the impact of international conflict on Maine shipowners and merchants is found in Joyce Butler, "Rising Like a Phoenix: Commerce in Southern Maine, 1775–1830," in Laura Fecych Sprague, ed., *Agreeable Situations: Society, Commerce, and Art in Southern Maine, 1780–1830* (Kennebunk, Me.: The Brick Store Museum, 1987), 15–31; Mary Ellen Chase, *Jonathan Fisher, Maine Parson, 1768–1847* (New York: Macmillan, 1948), 236; Smith, *Studies in the Land*, 3–5.

is but ½ of our usual supply, and, therefore, we eat with particular relish what we have." Fisher also copied into his commonplace book newspaper articles on both the War of 1812 and on contemporary political events in Europe, particularly the Napoleonic wars. In his journal he made explicit the connection between his two favorite topics: "I believe [the War of 1812] to be unjust on our part and greatly impolitic, a war which, I fear will issue in the subjection of America to Bonaparte, the despot of Europe [. . .]" Later, Fisher exclaimed to his journal in 1815 that he was "In consternation through a report that our vessels are condemned and to be taken by the British to Halifax,"[15] underscoring the centrality of maritime trade to the District of Maine. Fisher was undoubtedly troubled by the international conflict that disrupted the flow of settlers to the eastern frontier and the livelihoods of those who were already there, and he remained conservative in his politics. He was among those Maine residents whose opposition to Jefferson's Embargo and whose horror at the seizure of the nearby town of Castine by the British in 1814 sealed his association with the Federalist party.[16]

Fisher's painting of Blue Hill village constitutes a very persuasive argument for the parson's centrality in the place to which he devoted most of his life, not the least of all because he uses perspective to represent metaphorically his social and religious authority in spatial terms. Taking up a position from which to sketch on the hill opposite his house, Fisher was able to construct a scene that put his own residence at its center. Indeed, in the painting his farm occupies a spot very near to—if not dead on—the vanishing point of the composition. The orthogonal lines of the perspective system Fisher employed all recede to that single vanishing point. The Jonathan Fisher house sits, in the painting, just to the right of the center of the horizon line, at the top of what is now known as Tenney's Hill, at a higher point than even the spired meeting house. By setting up his camera obscura near Mr. Treworgy's house, Fisher was able to compose his view of Blue Hill so that it would emphasize his own crucial

15. The commonplace book was titled "National and Political" by Fisher and is now in the collection of the Jonathan Fisher Memorial, Blue Hill, Me. Also see: Diary entry of 1813 or 1814, quoted in Chase, *Jonathan Fisher*, 247, and Diary entries of 6/27/1812 and 4/7/1815.

16. On Federalist opposition in Maine to the War of 1812, and its impact on the statehood movement, see Ronald F. Banks, *Maine Becomes a State, The Movement to Separate Maine from Massachusetts, 1785–1820* (Somersworth, N.H. and Portland, Me.: New Hampshire Publishing Co. and Maine Historical Society, 1973), 57–66.

position in the place, if not his panoptic view of the village and its inhabitants. The fact that Jonathan Fisher painted his town at the moment at which he did, at the point when it had accumulated the institutions and fine residences that made a place a "village" in the Federal period, suggests his awareness of the process of establishing a settlement. The painting also demonstrates the degree to which its artist considered himself central to that process.

While in the Blue Hill painting Fisher captured the experience of view- ing the village, the 1814 addition to his house enhanced the prospect over the settlement at the head of the bay. Fisher's first house had been oriented in the traditional way, facing south, and thus away from Blue Hill. The addition, however, shifted the orientation of the main façade to the road (at the west). Nevertheless, in the addition Fisher made far more of the view of the village since the new parlor at the front enjoyed an elevated prospect over the town to its north. The rows of apple trees in the orchard to the north of the house seemed to trace the sight lines from the parlor windows over the settlement at the head of Blue Hill Bay. In other words, the view from the north side of town toward his own house, which Fisher captured in the painting, was returned by the gaze of the house's inhabitants over the village below.

The dynamics of viewing, as captured in Fisher's painting of the new settle- ment of Blue Hill, a growing commercial juncture on the edge of the Atlantic, reflected the young Jonathan Fisher's conception of himself as an important, if not *the only*, cultural and religious authority in the place. What distinguished Fisher from other settlers of the eastern frontier were precisely his cultural ambitions and the kit of intellectual and artistic tools he brought with him to Blue Hill. In a newly-established place, and at a politically and economically precarious moment, Fisher deployed an array of self-representations to posi- tion himself as a member of the local elite. Understanding how those projec- tions of the self succeeded or failed to establish Fisher's place in the commu- nity provides a window onto the larger question of how space was mobilized in contests for authority in early America.

A Morning View of Bluehill Village was the most succinct statement Jona- than Fisher ever provided of his view of the ideal Puritan settlement. In it, he makes order out of a landscape which—even if it wasn't quite in a state of chaos—was nonetheless a place that was changing in every possible way during the eventful decades in which he was the parson there. In some respects, Fisher was resilient to change, for instance, when he capitalized on growing markets for the home products he sold to advance his family's economic standing. In other ways, for example with respect to his Federalist politics and with regard to church discipline, he refused to soften his positions and ended up by driving members of his congregation away from the Church and failing to respond to political and religious transformations. Fisher could not, as the picture of Blue Hill illustrates, relinquish his image of the harmonious Puritan village. The new houses, the vessels under construction, the churches springing up in opposition to the Congregational meetinghouse, all of these elements of the growing, changing and prospering village are held in place in Fisher's picture of Blue Hill thanks to his use of perspective; none of them to any great degree disrupts the fundamental order of the place. The painting is the visual fulfillment of Jonathan Fisher's wish for how Blue Hill would develop, of how a traditional view of place could accommodate change.

Maine's elite of the Early National period were well aware of the influence that material things could wield in a bid for authority on the local level. However, Jonathan Fisher was quite rare—with respect to those who deployed imagery for political, social, and religious purposes—in that he made landscape paintings. Other members of the elite had their portraits painted, built high-style houses and laid out elaborate grounds around them as ways of claiming status locally, both in Maine's more established towns and on the frontier. In the older settlements, for instance in southern and coastal York County, such architectural and landscape statements were incorporated into village improvements of the Early National period. On the frontier, ambitious buildings and grounds produced jarring juxtapositions with the generally modest architecture that had been planted on the newly-cleared land.[17]

The great frontier houses enjoyed a relationship to the surrounding buildings that recalled the ways that grand eighteenth-century houses had related to their neighbors: "The eighteenth-century mansions," writes Richard Bushman, "had risen like bright sentinels of culture above the surrounding rough, dark houses of the common people." By the nineteenth century, Bushman

---

17. The generally modest character of American houses, and particularly those in frontier regions, is discussed on the basis of the 1798 direct tax lists by Carole Shammas, "The Housing Stock of the Early United States: Refinement Meets Migration," *William and Mary Quarterly* 3rd Series, Vol. 64 (July 2007): 549–89.

Fig. 3. Coventry Hall, York, Maine (1794–6) and the Judge Jonas Clark House, Kennebunk, Maine (addition, 1800–03), from William E. Barry, *Pen Sketches of Old Houses* (1874).

suggests, the general level of refinement in houses of all ranks had increased. Mansions were thus, in many places, not the anomalies that great eighteenth-century houses had been, but simply larger versions of what people at different economic levels all aspired to, and to some degree attained.[18] Bushman's generalization may apply to the early nineteenth-century mansions of Maine's more established port towns, Portland among them, but on the eastern frontier the eighteenth-century model seems to have persisted. There, in the absence of well-established settlements, the grand houses of the Early National period stood for exceptional wealth and cultural ambition well beyond the means of most settlers. Moreover, they show how the spaces of the frontier settlements became battlegrounds in contests over economic resources, as well as cultural, social, and political authority.

Of the many examples of ambitious village seats that might be understood as concretizations of status claims made in the long-standing communities of southern Maine during the Early National period, several houses designed and built by the housewright Thomas Eaton (active 1794–1831) in York County stand out. The first of these (in this case, only attributed to Eaton) is Coventry Hall (1794–6, fig. 3), the residence of Judge David Sewall and "York Village's only elaborate, completely new mansion of the Federal era."[19] Architectural historian Richard M. Candee has compared Coventry Hall to the elaborate

18. Richard L. Bushman, *The Refinement of America: Persons, Houses, Cities* (New York: Alfred A. Knopf, 1992), 142.

19. Richard M. Candee, "'The Appearance of Enterprise and Improvement': Architecture and the Coastal Elite of Southern Maine," in Sprague, ed., *Agreeable Situations,* 75.

urban houses designed around the same time by Boston architect Charles Bulfinch (1763–1844) and Connecticut architect and author Asher Benjamin (1773–1845). In York, Eaton followed the lead of these city architects in interpreting for the New England context the Roman neoclassicism developed during the eighteenth century in Great Britain by the Adam brothers and other designers. Thus Coventry Hall possesses a five-bay façade with center entrance surmounted by a fanlight, a balustrade at the roof, and ionic pilasters that run from basement to roof cornice and divide the elevation into three parts, all Adamesque elements. These neoclassical features are constructed, however, of the locally-favored building material—wood—rather than the masonry used for ambitious houses by urban architects in Britain and North America.

Even though he was building in a village, Eaton drew more directly from designs for country seats than from townhouse plans. This tendency is seen in the forms of the house itself, but more significantly, in its placement on the landscape. Judge Sewall signaled his social position through the sheer scale of the house, with its stylishness that associated it with the recent residences of other wealthy New Englanders, and through the way his house was sited in relation to the village center. Coventry Hall sat just outside the village—which already in the Early Republic had the reputation of being an old, established place—on the northeast side. Situated on a slight rise, the house addressed the village across a terraced yard, surrounded by a fence with posts surmounted by urns. The orientation of the house was not to the road but instead to the southwest towards the village, which comprised a cluster of houses and public buildings, including the famed eighteenth-century gaol, which it faced more or less directly. A few years after the completion of Coventry Hall, a debtor's cell would be added to the gaol and a new courthouse built nearby in recognition of the town's status as the county seat, a role that it played until 1832. A visual connection was thus established between the house and the expanding village, and the position of Coventry Hall on a rise above the town center metaphorically represented the relationship Judge Sewall occupied with respect to the townspeople: he was in the top two percent of taxpayers in York County in 1816, hence somebody of substantial means,[20] and he had a socially authoritative and prestigious occupation. The siting of Sewall's elaborate resi-

20. Candee, "'The Appearance of Enterprise and Improvement'," 71, 75; Candee, "Maine Towns, Maine People," 41, 45–46.

dence made materially manifest his position of superiority with respect to the community in York Village; in other words, it spatialized his standing in relation to other townspeople who could scarcely have ignored his house, which was an important component of the group of new buildings that added to the significance of the town center.

It is certainly plausible to assume that the house's formal qualities—its refined classical details, smooth wood façade and more—and its self-conscious siting with respect to the village center would have been understood by others to embody a claim for its owner's importance and authority. Indeed, the multiple implications of having an elevated view had been understood since the mid-seventeenth century, and the topic of commanding views had been discussed in "country house painting, poetry and landscaping throughout the seventeenth and eighteenth centuries." The command implied by the term "prospect," "was as much social and political as spatial."[21] Thus, Judge Sewall's gaze from his fine residence, across his fenced yard, and over the village would have been understood as a metaphor for his role as a legal overseer of the town and county and for his economic superiority in the community.

Similar to Coventry Hall in design and relationship to its site is the major addition made by another judge, Jonas Clark, to his house in Kennebunk between 1800 and 1803 (fig. 3). Local tradition that credits Eaton with the design is substantiated by formal similarities between the two buildings. The addition, which was like Jonathan Fisher's 1814 project in that it really constituted the construction of a new house for which the existing one became an ell, resembles Coventry Hall in having a façade divided into three parts by pilasters, a fanlight over the door, and in this case a flat-head Palladian window above the door and a louvred fan in a projection above the center bay at the roof level. Just as does Judge Sewall's house, Judge Clark's sits on a rise outside the village, which affords it a prospect across a terraced lawn toward the center of town. And as Fisher's addition did, so too Clark's reconfigured the relationship between his house and the village that it faced instead of the road after the expansion. Eaton is known to have substantially remodeled and added a spire to Kennebunk's meeting house in 1803–4, making it an even more prominent marker at the intersection of the north-south turnpike (now Route One) and

21. Denis Cosgrove, "Prospect, Perspective and the Evolution of the Landscape Idea," *Transactions of the Institute of British Geographers*, New Series, Vol. 10, No. 1 (1985): 55–56.

Summer Street, which ran east from the village of Kennebunk to Kennebunk Landing (on the Kennebunk River where much shipbuilding took place in the nineteenth century) and then to Kennebunkport on the coast. Judge Clark's house enjoyed an uninterrupted view toward the church and this major intersection. The siting of the house thus visually emphasized the owner's prominent social and economic position at the same time that it gave Clark a fine prospect over the village, which was just then being monumentalized in consequence of its prosperity that had come from shipping and shipbuilding.[22]

Clark, who came to Kennebunk from Portland in the mid-1790s, was considered one of the major investors in shipbuilding during the period. He also ran a store with a partner and became a special justice in the Court of Common Pleas around 1800. Although it is difficult to attribute Clark's professional success strictly to his house, it is the case that following the construction of the major addition to it, he was made a standing justice of the Court of Common Pleas (in 1808), collector of customs in 1810, and Judge of Probate in 1815.[23] While his spatial position with respect to the rest of the community may not have guaranteed him unchallenged authority, it did make it absolutely impossible for others *not* to literally look up to him as they moved through the principal nodal point in the village.

Both of these judges' houses stood out from their neighbors by virtue of scale and design sophistication. Despite drawing on the models of country seats, with their long prospects over fenced yards, these houses nonetheless belonged to established villages where there were other large residences and public buildings. Much more ostentatious standouts were built on the Maine frontier in the Early National period, including the house of Gen. Henry Knox (1750–1806) in Thomaston, known as Montpelier (fig. 4). Along with Coventry Hall, Candee considers Montpelier "one of the first high-style neoclassical seats in the District of Maine."[24] Like the judges' houses in York and

22. Candee, "'The Appearance of Enterprise and Improvement'," 79; Kevin D. Murphy, "The Architecture of Summer Street, Kennebunk, Maine," *Magazine Antiques* 168, No. 2 (August 2005): 55–58; Arthur J. Gerrier, "Thomas Eaton (Active 1794–1831)," in *A Biographical Dictionary of Architects in Maine* Vol. 5, No. 8 (1988): 3–4.

23. Edward Emerson Bourne, *History of Wells and Kennebunk, from the Earliest Settlement to the Year 1820: At which Time Kennebunk was Set Off, and Incorporated* (Portland, Me.: B. Thurston & Co., 1875), 576, 758–59.

24. Candee, "Appearance of Enterprise," 75.

Fig. 4. Montpelier, Daguerreotype, c. 1865. Collections of Montpelier, the General Henry Knox Mansion, Thomaston, Me.

Kennebunk, Montpelier bears many similarities to elaborate residences of the period, and especially to those designed by Bulfinch, to whom the design of Montpelier has been attributed. Like others of Bulfinch's houses, especially those constructed in semi-rural locations, Montpelier (built in 1794) featured an elliptical salon that provided access to elaborately laid-out grounds. As the Reverend Paul Coffin reported on Montpelier in 1796: "The General has a garden fenced ovally. Indeed circles and semi-circles in his fences &c., seem to be all the mode here."[25] These curved forms—appearing in the plans of rooms and gardens, as well as in decorative details in buildings and furnishings— were part of the vocabulary of stylish residences of the Early National period;

25. Paul Coffin, "Memoir and Journals of Rev. Paul Coffin, D.D.," *Collections of the Maine Historical Society*, 1st ser., 4 (1856): 327; Carolyn S. Parsons, "'Bordering on Magnificence': Urban Domestic Planning in the Maine Woods," in Clark, Leamon, and Bowden, eds., *Maine in the Early Republic*, 62–68.

ultimately, the forms were derived from British and Continental models. For Knox, George Washington's Secretary of War, who had gained possession of the Waldo Patent—a tract of Maine land more than a half-million acres in size—through his wife Lucy Flucker whose Loyalist parents had controlled three-fifths of it before the Revolution and through a series of surreptitious post-revolutionary land purchases,[26] an oval salon overlooking a fenced garden and the St. George River beyond contributed to his ambitious architectural and landscape statement on the frontier. Although it was to be built on a large scale and following a stylish plan, Montpelier—according to the contract Knox made with his Boston housewrights—was to be "plain without carving or other expensive ornament."[27] Its impressiveness was to have derived from sheer bulk and its visual association with Bulfinch's grand domestic projects built closer to New England's urban centers.

Like Blue Hill, Thomaston saw the construction of its first houses by white settlers in the 1760s. Thirty or so years later, when construction of Montpelier was begun, there were only two other houses there of two stories in height. Nineteenth-century historian Cyrus Eaton described the Thomaston area in 1796 as

> ...still a woody region, interspersed with straggling clearings, dotted here and there with small low, unpainted houses, many of them of logs and some few of hewn timber, distant from each other, along half made or newly laid out highways scarcely fit for wheel vehicles of any kind.[28]

In such a setting, the fashionable Montpelier stood out at the same time that it stood for Knox's high expectations for his place in the community. Moreover, the house (although only used for part of the year, in the warmer months) was the place in which the Knox family staged their refinement and their cultural distance from the community around them. What the Rev-

26. Alan Taylor, *Liberty Men and Great Proprietors: The Revolutionary Settlement on the Maine Frontier, 1760–1820* (Chapel Hill, N.C.: University of North Carolina Press, 1990), 39–40.

27. Contract made between Henry Knox and Ebenezer Dunton and Tileston Cushing, April 7, 1794; Knox Papers, Maine Historical Society, Portland, Me. Transcribed in James H. Mundy, "Two Early Building Specifications in Maine," *Bulletin of the Association for Preservation Technology* Vol. 7, No. 1 (1975): 103.

28. Cyrus Eaton, *History of Thomaston, Rockland, and South Thomaston, Maine*, 2 vols. (Hallowell, Me.: Masters, Smith & Co., 1865), vol. 1, 231; quoted in Parsons, "Bordering on Magnificence," 65. Also see: Samuel M. Green, "The Architecture of Thomaston, Maine," *Journal of the Society of Architectural Historians* Vol. 10, No. 4 (Dec. 1951): 24–25.

erend Coffin remembered from his visit to Montpelier in mid-August 1796 (besides the chilliness of the house) was his dinner with Lucy Flucker Knox, her daughters, and Mrs. William Bingham (the wife of Knox's wealthy partner, William Bingham of Philadelphia) and her sister and daughter. "We had a merry dinner," recalled Coffin, "the little Misses talking French in a gay mood. Mrs. Bingham was sensible, and had been in France, could talk of European politicks, and give the history of the family of the late King of France & c."[29] Following the general's death in 1806, the family's financial fortunes declined, but Lucy Flucker Knox maintained her sense of their genteel status. Her local reputation for aloofness outlived her by decades: even into the early twentieth century it could still be recalled that "Widow Knox, whose tastes in society were so exalted that she had never entered the house of anyone in Thomaston, always [sent] her coachman on any errand while she remained in her carriage."[30]

As Alan Taylor has argued, Montpelier perfectly expressed the absurd grandiosity that characterized Knox's economic exploitation of his Maine lands. He started numerous undercapitalized enterprises along the St. George River in Thomaston that produced everything from barrels to bricks, and operated mills as well as West India vessels, among many other businesses. Teetering on the brink of bankruptcy did not stop—and may even have encouraged—Henry and Lucy to "obsessively [squander] their resources to demonstrate their wealth, power, taste, and enlightened benevolence to the watching world." With its paired crescents of outbuildings, the landscape around Montpelier was a material expression of Knox's intention to put himself at the center of the region's economy.[31] In that the entire complex of buildings was subjected to an over-arching neoclassical aesthetic—the curved fencing, for example, echoing the plan of the oval salon—Montpelier emulated the country residence of prominent families further south in New England. The house was conceived of as an instrument for convincing the local population of the Knox family's superiority and hence of silencing any objections to Gen. Knox's autocratic control over the land and the economy.

Other, albeit more modest examples of houses that visually dominated the

29. Coffin, "Missionary Tour in Maine," 327.

30. Green, "Architecture of Thomaston, Maine," 26. Among Green's sources were two elderly women who preserved local oral traditions from the nineteenth century: Mrs. Richard Eliot of Thomaston and Mrs. William R. Tobey who was 90 years old in 1948.

31. Taylor, *Liberty Men*, 41–44. The quotation is from page 43.

Fig. 5. Ruggles House, Columbia Falls, Maine (1818), Historic American Buildings Survey, Library of Congress, Washington, D.C. Cervin Robinson, Photographer October 1960.

spaces around them as a means of demonstrating gentility, in addition to social, cultural, and economic authority, sprang up even further east on the frontier than Thomaston and they drew on both rural and urban models of how an ambitious house should occupy its setting in order to suggest its owner's prominence. An outstanding example is the house of Judge Thomas Ruggles in Columbia Falls (fig. 5) in Washington County northeast of Blue Hill, which was modeled on an elaborate urban house, despite having been built in a relatively new settlement. Like Jonathan Fisher, Ruggles came to the District of Maine from further south in Massachusetts in 1796. Settling in what had been Plantation 13 before 1796 and Columbia afterwards, Ruggles amassed a fortune by selling the timber from the vast tracts of land he purchased in Washington County and by exporting it in his own ships. At the time of Ruggles's arrival, Columbia possessed several substantial houses, a two-story inn, and saw and grist mills that created economic opportunity for the community of a little more than two hundred, clustered around the Pleasant River. The area was also home to a vigorous shipbuilding industry, and Ruggles acquired part interest in nearly a dozen ships constructed locally between 1802 and 1815. Ruggles's business interests undoubtedly colored his political views, which were Federalist, and led him, like Fisher, to oppose officially the Embargo Act.[32]

In recognition of his growing wealth, Ruggles acquired several important government posts, including chief justice of the Court of Sessions in Washington County. Like Fisher, Ruggles was conservative with respect to the timing of his investment in an ostentatious house. Both Fisher and Ruggles waited out the economic vicissitudes that accompanied the Embargo and the War of 1812 before constructing large residences. While Fisher chose to make a major addition to his existing house, Ruggles built an entirely new one with the assistance of Massachusetts housewright Aaron Sherman in 1818. The Ruggles house shares much with other large Maine residences of the Federal period. It has a five-bay façade, center entrance, hip roof, fanlight over the front door, and Palladian window in the second story. For Washington County, however, the Ruggles house was extraordinary, especially its elaborate exterior window details and its freestanding staircase in the center hall.[33] Like the houses of southern Maine judges, Ruggles's stood out from the buildings around it by virtue of its unique design, in which Ruth Clapp Ruggles, Thomas's wife, may have had a hand. Corresponding in some of their details to widely-known builders' guides by Asher Benjamin, and in certain concepts to the elaborate Boston-area residences designed by Bulfinch, the judges' houses emphasized their local standing by architectural means. Like Sewall and Clark, Ruggles positioned his house to provide an elevated view of his community. Where most of the standing houses were then clustered on the east side of the Pleasant River, Ruggles built on the west side, on an elevated site oriented to the south. As architectural historian Roger Reed suggests, "[T]he visual prominence of the house would have been especially evident to anyone arriving by water."[34] The Ruggles house also had an entrance portico, which no other in

32. Roger G. Reed, unpublished study of the Ruggles House, 2007–8, 4–6. The author kindly made his manuscript available to me for consultation.

33. "Wilderness Elegance Restored: The Thomas Ruggles House," *Early American Homes* (April, 1998): 45–52; personal correspondence (3/1/2006) with Roger Reed. Also see the documentation of the Ruggles House produced by the Historic American Buildings Survey (HABS) in the Library of Congress, Washington, DC and available online at http://memory.loc.gov.

34. Reed, Ruggles House, 9.

town had, as well as an exceptionally spacious stairhall. Its kitchen was located in the basement of an ell to the north side, an arrangement more common to urban residences of the period. The Ruggles family's decisions about the site of the house and its design reflected an overarching concern with how the building would be perceived. A visitor who came by water, which many likely did, who saw the house from a distance, would have understood from the presence of the porch that being received by the Ruggleses was a matter of some formality, and finally, if he or she were admitted, the first impression of the hall and stair would have been incredibly impressive.

As an economic enterprise, capitalizing on Maine's natural resources—especially her vast reserves of timber—as Ruggles did, was a controversial one. Alan Taylor has shown that the land claims of Maine's great proprietors in the Early National period were frequently disputed by poor settlers who had come to the District specifically to avail themselves of the property that was in short supply in more settled parts of Massachusetts. Social and economic conflict erupted over competing land claims and was expressed politically by the struggle between Federalists and Democratic-Republicans, and religiously between Congregationalists and members of Protestant sects.[35] In such an environment, making an authoritative architectural statement such as the one embodied in the Ruggles house would have been strategic. It would have made material Ruggles's bid to control and profit from the timber trade, and it would have shown his cultural ambition in three dimensions. At the same time, this astonishingly elaborate house would have turned the village into a space where the disparities between rich and poor, powerful and powerless were articulated by the elements of the built environment itself.

Maine proprietor William Bingham, in addition to parts of Knox's holdings and others previously owned by Henry Duer of New York, purchased more than two million "unsurveyed, unexplored, and uninhabited" acres of land in two tracts in 1793.[36] One, the Kennebec Purchase, comprised much of present-day Somerset County. The other, the Penobscot Purchase, was located in Hancock and Washington Counties, and included the present seacoast towns

35. The fundamental treatment of this conflict is found in Stephen A. Marini, *Radical Sects in Revolutionary New England* (Cambridge, Mass.: Harvard University Press, 1982).

36. Anon., *The Black Mansion: Historical Introduction* (n.p.: n.d.), 10; quoted in Woodlawn Museum, "Woodlawn: An Estate of History" (2008); http://www.woodlawnmuseum.com/historyfull.html. Accessed 12/8/2011.

of Gouldsboro, Trenton, Ellsworth, and Mt. Desert Island. Bingham's claims were disputed by the previous settlers of the land and he therefore appointed (in 1795) an agent, General David Cobb of Taunton, Massachusetts (a former aide to George Washington), to defend his interests on-site. Cobb traveled back to Philadelphia in late 1795 to meet Alexander Baring (later Lord Ashburton), the son of Sir Francis Baring, who was part of a group of British and European investors who in 1796 would purchase a substantial interest in Bingham's Maine lands. Bingham's death in 1804, the Embargo, the War of 1812, and ongoing conflict with timber "thieves" made it impossible for Cobb to bring about the agricultural development of downeast Maine that he had imagined and he returned to Massachusetts in 1822. [37]

The English-born Col. John Black (1781–1856), General Cobb's clerk and Sir Francis Baring's agent, arrived in Gouldsboro in 1799 to take over. Several years later he married Cobb's daughter Mary and the couple moved to Ellsworth in 1810. Despite his English origins, Black fought in the War of 1812 on the American side[38] and rose to the rank of general agent of the Bingham estate's Maine properties. Black's method diverged from Cobb's approach to the management of the Maine lands in that he successfully developed their timber resources. Black received a commission on the timber that settlers delivered to the landowners as payment for their tracts, logs that were then "saw'd or hew'd for the European market" and loaded onto the proprietors' ships for export.[39] Black's success, but also the perceived need to articulate his position through a carefully-sited house, was expressed in Woodlawn, built between 1824 and 1828 (fig. 6). Like the Ruggles house, Woodlawn dwarfed most everything around it, and like all three judges' houses, stood slightly beyond its village to enjoy a commanding view of the settlement. Woodlawn was originally located on a

37. Woodlawn Museum, "Woodlawn: An Estate of History" (2008); http://www.woodlawn-museum.com/historyfull.html. Accessed 12/8/2011.

38. Some of Black's neighbors doubted his patriotism, and prior to leading his military company on a march to Mt. Desert Island, the site of a feared British attack, Black assured the men that despite any rumors as to his allegiances, "I will defend *your* wives, children, and property, and the Constitution of our country, as far as my abilities permit, against the attacks of all enemies whatsoever" (emphasis present in the original). *Biographical Encyclopedia of Maine of the Nineteenth Century* (Boston: Metropolitan Publishing and Engraving Co., 1885), 214–15; quoted in Rebecca Robbins, *Colonel John Black of Ellsworth (1781–1856)* (np: nd), np, reprint from the *Maine Historical Society Quarterly* Vol. 17, No. 3 (Winter 1978).

39. David Cobb to C. W. Hare, 11/10/1810; quoted in Robbins, np.

Fig. 6. East Front and Office Wing, "Woodlawn," Ellsworth, Maine (1824–28), Historic American Buildings Survey, Library of Congress, Allen L. Hubbard, Photographer April 30, 1936.

property of about 300 acres, and the house perched nearly at the crest of a hill that slopes upward from the Union River.[40] From there it had a view over the river as well as the buildings of Ellsworth. The townspeople would also have had a good view of the house; it would have been an always visible reminder of Black's presence there as the agent of the major landholders in the area.

The distinctive design of Woodlawn enhanced the experiences of both overlooking the river and town from the house, and of seeing the building from the road below or from a further distance away. The plan, uncommon in the area, has been compared to a plate in Asher Benjamin's *The American Builder's Companion,* the first edition of which was published in 1806 and in subsequent editions in 1811 and 1827. Adopting almost verbatim Benjamin's "Plan and Elevation for a House which is intended for a country situation," the builder of Woodlawn placed four openings on the east front of the main block of the house and shifted the principal entrance from its customary spot at the center of the façade to the south wing. This wing, matched by another on

40. "Woodlawn Museum." The property has subsequently reduced to about 180 acres.

the north side of the main block, contained an entrance hall and office, while the main block of the house had double parlors running along the east with a stairhall and other secondary spaces at the back. Breaking from Benjamin's plan, the designer added a porch running the length of the east façade of the main block, with details that nevertheless corresponded to Benjamin's published drawing of the Ionic order.[41] The four front windows, again in contrast to Benjamin's design, extended all the way to the level of the porch floor, somewhat in the manner of Bulfinch's contemporary country seats where similar windows enabled movement from the interiors to the porches, terraces, and landscapes beyond. Moreover, they enlarged the prospect over the property, the river, and the great expanse of the frontier to the east.

The prestige of Woodlawn thus derived from a number of sources. It was a visually prominent part of the landscape, it was large, and it was stylistically sophisticated. At the same time that the design referenced a well-circulated pattern book, it also evidenced some creativity on the part of the builder, in the way that he had added the long piazza and carefully fitted its detailing to Benjamin's neoclassical aesthetic through the use of the Ionic order for the columns and entablature. The local viewers of the house could only have appreciated its difference from the smaller and less carefully detailed buildings nearby in Ellsworth—even the relatively large Federalist residences—which it completely outclassed. Situated on a large property, Woodlawn must also have been understood in relation to the eighteenth-century discourse of the country house in which, as we have already observed, the politics of the prospect were central.

But were houses like Woodlawn significant as anything other than metaphors for what their builders considered to be their positions in the communities around them? Did their domination of the landscape—on the bases of size, stylishness, or siting—have real significance with respect to how local struggles over religion, culture, economics, and politics were resolved? The District (and later the State) of Maine in the Early National period was an unstable place and from the perspectives of the white settlers, its eastern frontier was barely civilized. It is impossible to know how the contests there between Congregationalists and Baptists (and other members of Protestant sects), Federalists and

41. Walter Knight Sturges, "The Black House, Ellsworth: An Asher Benjamin House in Maine," *Magazine Antiques* Vol. 56 (May 1954): 398–400.

Democratic-Republicans, proprietors and squatters, and others would have been resolved in the absence of Montpelier, the Ruggles house, Woodlawn, the Fisher house, and other buildings that constituted architectural propositions about how the somewhat fluid society of settlers should be definitively organized. What can be said, however, is that these houses powerfully embodied a set of claims about where authority should reside, and that they inscribed those claims in space. They were sites for self-fashioning in which members of the elite staged their identities as religiously, socially, culturally, or economically dominant—or some combination of all four.

To compare this handful of ambitious houses is not to minimize the significant differences between the intentions and aspirations of their various builders. As we have seen, constructing an ambitious house in an existing village that was undergoing rebuilding was a different undertaking than building one on the frontier, and called for different architectural and landscape strategies. Both Knox and Black built houses, at least in part, as a means of insuring that settlers would acquiesce to their economic projects which were seen by some (especially the landless and impoverished) as exploitive. Other builders of ambitious houses, notably Jonathan Fisher, were not angling so much for economic preeminence as for cultural or religious authority over their communities. What all of these builders shared, however, was an implicit belief in the effectiveness of landscapes and buildings as both signs of the men's positions in their communities and as guarantors of their places in local hierarchies.[42] These houses were also significant to local struggles from a material point of view, not just as metaphors. Whereas Knox made Montpelier the center of an economic empire that was intended to engage a significant proportion of the local population in his web of patronage, Fisher's fancy house provided accommodations for boarders as well as the spaces in which they and the parson could study and recite, thus increasing his income from teaching.

However much social and economic relations may have been legible in the

42. The discipline of cultural geography has been effective in describing the ways in which landscape and architecture were manipulated (in early America and elsewhere) as means of reproducing social relations. See, for example: Richard Peet, "A Sign Taken for History: Daniel Shays' Memorial in Petersham, Massachusetts," *Annals of the Association of American Geographers* Vol. 86, No. 1 (March 1996): 21–43; and for an overview, Donald Mitchell, *Cultural Geography, A Critical Introduction* (np: Blackwell, 2000), especially Part II, "The Political Landscape" (89–144).

landscapes and buildings that the Federalist elite constructed for themselves, the built environment never effectively squelched opposition. Montpelier, for instance, "the largest and most ornate private building north of Philadelphia," according to Taylor, was not capable of convincing settlers of Knox's "taste and magnificence," nor of his benevolence that would have guaranteed deference from social and economic inferiors. Taylor considers Knox one of the "Federalists [who] eloquently preached the importance of a hierarchical and stable society" but who were unable to make others subservient to themselves merely by "parading their personas of genteel superiority." Ultimately, argues Taylor, Federalists like Knox failed to recognize (in the 1780s and 1790s) "the enduring potential of the American Revolution's legacy to legitimate upstarts unwilling or unable to achieve or to endure genteel authority." The self-perception of Federalist leaders as "Fathers of the People" was untenable in a political environment in which "Friends of the People"—social equals—had staked out a position more in keeping with Revolutionary ideology.[43]

Calvinist theology shared with Federalism an emphasis on order. Thus Jonathan Fisher's paternalistic view of his place in the community, although acceptable to other members of the elite, gained little traction with the broader group of settlers from less affluent and educated backgrounds. Increasingly, they were drawn to seemingly less elitist and more equalitarian and engaging Protestant sects, as well as to less conservative political positions. If Jonathan Fisher, like other conservative leaders on the eastern frontier, was ultimately ineffective in securing his place in the community through representations, his attempts to spatialize his claims for authority are nevertheless revealing. They demonstrate just how important landscapes and buildings were to the struggles that characterized the eastern frontier of the Early National period. To this extent, the spatial turn in cultural studies and other disciplines provides a crucial justification for the focus on material things that art and architectural history have always maintained. At the same time, however, it demands that we rethink our understanding of space. As Foucault writes, "[W]e do not live in a kind of void, inside of which we could place individuals and things. We do not live inside a void that could be colored with diverse shades of light, we live inside a set of relations that delineates sites which are irreducible to one

43. Alan Taylor, "From Fathers to Friends of the People: Political Personas in the Early Republic," *Journal of the Early Republic* Vol. 11 (Winter 1991): 466–91.

another [...]"[44] So it is with the eastern frontier. Relations between its inhabitants of varying class, social, religious, and political positions were played out in spaces that were punctuated with the material manifestations of their self-conceptions. The central struggles that characterized frontier life, or life in the more established towns, were not played out in some airless discursive realm, but instead in the very real spaces of new or newly-monumental villages.

44. Michel Foucault, "Of Other Spaces," trans. Jay Miskowiec, *Diacritics* Vol. 16, No. 1 (Spring 1986): 23. The text originated as a lecture given in 1967 but not published until October 1984 as "Des Espaces Autres" in *Architecture-Mouvement-Continuité*.

Domestic Exchange and Regional Identity

"The Remainder of Our Effects We Must Leave Behind": American Loyalists and the Meaning of Things

KATHERINE RIEDER

IN MARCH 1776, Peter Oliver, former Chief Justice of the colony of Massachusetts, embarked upon an evening ride through the countryside south of Boston. His trip shares some similarities with the now epic journey made nearly a year earlier by Paul Revere. Like Revere, Oliver traversed an area rife with hostile troops and weaponry while the darkness of the early-falling March night helped to conceal his maneuverings. But if the patriotic need to extend a warning prompted Revere's risky ride, what compelled Oliver to make a similarly dangerous trip? The answer: a silver sugar box made for the Oliver family in 1702 by renowned Boston silversmith Edward Winslow (fig. 1).[1] Oliver, as a loyalist, was preparing to enter into exile and his trip that night recovered a number of pieces of his family's substantial silver set, which he had left at his country home. The rescue of the silver kept objects like the sugar box out of enemy hands while simultaneously enabling Oliver to take a piece of convertible currency and his family's history with him into exile.

At least sixty thousand loyalists, or as many as one in forty late-eighteenth-century Americans, fled from Great Britain's thirteen rebellious colonies during the Revolutionary War.[2] And all of these political refugees were forced

1. For a dramatic account of Oliver's midnight ride as told by a descendent, see Peter Oliver, "Judge Oliver and the Small Oliver House in Middleborough," in Colonial Society of Massachusetts, *Transactions, 1947–1951*, 38 (1959): 302. For information regarding the sugar box crafted by Winslow, see Jonathan L. Fairbanks and Robert F. Trent, *Style*, vol. 3 of *New England Begins: The Seventeenth Century* (Boston: Museum of Fine Arts, Boston, 1982), 498–99.

2. This figure is the most conservative within the recently published literature on the loyalists, and another 15,000 can be added to the total if one counts slaves that were brought with fleeing loyalists. See Maya Jasanoff, "The Other Side of Revolution: Loyalists in the British Empire," *William & Mary Quarterly*, 3rd ser., 65 (April 2008): 208. Peter Coldham has recently set the figure at 70,000, although both historians agree that quantifying the number of loyalists that entered into exile is extremely difficult given the numerous destinations of flight and the ambiguities surrounding definitions of loyalism. See Peter Wilson Coldham, *American Migrations, 1765–1799: The Lives, Times and Families of Colonial Americans who Remained Loyal to the British Crown Before, During and After the Revolutionary War, as Related in their own Words and through their Correspondence* (Baltimore: Genealogical Publishing Co., Inc., 2000), ix.

Fig. 1. Edward Winslow, Sugar Box. Boston, 1702. Silver. Gift of Henry Francis du Pont. Courtesy, Winterthur Museum, Winterthur, Del.

to make choices like Oliver's in regard to their possessions. Crammed onto tightly packed ships, most could take only as much as they could carry with them. Many attempted to protect abandoned possessions by leaving them in the care of family members who stayed behind, while others entered into long legal battles to retrieve lost items. Still others replaced lost possessions with newly-fashioned substitutes.[3] This essay examines instances of each of these

3. For a case of a loyalist leaving possessions with patriot family members, see Elizabeth Gray Otis to Harrison Gray, undated, as quoted in Mabel Swann, "Furniture of the Boston Tories," *Antiques* 41 (March 1942): 187. For an attempt at retrieving abandoned property, see Andrew Spooner to Thomas Hutchinson, April 12, 1786, Hutchinson and Oliver Papers, Vol. 3, 1775 – 1811, Massachusetts Historical Society, Boston, Mass. Many loyalist refugees also filed claims requesting compensation for lost property from the British government; for a summary of these claims, see Mary Beth Norton, *The British Americans: The Loyalist Exiles in England, 1774–1789* (Boston: Little, Brown and Company, 1972), 196–222. These three strategies operate at the center of my dissertation, and this essay serves as an overview of the predominant themes of the larger project. See Katherine Rieder, "'The Remainder of Our Effects We Must Leave Behind': American Loyalists and the Meaning of Things, 1765–1800" (PhD diss., Harvard University, 2009).

strategies—rescue, protection, and replacement—in order to elucidate the role of objects within the circumstances of spousal abandonment, personal loss, and familial fragmentation that the loyalists confronted. As Massachusetts loyalist Samuel Quincy wrote from his exile in London, where he was physically separated from his wife, children, and home, the situation had "something in it so unexpected, so unprecedented, so complicated with evil & misfortune" that it had become "almost too burthensome for my spirits, nor have I words that can reach its description."[4] Paint, silver, and mahogany provided a vehicle for processing the upheaval attendant upon loyalism that other means could not adequately capture, making objects the central rather than secondary source for understanding the loyalist experience.

This is not to suggest, however, that the objects at the center of this material history of the loyalist experience operated in a unique manner. Rather, loyalist possessions were entangled in circumstances, although incredibly intensified, common to eighteenth-century objects at large. Temporal and spatial dislocations shared by people and things drove inheritance patterns and the organization of transatlantic networks, social systems that in turn contributed to the structuring of eighteenth-century existences.[5] Yet scholars have only recently begun to consider the transformative power of the object's imbrication in these networks during the colonial period. Anthropologist Igor Kopytoff's concept of the "cultural biography of things" has largely driven these new perspectives, which focus upon the pre-revolutionary object's movement through space and time rather than its significance as a relatively static signifier of status, a view that previously dominated studies of eighteenth-century art and material

4. Samuel Quincy to Hannah Hill Quincy, 1 January 1777. Papers Relating to the Quincy, Wendell, Holmes, and Upham Families, Massachusetts Historical Society.

5. For inheritance patterns in the eighteenth century, see Carole Shammas, Marylynn Salmon, and Michael Dahlin, *Inheritance in America From Colonial Times to the Present* (New Brunswick, N.J.: Rutgers University Press, 1987), 3–79; Laurel Thatcher Ulrich, "Furniture as Social History: Gender, Property, and Memory in the Decorative Arts," in *American Furniture*, Luke Beckerdite and William Hosley, eds. (Hanover, N.H.: Chipstone Foundation, 1995), 39–68; Amanda Vickery, "Women and the World of Goods: a Lancashire Consumer and her Possessions, 1751–81," in *Consumption and the World of Goods*, John Brewer and Roy Porter, eds. (New York: Routledge, 1993), 247–301; and the classic text on inheritance in colonial New England, Philip Greven Jr., *Four Generations: Population, Land, and Family in Colonial Andover, Massachusetts* (Ithaca, N.Y.: Cornell University Press,1970). For the structure and unreliability of transatlantic networks, see Ian K. Steele, *The English Atlantic, 1675–1740: An Exploration of Communication and Community* (New York: Oxford University Press, 1986), 26–27, 50–51.

culture.[6] The loyalist experience of loss and exile only served to personalize and heighten the impact of these spatial and temporal dislocations, causing them to become more evident in both the form and meaning of their things. Throughout this essay, I label these objects as "loyalist" due to their provenance and entanglement in these heightened circumstances, but it is important to remember that they speak on a general level to spatial and temporal upheavals that were not limited to one political party, or the immediate period of the revolution. The paintings, pieces of silver, and mahogany furniture I consider in this essay serve as a lens through which to better view and understand eighteenth-century objects in general.

It also bears stating that although my work is indebted to the recent scholarly interest in movement mentioned above, it is not limited to an investigation of a possession's literal mobility at the expense of explorations of transitions in ownership over time, or vice versa. Instead, it combines an examination of spatial and temporal movement in order to explain how loyalist objects worked as agents responsible for structuring personal relationships that could, in turn, persist *across* space and time. Theories that posit the object as a collector of meanings, such as Walter Benjamin's conception of the obdurate object that conceals its multiple meanings beneath its opaque surface, are crucial to this endeavor.[7]

6. Igor Kopytoff, "The Cultural Biography of Things: Commoditization as Process," in *The Social Life of Things: Commodities in Cultural Perspective,* ed. Arjun Appadurai (Cambridge, Eng.: Cambridge University Press, 1986), 66–67, 83. For recent works relating to the movement of colonial objects through space and time, see Margaretta Lovell's consideration of John Singleton Copley's c. 1770 portrait of Joshua Henshaw; the author follows the portrait through the circumstances leading to its production, to the interaction of Henshaw and Copley, and then through its progression through a line of descendents and institutions. See Margaretta Lovell, *Art in a Season of Revolution: Painters, Artisans, and Patrons in Early America* (Philadelphia: University of Pennsylvania Press, 2005), 94–140. Jennifer Roberts has taken the issue of movement more literally, proving the centrality of spatial issues such as transmission and mobility in the Atlantic world, especially in relation to the objects that connected the widely dispersed subjects of the British crown; see Jennifer L. Roberts, "Copley's Cargo: *Boy with a Squirrel* and the Dilemma of Transit," *American Art* 21 (Summer 2007): 20–41. For readings of portraiture and other objects as inert objects in schemes of self-fashioning and social emulation, see Paul Staiti, "Character and Class," in *John Singleton Copley in America,* by Carrie Rebora et al. (New York: Metropolitan Museum of Art, 1995), 53–77; T. H. Breen, "The Meaning of 'Likeness': American Portrait Painting in an Eighteenth-Century Consumer Society," *Word and Image* 6 (October–December 1990): 325–50; and Richard L. Bushman, *The Refinement of America: Persons, Houses, Cities* (New York: Vintage Books, 1993).

7. Walter Benjamin's musings on the object's use by "primitive society," the collector, and the allegorist are indicative of his conception of the obdurate object, which conceals its many mean-

Gift theory, that articulated by Marcel Mauss in particular, also plays a central role. Like Benjamin, Mauss posited that objects are imbued with an inalienable spirit, a spirit that enmeshes the object within a never-ending cycle of giving and receiving.[8] A self-perpetuating network is created as a result, pushing the gift/object and its accompanying accrual of meanings forward through time, signifying a sense of evolution that often, though not always, involved a spatial shift as well. What is at stake here is an understanding that the object's potential to take on multiple and even conflicting meanings and simultaneously move and evolve casts it as an agent active within the loyalist experience.

As family lore has it, Peter Oliver, "travel-stained and weary" after riding rapidly over 40 miles "at the edge of evening," entered his Middleborough home that aforementioned March night, "collected a few valuables from a secret drawer and, bidding farewell to his housekeeper, left, not to return again."[9] Yet the story of the sugar box, the only object amongst these "valuables" to be identified with some certainty, truly begins in 1702. Boston silversmith Edward Winslow raised, cast, and chased the box that year at the bequest of William Partridge, who gave it as a gift to Daniel Oliver and his niece-in-law Elizabeth Belcher Oliver on the occasion of the birth of a son. The box's inscription reads as much; "O/D·E/Donum W:P 1702" is found on its underside, which is a glyph for "To Daniel and Elizabeth Oliver, Given by William Partridge, 1702."[10]

ings; see Walter Benjamin, *The Arcades Project,* trans. Howard Eiland and Kevin McLaughlin (Cambridge, Mass.: The Belknap Press of Harvard University, 1999), 210–211.

8. For a discussion of the inalienable spirit, or *hau,* at the center of gifts and the social networks they create, see Marcel Mauss, *The Gift: the Form and Reason for Exchange in Archaic Societies,* trans. W. D. Halls (New York: W. W. Norton, 1990), viii, 11–12, 18. Mauss's work has become a seminal text in anthropology and cultural studies, producing a number of further meditations on the *hau* of objects and the function of gifts within contemporary and historical societies. See, for example, Marshall Sahlins, "The Spirit of the Gift," in *The Logic of the Gift: Toward an Ethic of Generosity,* Alan D. Schrift, ed. (New York: Routledge, 1997), 70–99; Nicolas Thomas, *Entangled Objects: Exchange, Material Culture, and Colonialism in the Pacific* (Cambridge, Mass.: Harvard University Press, 1991), 14–34 in particular; and Annette Weiner, *Inalienable Possessions: The Paradox of Keeping-While-Giving* (Berkeley, Calif.: University of California Press, 1992). Weiner's introductory discussion of the "paradox of keeping-while-giving," or forcing common memory into the future through the repeated inheritance of an object, is particularly relevant, see Weiner, 6–8.

9. Oliver, "Judge Oliver and the Small Oliver House in Middleborough," 302.

10. Fairbanks and Trent, *Style,* 498–99 and Ian M. G. Quimby, *American Silver at Winterthur* (Charlottesville, Va.: Winterthur Museum in association with the University Press of Virginia, 1995), 184. The above sources disagree, however, in relation to the name of the female recipient

Replete with iconography referring to "chivalry, courtly love, marriage, and fecundity," the function as well as the impetus behind the box's production mirrored these themes as the consumption of sugar often occurred as a part of courtship rituals. The birth of a child was such ritual's most propitious consummation.[11]

Peter Oliver, the original owner's third son, eventually inherited the box as well as the enmity of Massachusetts' patriot colonists.[12] Although the box commemorated the birth of Daniel Oliver Jr., he did not survive infancy, and as a result it was likely bequeathed to Andrew Oliver, the couple's eldest son surviving at the time of their deaths. At some point, possibly at the time of Andrew's death in 1774 when Peter became the family's patriarch, the box entered the latter's possession. Peter had acquired the reputation as a rather vehement "tory" as the box progressed along its path of inheritance to him and, as the brother of a former Lieutenant-Governor and himself the Chief Justice of the colony, his loyalty to the British and the animosity it caused hardly comes as a surprise.[13] By the time of Oliver's midnight ride then, the box carried a web of intricate family associations at a moment when its owner

---

of the sugar box; Fairbanks and Trent stated it was Mary Belcher Oliver while Quimby named the recipient as Elizabeth Belcher Oliver. Given the inscription on the box: "O/D·E/ Donnum W:P 1702," and the fact that Elizabeth Belcher Oliver (not Mary Belcher Oliver) is listed in family genealogies, Quimby's account is likely correct. For a genealogical chart of the Oliver family, see Andrew Oliver, *Faces of a Family: An Illustrated Catalogue of Portraits and Silhouettes…* (Privately Printed, 1960), 34–35. Such an elaborate gift between in-laws—Elizabeth Oliver's brother Jonathan married William Partridge's daughter Mary—may seem strange, but as Ian Quimby described it, "Given the Puritan habit of not distinguishing between blood relatives and those acquired by marriage, the relationship was more important than it might appear to today's readers." See Quimby, *American Silver at Winterthur,* 183.

11. Fairbanks and Trent, *Style,* 498. The catalogue entry for the object describes the iconographic elements as follows: "The mounted knight, bands of myrtle, *amorini,* and allegorical busts are all derived from illustrations in editions of Tasso's *Gerusalemme Liberata,* Spenser's *Faerie Queene,* and Homer's *Iliad,* where they accompany texts dealing with martial prowess and courtly love."

12. The box was likely given to commemorate the birth of Daniel Oliver, born June 13, 1702, who did not survive infancy. See "Object Report, Sugar Box," Silver Sugar Box (1959.3363), Curatorial Files, Winterthur Museum, Winterthur, Del. Peter Oliver, although the couple's third son, inherited the sugar box as both his elder brothers—another Daniel and Andrew—predeceased him. For information regarding the Oliver family genealogy, see Oliver, *Faces of a Family,* Appendices 5 and 6.

13. Linda Ayres, *Harvard Divided* (Cambridge, Mass.: President and Fellows of Harvard College, 1976), 20–21.

faced political exile and leaving the place, perhaps permanently, where these associations were fostered.

Silver, of course, stood as one of the objects fleeing loyalists favored; in addition to being highly portable, it could easily be converted to currency.[14] Yet as Oliver's mythic adventure alludes, something powerful lured him into the countryside that night. Whether it was the need to grab something that would be easy to carry, a preemptive move to insure the availability of quick cash, or the pull of the personal value and inalienable spirit intrinsic to an object passed down from generation to generation remains obscure, but his gesture further destabilizes the notion that eighteenth-century objects acted largely as signifiers of status.[15] If that were their sole or even primary function, Oliver would not have risked his life riding through a landscape teeming with patriots to secure the sugar box and the accompanying pieces of silver; he would have simply replaced the lost objects, at least for status's sake, as soon as financial circumstances allowed. Furthermore, that the sugar box somehow made it to Boston and eventually crossed the Atlantic, where it contributed to the establishment of a patrimony for the family in its new home in England, combined with the fact that it remained in the Oliver family's possession until at least the late nineteenth century, suggests that it was the sugar box's intimate family meaning that served as the primary motivation for its retrieval.[16]

For every object like the silver sugar box that loyalists "rescued" before venturing into exile, however, many more were left behind. Loyalist families often

14. For the inherent liquidity of silver objects, see Mark A. Peterson, "Puritanism and Refinement in Early New England: Reflections on Communion Silver," *William & Mary Quarterly,* 3rd ser., 58 (April 2001): 327, 331–34 and Lovell, *Art in a Season of Revolution,* 106. Given silver's complex role as both money and a material used to constitute decorative objects, it is important to note that prior to the advent of "modern banking," silversmiths and goldsmiths often took on the "many of the functions of a banker and a broker." See Fairbanks and Trent, *Style,* 480.

15. For a discussion of the inalienable spirit of objects enmeshed in social networks, see Mauss, *The Gift,* 11–12 and Weiner, *Inalienable Possessions,* 4–6.

16. There is some disagreement as to when the sugar box left the Oliver family's possession. The *New England Begins* catalogue posits that the English branch of the Oliver family sold the sugar box to a dealer in 1937, who subsequently sold it to American collector Henry Francis du Pont, upon which it became part of the Winterthur Museum's collection. See Fairbanks and Trent, *Style,* 498. The provenance of the object at Winterthur, however, maintains that it left the family at some point in the nineteenth century and entered the collections of a Scottish Church, where the same American dealer found it in the 1930s. See "Object Report, Sugar Box," Silver Sugar Box (1959.3363), Winterthur Museum Curatorial Files, Winterthur, Del.

attempted to secure these abandoned items by entrusting them to relatives remaining in the colonies, and married women were the likely candidates for such a task for a number of reasons. Their role as the primary caregivers of young children, the latter of which were thought incapable of enduring long sea voyages, often led them to stay in the colonies, as did their own fears regarding the harrowing experience of transatlantic passages.[17] Yet another factor contributed to the likelihood of their remaining at home—the ambivalent political position of women rendered them ideal protectors of loyalist property.

Eighteenth-century legal codes linked political agency with property ownership, and property ownership was bound with gender. A complicated triangulation resulted in which women forfeited the right to own property when they entered marriage and simultaneously lost their political agency as the latter depended on the former. The roots of this legal practice lay in English precedent, which defined politics and society in the North American colonies until after the Revolution. According to English law, property ownership was the condition that defined each citizen's relationship to the state. Propertied upper-class men residing in England constituted the only group possessing a demonstrable relationship to the state as they could vote for political representation in Parliament. Property-less men in England and male colonists enacted an indirect relationship as they could negotiate contracts and, in the case of propertied male colonists, serve in crown-appointed and elected office. Single women owning property also possessed a similar relationship as they paid taxes on that property, although voting rights certainly did not extend to this group of taxpayers. But married women were completely removed from these forms of citizenship through the law of coverture. Originating in medieval English legal tradition in which the conception of "Baron and Feme" or "lord and woman" defined domestic relations, a woman, upon marriage, relin-

17. Mary Beth Norton, "Eighteenth-Century American Women in Peace and War: The Case of the Loyalists," *William and Mary Quarterly,* 3rd ser., 33 (Jul. 1976): 398. As Samuel Quincy wrote to his wife in regard to her fear of transatlantic travel: "If therefore Things sh[d] not wear a more promising aspect upon the opening of the next year, by all means summon resolution enough to cross the Ocean. M[rs] Hutchinson tells me this was your greatest dread. Believe me you will find it infinitely less dangerous & terrifying than your imagination suggests. The recompence which awaits you, shall be the careful attention of friendship & the embrace of a faithful partner," see Samuel Quincy to Hannah Hill Quincy, 15 October 1777, Papers Relating to the Quincy, Wendell, Holmes, and Upham Families, Massachusetts Historical Society.

quished her limited civic identity to her spouse. Thus her interests were "covered" by those of her husband, who gained control of any property she brought to the marriage. The only right to property that remained to a married woman was dower, a one third share in her husband's estate claimed after his death and only available to the widow during her lifetime.[18] The temporary nature of property ownership under dower did not suffice for civic inclusion, and as property served as the means for entry into a relationship to the state, marriage severed that connection for many women and cast them as apolitical.[19]

It is important to note, however, that coverture and the resulting political alienation of women existed as an ideology, the way things were supposed to function in an ideal Atlantic world. As historian Marylynn Salmon described it, coverture was a "benchmark," a "goal of the law" that was "hoped for but never realized."[20] Several colonies allowed for "separate estates," or provisions in marriage contracts that enabled married women to own and control property separately from their husbands, while historiography has long established that women developed and actively advocated their own political opinions throughout the Revolutionary period.[21] Although the aforementioned instances of

18. Marylynn Salmon, *Women and the Law of Property in Early America* (Chapel Hill, N.C.: The University of North Carolina Press, 1986), 141–43.

19. See Linda Kerber, *Women of the Republic: Intellect and Ideology in Revolutionary America* (Chapel Hill, N.C.: University of North Carolina Press for the Omohundro Institute of Early American History and Culture, 1980), 120; Joan R. Gundersen, "Independence, Citizenship, and the American Revolution," *Signs* 13 (Autumn 1987): 59–61, 63; Linda Kerber, *No Constitutional Right to Be Ladies: Woman and the Obligations of Citizenship* (New York: Hill and Wang, 1998), 11–15; and Linda Kerber, "Paradox of Women's Citizenship in the Early Republic: the Case of *Martin v. Massachusetts*, 1805," *American Historical Review* 97 (Apr. 1992): 349–78. Coverture has also been defined in legal terms as "unity of person," meaning that the husband and wife together formed one legal entity rather than two. See Marylynn Salmon, *Women and the Law of Property in Early America*, 14–15.

20. Salmon, *Women and the Law of Property*, 14.

21. Salmon, *Women and the Law of Property*, xv. The adoption of the principle of separate estates largely depended on a colony adopting the dual system of English law, which involved establishing both courts of law and courts of equity (chancery courts). These equity courts then enforced the right of families to endow women with separate estates, which were meant to remain in their control rather than their husband's, a precedent that was based on the example of English chancery courts. While Salmon states that the Puritan bias against chancery courts prevented them from being established in New England, New York, Maryland, Virginia, and South Carolina did establish chancery courts. Pennsylvania did not, but did give its courts of law the ability to rule in cases of equity, giving the courts some teeth in terms of enforcing separate estates. See Salmon, *Women and the Law of Property*, 81–84, 120–23. For colonial women who articulated political opinions, particularly in opposition to those of their spouse, see Cynthia

property protection involved male relatives, other loyalists recognized the power of the legal ideology of coverture and used it to their advantage. The logic is easy to follow. Because married women could not legally own property as an individual, they were incapable of asserting political identities independent of those of their husbands.[22] And because they could not legally assert a political identity, the lands and goods in their possession, particularly the one-third share of their husbands' property guaranteed by the right of dower, could not be defined by the state as either patriot or loyalist in the absence of those husbands. Fleeing loyalists therefore hoped that the objects they entrusted to their wives who stayed behind would remain immune to the confiscation laws enacted by fledgling state legislatures in order to punish loyalist traitors and shore up the coffers of struggling revolutionary governments.[23]

Kierner, *Southern Women in Revolution, 1776–1800: Personal and Political Narratives* (Columbia, S.C.: University of South Carolina Press, 1998), 100, 151–58; Kerber, *Women of the Republic*, 119–55; and Gundersen, "Independence, Citizenship, and the American Revolution," 68–71.

22. The exception of course, is the aforementioned settlement of a separate estate within a marriage contract. Separate estates, however, were not available to women in all thirteen colonies (see n21, above), and were employed by only a few families. Salmon labels them "not numerous", and Gunderson states that they failed to grant women any real measure of economic independence. Furthermore, even if a colonial woman was endowed with a separate estate, her husband's political opinions still "covered" her own. The separate estate did not translate into an opportunity for political agency, which a woman's marriage continued to nullify. See Salmon, *Women and the Law of Property*, 83 and Gunderson, "Independence, Citizenship, and the American Revolution," 72–73.

23. Confiscation laws varied by state, although all state governments acted against the estates of loyalists in some manner. For confiscation law in Massachusetts, see Richard D. Brown, "The Confiscation and Disposition of Loyalists' Estates in Suffolk County, Massachusetts," *William and Mary Quarterly*, 3rd ser., 21 (Oct. 1964): 534–50; Andrew McFarland Davis, "The Confiscation Laws of Massachusetts," Colonial Society of Massachusetts, *Transactions, 1902–4*, 8 (1906): 50–72; and David Edward Maas, *The Return of the Massachusetts Loyalists* (New York: Garland Publishing Inc., 1989), 270–337. For Connecticut, see Oscar Zeichner, "The Rehabilitation of the Loyalists in Connecticut," *New England Quarterly* 11 (June 1938): 308–30. For New York, see Harry B. Yoshpe, *The Disposition of Loyalist Estates in the Southern District of the State of New York* (New York: Columbia University Press, 1939), 13–27. For Pennsylvania, see Anne M. Ousterhout, *A State Divided: Opposition in Pennsylvania to the American Revolution* (New York: Greenwood Press, 1987), 148, 172–73, 279, 288 and Anne M. Ousterhout, "Pennsylvania Land Confiscations During the Revolution," *Pennsylvania Magazine of History and Biography* 102 (July 1978): 328–43. For Georgia, see Robert S. Lambert, "The Confiscation of Loyalist Property in Georgia, 1782–1786," *William and Mary Quarterly*, 3rd ser., 20 (Jan. 1963): 80–94. For an excellent summary of the confiscation policies of the four southern states—Virginia, North Carolina, South Carolina, and Georgia—see Kierner, *Southern Women in Revolution*, 7. For the hope that loyalist objects entrusted to women would remain safe from confiscations, see Kerber, *Women of the Republic*, 9–10.

Loyalist Harrison Gray relied upon this legal lacuna. As Gray shut up his home in Boston in preparation to embark with the British troops, he did so with the knowledge that his daughter, Elizabeth Gray Otis, would fill his place, taking up residence in the house and protecting the goods he had left behind.[24] Although several sources deem Gray a "moderate" Tory, the Massachusetts government acted quickly against his property because Elizabeth, as Gray's daughter rather than wife, exercised no legal right to its possession.[25] On July 6, 1776, Elizabeth wrote her father that "the Committee has taken most of your Estate into their hands." "[I] wish you had carried more of your Effects with you," she continued, and "hope and pray you may be well provided for, to say the least I think Colo. Murray treated me very ungenteelly in carrying off so many of our things, but these are strange times."[26] The items Elizabeth watched the specially-appointed committee remove from the house were never returned to either her or her father. The only restitution Gray received from the state of Massachusetts resulted from intricate legal maneuvering regarding outstanding debts owed to him when he entered exile.[27]

Some instances of loss were expected during the eighteenth century. The influx of many finished goods into the colonies depended on the capricious nature of transatlantic shipping. Loss, damage, and delayed arrivals seemed unavoidable, and the expectations of those buying or receiving the goods were adjusted accordingly.[28] The nature of life in the eighteenth century—particu-

24. Samuel Eliot Morison, *Harrison Gray Otis, 1765–1848: The Urbane Federalist* (Boston: Houghton Mifflin Company, 1969), 28.

25. If Gray were dead, the case for Elizabeth's possession would have been stronger, although the property would have most likely devolved to her brother or her son. Morison, *Harrison Gray Otis,* 18; Samuel Eliot Morison, "The Property of Harrison Gray, Loyalist," Colonial Society of Massachusetts, *Transactions, 1911–13,* 14 (1913): 324–27. Art historian Ellen Miles has also noted that Gray initially "opposed the use of violence by either side," see Ellen G. Miles, *American Paintings of the Eighteenth Century* (Washington, D.C.: National Gallery of Art, 1995), 34.

26. Elizabeth Gray Otis to Harrison Gray, 6 July 1776 as quoted in Morison, "The Property of Harrison Gray," 328.

27. For one of the Gray homes remaining in the possession of Elizabeth Gray Otis and her husband, Samuel Alleyne Otis, see Morison, "The Property of Harrison Gray," 330–31. Morison declared Gray's other real estate, and the implied goods within it, "long past recovery" by the end of the Revolution. The outstanding debts were recoverable because Gray's grandson, Harrison Gray Otis, had them assigned to him, thus preempting the appeal that would undoubtedly arise—that the debts were owed to a loyalist and should therefore be exempt from repayment. See Morison, *Harrison Gray Otis,* 61 and Morison, "The Property of Harrison Gray," 336–50.

28. Roberts, "Copley's Cargo," 26–28.

larly in cities where crowded streets and public spaces invited pickpockets and where frequent vaults into and out of carriages loosened items secured to bodies (jewelry, watches, ribbons) and concealed in pockets (snuffboxes, pocketbooks, notes)—also gave rise to circumstances in which theft and loss became relatively commonplace. This was the era when the publishing of advertisements for lost items began to gain real strength, especially for the lost-person possession, the runaway slave. London even had its own broker of lost and stolen things during the first quarter of the eighteenth century, Jonathan Wild, who brought together thieves and victims to negotiate prices for the return of goods obtained through nefarious means.[29] These occurrences of loss disrupted the owner, who invested and recognized themselves in the object, creating, as literary scholar Jonathan Lamb has termed it, a "desire of owners to be reacquainted with a material portion of their selves."[30] For the loyalists, who lost almost all of their possessions rather than an earring here and a pocketbook there, the circumstances were enormously more unnerving. Not only had they lost parts of themselves, they had lost the parts of their history and their family members—both dead and living—that had also become invested in the objects they were forced to leave behind.

When protective strategies worked, then, the "rescued" objects became even more significant in the lives of their owners. A monumental desk-and-book-case, commissioned in 1749 from a highly-accomplished Boston cabinetmaking shop for the Deblois family, provides an example (fig. 2). Like the Oliver sugar box that carried heightened significance as a family heirloom well into the nineteenth century after its midnight recovery a hundred years earlier, the desk-and-bookcase became a venerated object. Unlike the sugar box, however, and in direct contrast to Gray's experience, a married woman's agency combined with her peripheral yet extremely useful legal position preserved the piece. Gilbert Deblois fled Boston in March 1776 while his wife, Ann Coffin Deblois, remained behind with the couple's youngest children. It was not until nearly three years after Gilbert's departure that Massachusetts acted against the family. "Gilbert Deblois, merchant" appeared prominently on a list of proscribed and banished persons passed by the legislature in the fall of

29. Jonathan Lamb, "The Crying of Lost Things," *English Literary History* 71 (2004): 949–58.
30. Lamb, "The Crying of Lost Things," 955.

1778 and the state confiscated his estate shortly thereafter.[31] Ann, however, as a wife or widow who had "remained within the jurisdiction" and "actual authority" of the United States, continued to exercise her dower rights as long as she resided therein.[32] As a result, Ann's presence in Massachusetts meant that the Debloises avoided the fate of many other loyalist families—the complete loss of their possessions and property. Yet while Ann's mere presence limited the impact of confiscation, her agency as a legal advocate for the family enabled her to reacquire the two-thirds share of the house and land that

Fig. 2. Desk-and-Bookcase, attributed to John Welch (carver). Boston, ca. 1756. Mahogany. Private collection. Courtesy, Sotheby's New York.

31. Massachusetts General Court, An Act to Prevent the Return to this State, of Certain Persons Therein Named, and Others, Who Have Left This State, or Either of the United States, and Joined the Enemies Thereof, (16 October 1778), *The Acts and Resolves, Public and Private, of the Province of Massachusetts Bay* (Boston: Wright & Potter, printers to the state, 1905), 5: 912 (hereafter *Acts and Resolves*).

32. Massachusetts General Court, An Act for Confiscating the Estates of Certain Persons Commonly Called Absentees, 4th sess. (1 May 1779), *Acts and Resolves*, 5: 971. The act went on to explain that "her dower therein shall be set off to her, by the judges of probate of wills, in like manner as it might have been if her husband had died, intestate, within the jurisdiction of this state."

the government did eventually seize; she repurchased it from the state after the war.[33]

One of the many objects Ann secured from confiscation and loss was the aforementioned mahogany desk-and-bookcase.[34] Standing more than seven-and-a-half feet tall, and spanning a width greater than three feet, the piece, although separable where the desk and bookcase meet, hardly fulfills eighteenth-century standards of easy mobility or storage. It follows that had the entire Deblois family fled, the desk-and-bookcase would have been amongst the "effects" they were forced to leave behind in Boston, where it would have been either stolen or confiscated and sold. Ann's advocacy in terms of protecting and repurchasing the confiscated portion of the estate is manifest materially in the desk and bookcase itself. It does not carry the plethora of physical bruises associated with constant shifts in ownership—the dents, the dings, the replaced panels, large swaths of missing ornamentation, or incomplete provenance typical of a piece that, although very large and cumbersome, would have changed hands repeatedly had it been left behind.[35] Here, what is absent is as significant as what is present. Ann's labor and its successful outcome—preservation—are invisible; they are only manifest in the absence of change.

33. There is some disagreement as to when Ann repurchased the property; one source states the purchase occurred in 1781, another cites Ann's intervention as taking place in October, 1785. See Tim Clark, "The Saga of Aunt Bessie's Chest-on-Chest," *Yankee* (April 1988): 81 and Wendell Garrett, "The Story of a Boston Merchant," in Sotheby's New York, Important Americana Sale, 19–21 January 2007, 150.

34. Although Gilbert died in England in 1791, he returned briefly to Boston in 1789 and while there, made a will. An inventory of his possessions followed in 1792 and included a large number of goods, all of which Ann Deblois likely played a role in preserving. See Gilbert Deblois Inventory, 13 March 1792, docket no. 19898, Suffolk County Registry of Probate. The Museum of Fine Arts, Boston also holds a c. 1740–1750 clothespress with a Deblois family provenance, as well as a portrait of Gilbert Deblois (1990.300) painted by John Singleton Copley while both men resided in London during the Revolution. See Clothespress (1987.254), Museum of Fine Arts, Boston Curatorial Files, Boston, Mass.

35. The desk-and-bookcase is missing some of its original ornament—the upper portion of the bookcase most likely included a finial and three small holes above the arched central prospect door indicate the possible presence of nail/sprigs that once secured a piece of carving—yet its overall condition is remarkable given its age. This is evidenced by the fact that all the original hardware is intact and most of the damage sustained has been the result of wood expansion and shrinkage related to natural shifts in climate. See Robert Mussey Associates, Inc., "Treatment Report," 26 March 2007. The fact that the desk-and-bookcase was constructed of a grade of particularly hard, dense mahogany also made it less susceptible to the dents, bruises, and dings that occur with the passage of time. Robert Mussey, email message to author, 15 June 2010.

Furthermore, Ann's fight to hold onto the desk-and-bookcase inspired subsequent generations of the family to follow her lead. Like the Oliver sugar box that carried heightened significance as a family heirloom well into the nineteenth century after its midnight recovery a hundred years earlier, the desk-and-bookcase became a venerated object that stood proudly in a series of family homes and figured actively in the family's lore as a result. Maintaining the desk-and-bookcase's unaltered condition over time required still more invisible work, and as a Deblois descendent advised his son in 1951 in a statement that conjured Ann's much earlier efforts, "hold tight to it [the desk-and-bookcase] through thick and thin!"[36]

Although any object—a silver sugar box, a mahogany desk-and-bookcase, or even a letter—could be implicated within these personal relationships strained by the realities of war, portraiture was a uniquely doubly-valent medium. As an object similar to the sugar box, it could carry multiple meanings and serve as a connector between family members separated by time, space, and death. Yet due to its representational program, it could simultaneously manifest those same meanings and connections visually. Portraiture's special status as both an object among other loyalist objects and a representation capable of crafting visual solutions leads to the focus of the remainder of this essay—the loyalist portrait.

In January 1777 Roger Morris, living in political exile in London, wrote his wife, Mary, who had remained in New York, that "tho you cannot conceive how much I think of you, you easily will how much I miss you . . . your constant proofs of tender love & Esteem, so daily occur to my mind, that in my present Situation I am totally unhinged."[37] The letter, which so poignantly described the anxiety the couple's two-year separation had caused, was just one of a series that crisscrossed the Atlantic, maintaining the couple's bond

36. Lewis Deblois to Steven Deblois, 10 March 1951, Private Collection. The Deblois desk-and-bookcase proceeded down a direct line of family descent until 2007. See Lot 294, Sotheby's New York, Important Americana Sale, 19–21 January 2007, 154. For a detailed description of the object's provenance to 1896, and its unique hold on the Deblois family's collective memory, see Wendell Garrett, "The Story of a Boston Merchant," 152–53. The Deblois clothespress, or chest-on-chest, has a similar provenance, remaining in the family until the Museum of Fine Arts, Boston acquired it in 1987. See Edward S. Cooke, "Boston Clothespresses of the Mid-Eighteenth Century," *Journal of the Museum of Fine Arts* 1 (1989): 94n15.

37. Roger Morris to Mary Philipse Morris, 1 January 1777, Roger Morris Letters 1775–1777, Folder 1.3, Reference Collection, Morris-Jumel Mansion, New York, N.Y.

despite their physical absence from one another. The letters themselves can be considered moving objects that connected the couple despite the ocean that lay between them; Roger worried ceaselessly about them becoming lost or waylaid, numbering the letters so Mary would recognize their place in the seriated dialogue.[38] Other objects also performed such work—including the gowns and shoes the couple trafficked back and forth—but none as powerfully as portraits. Roger wrote to Mary earlier in their separation, admitting that "There is one particular, I own, I wish much to see, & that is your miniature Picture." "You know my dear," he continued, "it had been for some time past, in one of your Band Boxes." Given its neglected state, he mentioned that "[I] should be extremely happy to have it sent," but only if a "very very safe Conveyance" was available as "[I] would by no means run the risk of losing it."[39] Roger continued to ask Mary for the miniature until he wrote that he had received "a little Box" the contents of which he had "placed where I always wished it to be, & where I purpose to continue it."[40] For Roger, this likely meant on his person, as most eighteenth-century men carried portrait miniatures in their pockets.[41]

The importance of the miniature, which is no longer extant, lay in its ability to connect Roger to Mary. As mentioned previously, although any object could create connections between displaced family members, portraits, especially miniature ones that embarked on transatlantic voyages relatively easily, added the significant dimension of presence.[42] Miniatures, which were designed to

38. Roger Morris to Mary Philipse Morris, 4 October 1775 and 23 December 1775, Roger Morris Letters 1775–1777. For additional considerations of the difficulty accompanying the receipt of transatlantic letters and the anxiety that accompanied such an uncertain exchange, see Jennifer Roberts, "Copley's Cargo," 26–27 and Sarah Pearsall, "'After All These Revolutions': Epistolary Identities in an Atlantic World, 1760–1815" (PhD diss., Harvard University, 2001), 92, 94–95, 104–6.

39. Roger Morris to Mary Philipse Morris, 4 July 1775, Roger Morris Letters 1775–1777.

40. Roger Morris to Mary Philipse Morris, 14 March 1775 and 23 December 1775, Roger Morris Letters 1775–1777.

41. Anne Verplanck, "The Social Meanings of Portrait Miniatures in Philadelphia, 1760–1820," in *American Material Culture: The Shape of the Field,* Ann Smart Martin and Ritchie Garrison, eds., (Winterthur, Del.: Henry Francis du Pont Winterthur Museum), 201–2; 206–7.

42. Art historian Marcia Pointon has noted the similarity between portrait miniatures—which she terms "portrait-objects"—and letters as agents of personal connection, a relationship I believe can be extended to other, larger objects as well. See Marcia Pointon, "'Surrounded with Brilliants': Miniature Portraits in Eighteenth-Century England," *Art Bulletin* 83 (March 2001): 65–67.

be held and worn, enabled the viewer to come into intimate contact with their absent loved one's representation through touch.[43] Furthermore, the hair of the sitter (or person being commemorated in the case of mourning miniatures) was often woven into elaborate motifs and enframed on the backs of miniatures during the late eighteenth century, making a physical aspect of that body present within the object and subsequently, the space of those who held or wore it.[44] While the larger size of wall portraits prohibited such a bodily interaction, they were said to enter into "conversations" in which the figure in the portrait "spoke" to the viewer from which they were physically estranged.[45] Yet as the above examples indicate, these intimate interactions depended upon absence—one did not need to hold a miniature or speak with a portrait if the person portrayed was present. This points to the dialectical nature of portraiture as a genre; while it enacts presence through representation, it simultaneously enforces the absence of the portrayed *because* it is a representation, or a painted substitute for the real. As art historian Hans Belting has relayed, portraiture encompasses "the ancient antithesis between representing and being present, between holding the place of someone and being that someone."[46] It follows that portraiture looks forward beyond the moment of its production, when the subject of the portrait was presumably present, to the future when separation or death subsequently created an absence the representation must

43. Pointon, "'Surrounded with Brilliants': Miniature Portraits in Eighteenth-Century England," 52–66.

44. In some cases the artist crafting the miniature mixed hair into the pigment used to create the image, inserting the body even further into the object's inextricable fabric. See Robin Jaffee Frank, *Love and Loss: American Portrait and Mourning Miniatures* (New Haven: Yale University Press), 109–17.

45. In 1735, William Byrd wrote his good friend John Perceval, Earl of Egmont, that he had had "the pleasure of conversing a great deal with your picture." See Marion Tingling, ed., *The Correspondence of the Three William Byrds of Westover, Virginia, 1684–1776* (Charlottesville, Va.: The Virginia Historical Society in Association with The University Press of Virginia, 1977), 487. Byrd also talked with another portrait in his home, that of his sister-in-law, Jane Pratt Taylor. Byrd wrote Pratt, "We often discourse with you in effigie, and call the painter a bungler for falling so short of the original." See David Meschutt, "William Bryd and his Portrait Collection," *Journal of Early Southern Decorative Arts* (May 1988): 26–27. I owe this citation to the collegiality of Jennifer Van Horn.

46. Belting credits the quote to Erhart Kästner via a parenthetical quotation, but does not provide a full citation in an endnote or bibliography. See Hans Belting, *Likeness and Presence: A History of the Image Before the Era of Art,* trans. E. Jephcott (Chicago: University of Chicago Press, 1994), 9.

fill.[47] This complicated oscillation between the intimate and reassuring aspect of a limned likeness's ability to substitute for an absent loved one and its concurrent re-enforcement of that absence led to the ambivalent role the genre played within the experience of a displaced loyalist in possession of a portrait. Not only did it provide comfort, the portrait constantly re-invoked the separation that needed to be bridged as well.

Yet the oscillating effect of presence and absence inherent to portraiture also had other implications. Because portraits carried a likeness and, as a consequence, acted as substitutions in situations where families were separated by space or death, they were objects with a uniquely referential relationship to a family and its members and required special protection as a result. It comes as little surprise then that Roger Morris, similar to his prodding regarding the miniature, urged Mary on several occasions to take "particular" care of "Copley's Performance."[48] The three-quarter length portrait in question, produced by the artist during his 1771 stint in New York City, had been placed in Mary's care with Roger's departure. She obviously heeded his request as it remained in the family's possession throughout the war, which required a concentrated effort on Mary's part as constant troop movements in and around Manhattan forced her to shuttle back and forth between four residences (fig. 3).[49] And this

47. Both Margaretta Lovell and Marcia Pointon have discussed this function of portraiture; Lovell, *Art in a Season of Revolution,* 29, 34–35 and Marcia Pointon, *Hanging the Head: Portraiture and Social Formation in Eighteenth-Century England* (New Haven: The Paul Mellon Centre for Studies in British Art in association with Yale University Press, 1993), 159–75. Pointon's consideration of the issue of absence is double-layered. Not only does she liken the conversation piece to a will, in which the person responsible for the object's creation is now (and necessarily) absent, but she also considers how literal absences are painted into conversation pieces, which highlights the complicated line drawn between the "real" and the "representation."

48. Roger Morris to Mary Philipse Morris, 2 September 1775, 4 October 1775, and 23 December 1775, Roger Morris Letters 1775–1777.

49. Mary Morris changed residences several times during Roger's absence, shifting possessions to and from the couple's two country estates—one in Harlem, the other in Dutchess County—a rented house in Manhattan, and her family home in Yonkers. The Copley portrait evidently made some, if not all, of these trips with her. Although the series of letters between husband and wife ceased before the couple's final move to England in 1783 (Roger had by then returned to British-controlled New York and the couple undertook the move together), the provenance of the painting has led scholars to believe that the portrait also undertook the Atlantic voyage. See Rebora et al., *John Singleton Copley in America,* 300 and Wendy A. Cooper, *An American Vision: Henry Francis du Pont's Winterthur Museum* (Washington, D.C.: Board of Trustees, National Gallery of Art, 2002), 112.

Fig. 3. John Singleton Copley. *Mrs. Roger Morris (Mary Philipse)*. 1771. Oil on canvas. Courtesy, Winterthur Museum.

impulse was not exclusive to the Morris family; many other loyalists displayed a similar mindset in their devotion to the portraits of their family members.[50]

While the likenesses present in portraiture made these objects particularly important within the loyalist experience, images produced in the war's wake had a unique opportunity to act as a bridge between family members driven apart by divergent political views, flight to far-flung locations, and even death. Not

50. For example, a pair of pendants painted in 1769 by John Singleton Copley for Massachusetts native Isaac Royall shared in their owner's political exile in London by 1778, see Jules Prown, *John Singleton Copley* (Washington, D.C.: The National Gallery of Art, 1966), 2: 266. The pendants of James and Susannah Boutineau painted by Robert Feke in 1748 are also believed to have made the trip from Massachusetts to Nova Scotia with fleeing loyalists; see Richard H. Saunders and Ellen G. Miles, *American Colonial Portraits: 1770–1776* (Washington, D.C.: Smithsonian Institution, 1987), 167–69.

Fig. 4. John Singleton Copley. *Colonel William Fitch and His Sisters Sarah and Ann Fitch.* 1800/1801. Oil on canvas. National Gallery of Art. Gift of Eleanor Lothrop, Gordon Abbott, and Katharine A. Batchelder. Image courtesy National Gallery of Art, Washington, D.C.

only could their materiality challenge these occurrences, which was enhanced by the effect of presence likeness offered, their representational program could create narratives that simultaneously acknowledged and contested these realities. John Singleton Copley's large-scale group portrait *Colonel William Fitch and His Sisters Sarah and Ann Fitch*, painted between 1800 and 1801, serves as a case in point (fig. 4). The largest of Copley's surviving group portraits, its vast size contributes to the overall sense of drama it presents.[51] Three figures—from

51. Art historian Ellen Miles calls the Fitch portrait the largest of Copley's surviving group portraits. Only *The Knatchbull Family* (c. 1800–01) was larger, and it has since been cut down. See Miles, *American Paintings of the Eighteenth Century*, 82, 86n9. For comparative purposes, *Colonel William Fitch and His Sisters Sarah and Ann Fitch* measures 101½ x 134 inches while two of Copley's other large group portraits, *Mr. and Mrs. Ralph Izard* (1775) and *The Copley Family* (1776–77), measure 69 x 88½ inches and 72½ x 90¼ inches, respectively.

left to right, Sarah, Ann, and William Fitch—stand amidst a rural landscape complete with autumnal foliage, a stream that flows quickly to the front of the image (indicated by its frothy white capped waters), and mountains in the distance that demarcate the painting's low horizon line. Swirling clouds fill a sky tinged with the pinks and golds associated with either a rising or setting sun, while Sarah's floating veil and the animated locks of the horse's mane and tail emphasize that the winds that whisk the clouds in the background also whistle through the foreground space occupied by the siblings and William's horse. The contrapposto stance of both William and his mount accentuates this sense of movement. Not only are winds flowing through the canvas from background to foreground, sky to earth, William is caught mid-turn as he begins to twist from his sisters to mount his horse and proceed across the stream and into the space of the canvas.

A network of outstretched arms attempts to make connections between the three figures situated in this swirling landscape. Sarah—who is in the midst of moving forward as her skirt and veil trail behind her—reaches her right arm toward the left arm of her brother, which grasps an overturned hat and a walk-ing stick. Ann, too, reaches toward her brother, resting her pale left hand on the brilliant scarlet coat of his military uniform. Establishing a connection with William's twisting figure drives the women's actions, who direct their glances as well as their arms toward their brother. In a reciprocal action, William's left hand disappears behind the hat he holds, merging into the blackness of Ann's skirt and connecting his body to hers. In fact, if one divides the canvas in half, the two figures on each side—Ann and Sarah at the left, and William and his horse at the right—also seem to merge. The arms of the two women intertwine, Sarah's left forearm and Ann's right uniting to form one side of an elegant X-shape, which is crossed by the more full extension of Sarah's other limb, connecting the bodies of the women in this intersection of arms. Furthermore, the manner in which the women stand—Sarah turned in three-quarter view against Ann's frontally positioned body—folds the bodies of the two women into each other. Two outstretched arms encompass one unified body rather than two separate entities.

This same sense of merger characterizes the figure of William with that of his horse. William's body presses against the horse's shoulder in an effort to still the stirring animal, exemplified by his taut left arm, which extends over the saddle as a steadying force. In fact, the Colonel's body aligns with the body of the horse, his head in mirrored profile with that of the equine, and perfectly placed within the confines of its neck and mane. This coalescing of man and animal continues as the eye moves down the curve of the horse's snout and neck and through William's head and torso as the man's legs double for those of his horse. Like the sisters on the opposite side of the canvas, two bodies connect and converge.

This theme of connection amidst a moving and shifting landscape visually manifests the Fitch family's intentions. According to family tradition, the Fitches commissioned Copley to paint the portrait as a gift for their maternal uncle, Dr. James A. Lloyd, a prominent surgeon in Boston, Massachusetts.[52] Although the Fitch siblings had resided in England for many years by the time Copley executed their portraits, they had spent their adolescence in Boston. Their father, Samuel Fitch, served as Advocate General for the colony of Massachusetts Bay and, because of his support of the British government as Revolutionary fervor spread, fled Boston with his family when the British evacuated the city in March 1776. As Fitch made clear in a claim he submitted to the British government in an attempt to garner compensation for his losses, his loyalty to the crown meant that he had been "compelled" to leave his home in Boston; he did not do so "voluntarily."[53] The political allegiance of James Lloyd, Elizabeth Lloyd Fitch's brother, was hardly as ardent or as unwavering and such equivocal politics caused tension when confronted by Fitch's absolute loyalist stance. When Samuel Fitch left Boston with his wife and 20-year-old William, 17-year-old Ann, and Sarah, the youngest at thirteen, in tow, their departure cemented a cleavage with family members that had been brewing for several years.

By the time Copley painted the portrait of the Fitch siblings, however, that

52. Memorandum, 26 August 1988, *Colonel William Fitch and His Sisters Sarah and Ann Fitch* (1960.4.1), Curatorial Files, National Gallery of Art, Washington, D.C. See also Miles, *American Paintings of the Eighteenth Century,* 82 and Prown, *John Singleton Copley,* 2:419. There is some debate regarding who was the intended recipient of the painting. Although both the artist and the donors of the portrait believed it was intended for Dr. James Lloyd, the Fitch sibling's uncle, earlier owners maintained it was intended for Lloyd's son, also James Lloyd. The fact that father and son had the same name has certainly contributed to this confusion. See Miles, *American Paintings of the Eighteenth Century,* 86n1. Whoever the intended recipient, however, the painting's function as a means to reunify strained family bonds remains the same.

53. Samuel Fitch Claim, undated, T 12/105/90, Public Records Office, Kew, Eng.

breach had begun to heal, and the image itself served as an active agent in that process. The Fitches commissioned the image with the explicit intent that it traverse the Atlantic as a gift to an estranged uncle in hope of repairing family ties strained by the war. The connections Copley so painstakingly emphasized in terms of the iconography of the portrait's merging bodies transformed the painting's purpose—the reconnection of the Fitch and Lloyd families—into a visual motif. Furthermore, the portrait also carries the sense of movement—brisk winds, shifting figures, quickly moving waterways—that it would encounter as an object being shipped from London to Boston. The goal of the image as object became encoded in its visual structure.

It remains important to note that it was the Fitch children that carried out this project of reunification with the Boston branch of their family. Samuel and Elizabeth Fitch had died a few years prior to the portrait's painting, and Sarah, dressed in what could be read as a bridal costume in the early nineteenth century, was set to marry a fellow loyalist expatriate, Leonard Vassall.[54] Although white bridal wear had yet to become ubiquitous, many brides during this period did choose to don the color for the occasion and, given the concurrent timing of the portrait's production and Sarah's impending nuptials, reading her ensemble as a reference to her upcoming marriage seems appropriate.[55] It follows that the portrait's commissioning occurred at an important moment of transition for the Fitch siblings; they now served as heads of the Fitch family line, and Sarah's forthcoming marriage marked the moment at

54. Miles, *American Paintings of the Eighteenth Century*, 82.

55. Most historians link the beginning of the cultural turn to the "white wedding," particularly in Great Britain and the United States, to the wedding of Queen Victoria of Great Britain and Prince Albert of Saxe-Coburg and Gotha that took place on February 10, 1840. Contrary to tradition, the young Queen eschewed state robes and court dress, wearing a white silk satin dress (made of English cloth no less) instead. While the Queen's sartorial choice cemented the widespread shift to the white wedding dress, some brides did choose to wear the color prior to 1840 and, like Queen Victoria, also wore veils. In 1801, the Peirce family of Salem, Massachusetts, initiated an extensive refurbishing of their east parlor in preparation for their daughter Sally's wedding, to which she wore a white muslin empire-waist dress and a lace veil "put on turban fashion," an ensemble that very closely resembles that of Sarah Fitch in the Copley portrait. See Paula Bradstreet Richter, *Wedded Bliss: The Marriage of Art and Ceremony* (Hanover, N.H.: University Press of New England for the Peabody Essex Museum, 2008), 117–20, plate 4, and Barbara Penner, "'A Vision of Love and Luxury': The Commercialization of Nineteenth-Century American Weddings," *Winterthur Portfolio* 34 (Spring 2004): 2.

which that line gained the potential to continue.[56] The portrait thus marked their successful attainment of majority, and all that meant for the perpetuation of the family into the future, as well as their effort to reconnect with family members divorced from them by the circumstances of the war.

While Sarah's white dress and bridal veil allude to the family's future line, Ann's black dress functions as a reminder of her parents' recent death, and serves as a portent of things to come.[57] The sense of movement that characterizes the portrait foreshadows the transatlantic trip the image was created to take, but it also serves another purpose. Like Ann's black dress that stands in such sharp contrast to the white of her sister's costume and the scarlet of her brother's coat, it too lends an air of unsettledness to the painting.[58] Overall, while connection constitutes a major theme of the painting, its opposing force—disconnection—also bubbles to the surface. The circle formed by the siblings' arms never truly closes and completes itself. While William's hand disappears behind his overturned hat and merges into the folds of Ann's skirt, it fails to meet with Sarah's pale and beseeching fingers. The glances of Ann, Sarah, and William also betray a broken connection. Ann and Sarah direct all their bodily and visual attention in William's direction while he fails to meet their glances, gazing off into the distance at the left of the painting. Furthermore, none of the figures look in the viewer's direction. All of the looking in the portrait—between the figures themselves and the figures and the viewer—is unacknowledged.

The Fitches, however, are separated by more than unreturned glances and diverted gestures. While they all stand upon an outcropping or "terrace" above the stream that flows rapidly into the foreground, the waterfall that marks its beginning constitutes the middle of a triangular region of space that separates William from Sarah and Ann.[59] William's arm and his hat perched atop his walking stick outline a zone through which the arms of the women cannot

56. Margaretta Lovell has argued that "almost all private portraits were made at the time an individual's achievement of majority, inheritance, marriage, or first issue—moments that mark the movement of family substance in an orderly, prescribed manner." See Lovell, *Art in a Season of Revolution*, 10.

57. Richter, *Wedded Bliss*, plate 4

58. Miles, *American Paintings of the Eighteenth Century*, 82.

59. For the description of the ground the Fitches stand upon as a "terrace" see Miles, *American Paintings of the Eighteenth Century*, 84.

Fig. 5. John Singleton Copley. *The Copley Family.* 1776–1777. Oil on canvas. National Gallery of Art. Andrew Mellon Fund. Image courtesy National Gallery of Art, Washington, D.C.

penetrate, and the water rushes forward, almost pushing the figures further apart. Copley employed the theme of water as an agent and metaphor of spatial separation in another group portrait of a loyalist family—that of his own painted in 1776–77 (fig. 5). The story of the Copley family's imbrication in loyalism, however, begins more than ten years earlier. Copley, as a Boston resident in 1765 when the enforcement of the Stamp Act first incited protest, saw much of the initial revolutionary activity first hand. His marriage to Susanna Clarke, the daughter of the city's leading importer, in 1769 implicated him even further. Richard Clarke's mercantile firm served as the consignee for the English tea that found its way to the bottom of Boston Harbor on December 16, 1773. Protests had taken place in front of Clarke's home the previous November, and Copley attempted to mediate during the conflict, delivering a letter from the consignees to the angry Bostonians that same month.[60] Yet Copley's mediation ultimately failed; rather than being viewed as a neutral party, Boston radicals, who were quickly becoming known as patriots, linked him with supporters of British colonial policy like his father-in-law. Copley's choice to sail for England in June 1774 in order to complete his artistic education and later forge a career there rather than the colonies confirmed to many that the artist had loyalist leanings, although he maintained his neutrality throughout the Revolution and its aftermath.[61]

Copley's embarkation on a Grand Tour while his family faced the trepidations associated with being labeled as loyalists caused a great deal of anxiety and unsettledness. The family was separated for a year and a half before Susanna and the children sailed for London, and *The Copley Family* was painted to commemorate their reunion.[62] In the image, Copley stands slightly outside the group composed of his young family and father-in-law; a stream of rushing water very similar to that in the Fitch portrait sets him apart spatially from his

60. Ann Uhry Abrams, "Politics, Prints, and John Singleton Copley's *Watson and the Shark*," *The Art Bulletin* 61 (June 1979): 267.

61. See Abrams, "Politics, Prints, and John Singleton Copley," 268, 276 and Maurie McInnis, "Cultural Politics, Colonial Crisis, and Ancient Metaphor in John Singleton Copley's *Mr. and Mrs. Ralph Izard*," *Winterthur Portfolio* 34 (Summer-Autumn 1999): 90. I, however, believe that Copley was much more of a loyalist than scholars tend to admit. The fact that he never returned to the United States after the Revolution, despite a more willing and established clientele in the former colonies, leads me to this conclusion. Although the financial situation of the colonies was precarious post-revolution, Copley had to struggle for a British audience and rely heavily upon the financial support of his father-in-law, putting him in a similarly unpredictable financial situation. See Prown, *John Singleton Copley,* 2:259n2.

62. It is important to note that Susanna left one of the couple's four children, Clarke Copley, in Boston under the care of Copley's mother, Mary Copley Pelham. It was not unusual for women to leave infant children behind with relatives while the remainder of the family embarked on a transoceanic trip as it was feared that their bodies could not withstand the physical difficulties associated with a long sea voyage. Clarke Copley, who had been born in January 1774, was simply too young to take with the family in May 1775. He was left in the care of Copley's mother, Mary Copley Pelham, who was expected to venture to London soon. Clarke died in January 1776 and Mary Copley Pelham could never be persuaded to make the trip to England; she died in Boston in 1789 after successfully serving as Copley's agent for his Beacon Hill property for nearly fifteen years; see Prown, *John Singleton Copley,* 2:262, 341. It is believed that the reaching infant in the portrait was initially conceived by Copley as Clarke, as the family did not learn of his death until after work on the portrait had begun. His wife was expecting, however, so the child was not omitted from the composition, and has since been referred to as Susanna, who was born in London in October 1776. See Miles, *American Paintings of the Eighteenth Century,* 48 and Prown, *John Singleton Copley,* 2:262.

wife and three of their four children. The image's emphasis on the seemingly contradictory aspects of inclusion and exclusion, mediated by a body of water, indicates the hesitancy of a family attempting to reconstitute itself after a harsh and uncertain separation. Of course, the water can be read as part of the natural landscape so often found in the background of individual and group portraits produced in the eighteenth century. In the case of both the Fitch and Copley images however, it also alludes to each family's dispersal across the Atlantic ocean, a spatial diffusion linked to loyalist politics and, in Copley's case, the practice of art. Furthermore, in relation to the Fitch portrait, the river, which the sisters and brother are united against in terms of standing upon the same bank, yet simultaneously separated by, also carries another metaphorical meaning. In Greek mythology, the River Styx acted as the symbol for the passage of death, the journey one took between Earth and the underworld.[63] Copley's engagement with mythology and his application of it in his paintings has been well demonstrated in terms of his 1775 portrait of *Mr. and Mrs. Ralph Izard*, yet another image heavily implicated within the experience of loyalism (fig. 6).[64] Interestingly, Copley situated the krater, another allusion to classical

63. The popularity and influence of antiquity in eighteenth-century arts and letters has been well demonstrated in recent years, and there is no doubt of its cultural force. See, for example, Colin B. Bailey, *The Loves of the Gods: Mythological Painting From Watteau to David* (New York: Rizzoli,1992), 99–515; Marcia Pointon, *Strategies for Showing: Women, Possession, and Representation in English Visual Culture, 1665–1800* (New York: Oxford University Press, 1997), 173–227; Caroline Winterer, *The Culture of Classicism: Ancient Greece and Rome in American Intellectual Life, 1780–1910* (Baltimore: The Johns Hopkins University Press, 2002), 40, 86; and Caroline Winterer, *The Mirror of Antiquity: American Women and the Classical Tradition, 1750–1900* (Ithaca, N.Y.: Cornell University Press, 2007), 26–27. While Hades and the River Styx were not often used as visual motifs in this period, they did serve as potent literary references ranging from Odysseus's visit to Hades in the *Odyssey* to Dante's discussion of his journey, accompanied by Virgil, down the River Styx into the *Inferno*. Such references would have resonated with those viewing the image who recognized William Fitch's portrait as posthumous. Notably, the River Styx was also supposed to ascend from a great height at its origin, as explained in Apuleius's tale of Venus's trials for Pysche in *The Golden Ass*, further likening the falls in the Fitch portrait with those of the mythical river.

64. According to art historian Maurie McInnis's analysis of the iconography of the Izard portrait—the elements of classical Greek sculpture and pottery in particular—the image presents a moment of contemplation on Ralph's part with symbols of both loyalism and patriotism included in the work. The eighteenth-century metaphor that figured the colonies as belligerent children who rebelled against their wise mother England serves as the basis of her argument, which she then relates to the antiquities present in the painting. McInnis identifies the mythical scene portrayed on the volute krater, located in the upper-right-hand corner of the image, as one of matriarchal tyranny. Leto, angered that Niobe boasted that her happiness outweighed

Fig. 6. John Singleton Copley. *Mr. and Mrs. Ralph Izard (Alice Delancey).* 1775. Oil on canvas. Museum of Fine Arts, Boston, Mass. Edward Ingersoll Brown Fund.

culture, at the left of the image of the Fitch siblings in a manner nearly identical to that in the portrait of the Izards, linking these two paintings visually as well as in their interest in mythological subject matter and, similar to *The Copley Family,* their shared loyalist context.[65]

The biographical facts of William's life cast the Fitch portrait's allusion

---

Leto's, ordered her children, Artemis and Apollo, to kill Niobe's sons and daughters. Conversely, the statue portrayed in the background of the canvas and on the sketch that Ralph holds relates to the story of Papirius and his mother, the former being a virtuous young man who refused to tell his mother the proceedings of the Roman senate, which he recently witnessed, despite her urging. The mother acts dishonorably in both narratives, but it is Papirius, in his virtuous immunity to his mother's wrongful appeals, that signifies patriotism while Artemis and Apollo's blind faith in their mother's request conveys loyalism. McInnis ultimately concludes, based on the double inclusion of *Papirius and His Mother* and the positive connotation of its narrative, that the painting evidences Ralph's ultimate alignment with the patriot cause. See McInnis, "Cultural Politics," 103–6.

65. Jules Prown has also noted the similarity of the vases in the Fitch and Izard portraits; see Prown, *John Singleton Copley,* 2:419–20.

to disconnection in a different light. Although William appears very much alive in the portrait, he had died nearly six years before Copley painted it. In fact, the portrait presents a moment in 1795 when the sisters bid farewell to William who, as an officer in the British army, was embarking on military duty to Jamaica. William received a mortal wound while engaged in combat there; as art historian Ellen Miles described the painting, it depicted a "literal and figurative farewell."[66] The painting's dialectical sense of connection and simultaneous disconnection emphasizes the ambiguity of the pregnant moment portrayed.

Contemporary reviewers of the portrait, which Copley submitted to the annual exhibition of the Royal Academy of the Arts before it departed London as a gift for Dr. Lloyd, reacted in tepid tones to the work. One bemoaned the "preponderance of portraits" at the exhibition in general, while another commented that the image was "well conceived," but the figures were "still and ill drawn" and the "wooden horse" was abominable."[67] Some of this negativity stemmed from the fact that several of the reviewers knew of William's fate and believed the Fitch portrait simply attempted to accomplish too much on one canvas; it was, after all, a "military image, a family group, and a memorial portrait" all at once.[68] The painting's equivocation in terms of the genres and narrative moments it set out to portray caused one reviewer to extend his analysis further in an attempt to elucidate the ambiguity at its core. "The fate of the Colonel," he stated, "attaches to this piece a degree of interest which it would otherwise have failed to produce." While the reviewer praised the figures as "well drawn," and the coloring as "natural and chaste," he found that the sisters' "countenances indicate too much a *presentiment* of their brother's fate, which at the time they cannot be supposed to have foreseen."[69] The two temporalities in the canvas—the moment of William's departure, and the hint of his impending death—disturbed the critic and ultimately caused him to

66. Miles, *American Paintings of the Eighteenth Century,* 82.

67. "Royal Academy," *Morning Post and Gazetteer,* 27 April 1801, 3 and "Exhibition of Paintings &c. At the Royal Academy, Somerset-Place," *The St. James Chronicle: or, British Evening-Post,* 7–9 May 1801, 4. Both are quoted in Miles, *American Paintings of the Eighteenth Century,* 85. See also *Colonel William Fitch and His Sisters Sarah and Ann Fitch* (1960.4.1), Curatorial Files, National Gallery of Art, Washington, D.C.

68. Miles, *American Paintings of the Eighteenth Century,* 84.

69. "Royal Academy, III," *Morning Herald,* 1 May 1801, 2; *Colonel William Fitch and His Sisters Sarah and Ann Fitch (*1960.4.1), Curatorial Files, National Gallery of Art, Washington, D.C.

review the portrait negatively. The image contained too much to be recognized as real—it referenced shifts in time that simply could not exist.

These seemingly impossible shifts in time, however, were integral to Copley's and the Fitch sisters' conception of the work. The portrait sought to memorialize and connect a dead brother with his sisters despite depicting a moment before that death occurred, and also served as a gift to an estranged family member in Boston meant to strengthen weakened ties of affection. Without these shifts in time—a reversal to a moment before William's death and a simultaneously advancement to that death through iconographic and narrative elements—the implied connection of the siblings *across* death would have remained incomplete. And without this connection of the siblings, however fraught it might have been, the portrait would have had difficulty serving as a bridge between family members divided by political views and physical space. After all, if the painting could connect a living yet simultaneous dead brother with his sisters, it certainly could repair family bonds strained by the distance created by the war and the Atlantic.

When families such as the Fitches became politically and spatially divided by the Revolution, and the death of family members permanently altered their composition, paint became the means for reunification and resurrection. The portrait Copley painted for Sarah and Ann Fitch resurrects William's body through the production of a posthumous portrait and also attempts to resuscitate the dying Fitch family by acting as a gift and connection between its divided branches. The concerns of Copley's wife regarding the painting's transatlantic journey affirm that those connected to the object recognized its capacity to perform such work. In an undated letter to her daughter, Elizabeth Copley Greene, who resided in Boston, Susanna Clarke Copley mentioned that "Miss Fitch has sent her picture to Mr. Lloyd. It went from this in very good order." She went on to instruct Elizabeth that "should it, by being shut up, or by the dampness of the sea, contract a fog, it will only be necessary to have it well rubbed with a warm, soft handkerchief, which will restore the varnish. I mention this, as perhaps they [the Lloyds] may be at a loss, and apply to you for information."[70] As Susanna described it, the portrait might corrode,

70. Susanna Clarke Copley to Elizabeth Copley Greene, undated, as quoted in Martha Babcock Greene Amory, *The Domestic and Artistic Life of John Singleton Copley, R.A.: With Notices of his Works, and Reminiscences of his Son, Lord Lyndhurst, High Chancellor of Great Britain* (Boston: Houghton, Mifflin and Company, 1882), 195–96.

or "contract a fog" when it crossed the ocean. That "fog" could be reversed, but her conception of the potential dangers of its journey alludes to the almost preternatural power of distance and space to harm both loyalist paintings and families. These damaged families had to be repaired and reborn—resurrected in paint—and the Fitch portrait combines allusions to the family's figurative death and its rebirth. Because the painting's iconography and narrative could capture both union and dissolution and the painting as an object could physically shift and move, it could enact these connections and resurrections that mere bodies could not achieve.

Portraits, with their ability to simultaneously function as objects and representations, acted with particular potency in the loyalist experience. Whether through the ambivalent intimacy created by likeness or a temporally ambiguous narrative that presaged a brother's death while facilitating his rebirth, the portraits of the Morris and Fitch families actively mediated and structured their experience of loyalism. While portraits are unique in their ability to both create and represent familial connections, reading other, less representational objects such as Peter Oliver's silver sugar box, the lost possessions of the Grays, and the monumental Deblois desk-and-bookcase with this agency in mind helps to reveal similar activities that often become obscured beneath the patina of mahogany or the shine of silver. And, as discussed previously, these readings of loyalist objects can be extended beyond the scope of particular political parties or the immediate years of the Revolution. The ability of the loyalist object—whether it be a portrait or a piece of silver—to engender persistent yet flexible family relationships across space and over time is an ability inherent to almost any object enmeshed in a close and reciprocal relationship with a subject. The loyalists, then, in this period of heightened relation to their objects, help us understand the multiple and shifting meanings embedded in eighteenth-century things.

Fig. 1. Susan Anne Livingston Ridley Sedgwick, Portrait of Elizabeth 'Mumbet' Freeman (c.1742–1829). Watercolor on ivory, 1811. © Massachusetts Historical Society, Boston, MA, USA/ The Bridgeman Art Library.

Fig. 2. Elizabeth Way Champlain, unfinished self portrait. Watercolor on ivory, n.d. Courtesy of Ramsay MacMullen.

The Color of Whiteness: Picturing Race on Ivory

CATHERINE E. KELLY

TWO WOMEN—one black, the other white—meet our gaze. The black woman is recessed into the picture plane, as though she has taken a step back, away from us. With a tilt of her chin, the white woman appears to project herself off of the ivory support and into our space. The painting of the black woman is finished and framed; her likeness has moved into the networks of affiliation that sustain and are sustained by portraiture. The painting of the white woman is unfinished. It never served as a surrogate for the sitter in its own time, although it does fulfill that purpose in ours. The paintings are conventional, immediately recognizable as miniature portraits painted in watercolor on thin sheets of ivory. In the first half of the nineteenth century, such likenesses were ubiquitous among affluent and middling Americans; today, they are ubiquitous at historical societies and museums, in antiques shops, and on eBay. Yet while the genre is familiar, these particular paintings are not. Portraits of nineteenth-century African-American women are rare, portraits on ivory all the more so. Unfinished miniature portraits from any period are also unusual. Yet these miniatures are set apart by more than the race of the sitter or the completion of the painting. Unlike the vast majority of extant ivory miniatures, they survive embedded in their stories, stories about the ties that bound sitters, artists, and viewers.

The painting of the African-American woman is a portrait of Elizabeth Freeman, a Massachusetts slave who claimed her liberty in 1781 (fig. 1). According to one story, after hearing the Declaration of Independence read aloud in a Sheffield church, she successfully sued for freedom in a case that challenged the constitutionality of slavery in Massachusetts. Freeman never learned to read or write. But even as a slave, she had been widely respected for her courage, integrity, and judgment. After gaining her freedom, she went to work in the household of Theodore Sedgwick, the attorney who had represented her. There, she was cook, housekeeper, nurse, and more. Sedgwick's first wife, Pamela Dwight Sedgwick, was regularly incapacitated, physically and emotionally. Elizabeth Freeman stepped into the vacuum left by her mistress's frailty and finally by her death in 1807. She left the Sedgwick household a year later, when Theodore remarried: according to Sedgwick family lore, Freeman balked at conceding her cherished authority to the new mistress. Instead, she retired to the small home she had purchased with her savings, worked as a nurse, and devoted herself to her grown child, grandchildren, and great-grand-children. But she never cut her ties to the Sedgwick family circle. Instead, she returned at regular intervals to care for the family when she was especially needed. Indeed, it may well have been one of these visits—part sociability, part support—that occasioned Freeman's portrait, painted in 1811 by Susan Livingston Ridley Sedgwick, the daughter-in-law of Freeman's former attorney and employer. Elizabeth Freeman died in 1829. Despite her own fondness for fine dress and what one contemporary described as the "reckless consumption" of her kin, she left not "a single debt" to encumber an estate that amounted to nearly $1,000.[1]

The white woman portrayed in the second painting is Elizabeth (Betsey) Way Champlain, a miniaturist from New London, Connecticut. She began this self-portrait in 1818 (fig. 2). Champlain was born into a middling mercantile family just before the Revolution. It isn't clear when or how she learned to paint, but by the time she was in her twenties, she had begun to paint miniature portraits of neighbors and kin. Her 1794 marriage to ship captain George Champlain did not bring her career to a halt. On the contrary. She continued to paint and teach throughout her marriage, perhaps to help stabilize the family's erratic income. From her husband's death in 1820 until her own, she lived mostly by her brush. Betsey Way Champlain worked diligently at her craft, learning when and where she could. Yet it would be a mistake to cast her merely as an earnest craftswoman, for she was an irrepressible culture vulture. She wrote sketches and especially poems on themes like "Viewing a

---

1. The life of Elizabeth Freeman is discussed in Catharine Maria Sedgwick, "Mumbet," unpublished mss., Catharine Maria Sedgwick Papers, Massachusetts Historical Society, Boston, Mass.; Mary Kelley, ed., *The Power of Her Sympathy: The Autobiography and Journal of Catharine Maria Sedgwick* (Boston: Massachusetts Historical Society, 1993), 69–71, 124–26; Theodore Sedgwick, *The Practicability of the Abolition of Slavery: A Lecture* (New York: J. Seymour, 1831). Freeman's legal case is discussed in Arthur Zilversmit, "Quok Walker, Mumbet, and the Abolition of Slavery in Massachusetts," *William and Mary Quarterly*, 3rd Ser. (Oct. 1968): 614–24. Quote is from Sedgwick, "Mumbet."

Comet," "On Flattery," "The Muse," and "Fancy." She associated herself with
a coterie of very minor poets who circulated between New London and New
York City. She played guitar and "flaggellett" and in her forties she took up
dancing, mastering the "five positions" and waltzing her husband—and his
cane—around their parlor. In 1825, Betsey Way Champlain died unexpectedly
after a brief illness.[2]

And what of the paintings themselves? However different the sitters were
from one another, their portraits confirm scholars' conclusions about the cultural and social contexts of women's artistic production on the one hand and
the significance of portrait miniatures in the Early Republic. We know nothing
about how, when, or why either Susan Ridley Sedgwick or Betsey Way Champlain learned to paint, much less how the women acquired the special skills
necessary to paint in miniature on ivory. But it is doubtful that either received
systematic training in the arts. That kind of instruction was notoriously hard
to come by, even for aspiring male artists; indeed, its absence has become a set
piece in art historical narratives. It therefore seems likely that both Sedgwick
and Champlain were introduced to the rudiments of watercolor painting as
part of their acquisition of the accomplishments that crowned elite and middling women's education in the Early Republic. The overwhelming majority
of female and coeducational academies and seminaries included some form
of artistic training in their curricula; when they did not, private drawing and
painting masters catering to young ladies and gentlemen stepped in to supply
the need. One component of a broader concern with aesthetics, accomplishments were calculated to cultivate taste. The creation of an embroidered picture, a water-colored landscape, or a bouquet of worsted flowers suitable for
display in the home was the training's byproduct rather than its end.[3] That

2. My discussion of Betsey Way Champlain's life is drawn from Ramsay MacMullen's invaluable collection of the Way-Champlain Family correspondence, *Sisters of the Brush: Their Family,
Art, Lives, and Letters, 1797–1833* (New Haven: Past Times Press, 1997). The original letters, and
many unpublished examples of Betsey Way Champlain's literary activities, can be found in the
Way-Champlain Family Correspondence, American Antiquarian Society, Worcester, Mass.

3. This argument is developed at length in my "Reading and the Problem of Accomplishment," Heidi Brayman Hackel and Catherine E. Kelly, eds., *Reading Women: Literacy, Authorship, and Culture in the Atlantic World, 1500–1800* (Philadelphia: University of Pennsylvania
Press, 2007), 124–43. A rare example of an ivory miniature painted by a "schoolgirl" who attended
Mrs. Morris's Philadelphia academy is included in Dale T. Johnson, *American Portrait Minia-*

said, advocates of the accomplishments also pointed out that the ornamental skills had market value; in a pinch, a woman could use her accomplishments for self-support. As one writer put it, the "fine arts or the sciences" that single women pursued for their "amusement or instruction" could become necessities depending on the "inactivity, folly, or death of a husband."[4]

For Susan Ridley Sedgwick, daughter of one prosperous man and wife of another, painting remained an avocation, an accomplishment. As a girl, she had attended schools in Boston and Albany, where she met Catharine Maria Sedgwick and where she likely met her future husband, Theodore Sedgwick II, an attorney and Catharine's older brother. Susan Ridley Sedgwick set enough store on art and on her own talent that she devoted time to mastering the painstaking technique demanded by a water-colored ivory miniature. She probably offered support, perhaps even instruction, to her daughter, Maria Banyer Sedgwick, another gifted amateur artist. But, like Betsey Champlain, Susan Ridley Sedgwick also enjoyed writing, a creative outlet and form of cultural production that offered distinct advantages over painting. For one thing, as a fledgling writer, Susan enjoyed the enthusiastic encouragement of her dear friend and sister-in-law, the renowned novelist Catharine Maria Sedgwick. For another, a writer could produce (and sell) her work from the privacy of her own home, shrouded in decorous anonymity. Portrait painters by necessity ventured into the public to secure sitters. In the nineteenth century, it was far easier to be a scribbling woman than a painting one. Personal connections and public sentiment all but guaranteed that when Susan Ridley Sedgwick entered

---

tures in the Manney Collection (New York: Metropolitan Museum of Art, 1991), 156. For general descriptions of the art made by female students, see Lynne Templeton Brickley, "Sarah Pierce's Litchfield Female Academy, 1792–1833" (Ed.D. Diss, Harvard University, 1985); Catherine Keene Fields and Lisa C. Knightlinger eds., *To Ornament Their Minds: Sarah Pierce's Litchfield Academy, 1792–1833* (Litchfield Conn.: Litchfield Historical Society, 1993); Suzanne L. Flynt, *Ornamental and Useful Accomplishments: Schoolgirl Education and Deerfield Academy, 1800–1830* (Deerfield, Mass.: Pocumtuck Valley Memorial Association, 1988); Betty Ring, *Let Virtue be a Guide to Thee: Needlework in the Education of Rhode Island Women* (Providence: Rhode Island Historical Society, 1983) and her *Girlhood Embroidery: American Samplers and Pictorial Needlework, 1690–1850* (New York: Knopf, 1993), vol. 1–2.

4. "RUDIMENTS OF TASTE and a POLITE FEMALE EDUCATION," *Juvenile Port-Folio and Literary Miscellany* 1:38 (July 3, 1813): 150. See also the letters of the fictional Miss Penelope Airy, who supports herself with her needle after the premature deaths of her parents in [Judith Sargent Murray] *The Gleaner. A miscellaneous production. In three volumes. By Constantia* (Boston: I. Thomas and E.T. Andrews, 1798), 176–78.

the cultural marketplace in the late 1820s, her aim was not to sell portraits but to publish didactic children's literature.[5]

Pushed by economic necessity and pulled by a love of art, Betsey Way Champlain turned her accomplishment into a saleable skill. This was no mean feat. Earning steady money as a female painter was far more difficult than promised by pundits touting the marketability of the accomplishments. In reality, it "required the greatest exertions to make both ends meet" as Champlain complained in 1822. More than once, she admitted that a "suppression of business" resulted in an "attack of hypochondriac." Confronted by fluctuating demand and slim profits, Champlain displayed enormous energy, resilience, and ingenuity. She painted kin, neighbors, and local notables. In the 1810s, she expanded her business by taking likenesses of corpses. All told, she painted enough of New London that by the end of the nineteenth century her portraits of "ladies"—marked by a "delicacy of treatment and purity of sentiment" —had come to stand for the best of "old time" society. When portrait commissions were few and far between, she gave lessons to young women. But despite her eventual status as New London's painter of record, Champlain deplored her spotty training, which consisted of poring over precepts included in letters from her sister, miniaturist Mary Way, and copying other paintings when they came her way. She and her family were always certain that her progress was hobbled by her ignorance of theory and by the lack of guidance that formal studio training could provide.[6]

5. Susan Ridley Sedgwick's titles included *The Morals of Pleasure: Illustrated by Stories Designed for Young Persons* (1829), *Allen Prescott: or, the Fortunes of a New England Boy* (1834), *Alida; or, Town and Country* (1844), and *Walter Thornley, or, a Peep at the Past* (1859). On Susan Ridley Sedgwick's life and place in the Sedgwick clan, see Kelley, *Autobiography*, 90–94; Timothy Kenslea, *The Sedgwicks in Love: Courtship, Engagement, and Marriage in the Early Republic* (Boston: Northeastern University Press, 2006), 48–50, 225 n. 48. On the fraught relation between creative women and publicity in the nineteenth century, see Mary Kelley, *Private Woman, Public Stage: Literary Domesticity in Nineteenth-Century America* (New York: Oxford University Press, 1984); Anne Sue Hirshorn, "Anna Claypoole, Margaretta, and Sarah Miriam Peale: Modes of Accomplishment and Fortune," in Lillian B. Miller, ed., *The Peale Family: Creation of a Legacy, 1770–1870* (Washington, D.C.: Abbeville Press in Association with the Trust for Museum Exhibitions and the National Portrait Gallery, Smithsonian Institution, 1996), 220–47.

6. Elizabeth Way Champlain to Mary Way, May 1822 and 1819 in *Sisters*, 242, 129. Lizzie W. Champney, "Sea-Drift from a New England Port," *Harper's Monthly Magazine*, Dec. 1879 (60:355): 62. Betsey Champlain's career is summarized in MacMullen, *Sisters*, 33–44; for a detailed description of taking the likeness of a corpse, see Betsey Way Champlain to Eliza Way, c. 1822, *Sisters*, 242–43.

Just as the artists' lives confirm our understanding of the gendered dimension of art production, their paintings confirm our understanding of the familial resonance of miniature portraits. As the art historian Robin Jaffee Frank has suggested, by the early nineteenth century, the growing importance of affection as a family value increased the popularity of ivory miniatures. Small and private, viewed and sometimes worn close to the owner's body, miniatures deployed physical proximity as a bid for emotional proximity. The sentiments symbolized by these paintings were also manifested by their disposition, for they were typically commissioned as gifts. Whether bestowed singly or as part of a mutual exchange, miniatures reified feeling, fusing it with an object that communicated status as well as sentiment. [7]

Initially, Anglo-American miniatures evoked sentiments associated with courtship and marriage. Given the price of high-style miniatures like the ones painted by Edward Malbone or Benjamin Trott, which could rival the cost of bust-size oil portraits, it is not surprising that there was often something distinctly dynastic about these unions. However companionate, such marriages were also political, social, and economic alliances between powerful families. Over the first quarter of the nineteenth century, however, the relationships represented and preserved by miniatures began to extend beyond the marital couple—dynastic and otherwise—to encompass wide-ranging networks of kin and friends. This shift surely reflected the growing influence of child-centered family ideals and the emergent culture of sentiment. But it also reflected the increasing availability and affordability of ivory portrait miniatures. By the 1810s, a celebrated miniaturist like Anson Dickinson could command as much

---

7. Robin Jaffee Frank, *Love and Loss: American Portrait and Mourning Miniatures* (New Haven: Yale University Press, 2000). For a different perspective on the psychological resonances of miniatures, see Susan Stewart, *On Longing: Narratives of the Miniature, the Gigantic, the Souvenir, the Collection* (Durham, N.C.: Duke University Press, 1993), 125–27. Katherine C. Reider astutely analyzes the gifting of miniatures in the construction and perpetuation of status in "Gifting and Fetishization: The Portrait Miniature of Sally Foster Otis as a Maker of Female Memory," unpublished paper in author's possession. On exchange and status more generally, see Chris Packard, "Self-Fashioning in Sarah Goodridge's Self Portraits," *Common-place* 4:1 (2003); Marcia Pointon, "'Surrounded by Brilliants': Miniature Portraits in Eighteenth-Century England." *Art Bulletin* 83:1 (March 2001): 48–71; Anne A. Verplanck, "The Social Meanings of Portrait Miniatures in Philadelphia, 1760–1820," in Ann Smart Martin and J. Ritchie Garrison, eds., *American Material Culture: The Shape of the Field* (Winterthur, Del.: Henry Francis du Pont Winterthur Museum; Knoxville, Tenn.: Distributed by University of Tennessee Press, 1997), 195–223.

as $50.00 for a likeness from a New York City patron. Yet other artists, especially women, charged only a fraction of that. Betsey Way Champlain's sister Mary Way, who was Dickinson's New York contemporary if not precisely his competitor, charged around $8.00 per painting. Betsey could charge New Londoners around $5.00.[8] Cheap labor, much of it women's labor, helped create an expansive art market in the first decades of the nineteenth century. Especially in urban areas, middle-class families took advantage of this market to amass multiple representations of multiple kin. Miniatures depicting children, parents, siblings, cousins—even the deceased—heightened the genre's domestic (as opposed to its conjugal) associations. By the early nineteenth century, ivory miniatures had become affordable luxuries, mementos that could be purchased at any number of junctures in a family's life course. The portraits of Elizabeth Freeman and Betsey Way Champlain operated in precisely this way. They commemorated and cemented relations among kin, real and fictive. They also captured the mixture of intimacy and interiority that marked the bourgeois family.

Champlain began her self-portrait at the request of and as a gift for her sister Mary Way. After more than seven years apart, Way had an "unconquerable desire" to see Champlain. In particular, she wanted to see her sister decked out in the costume she had only read about: A "sun-flower uniform" comprised of a "yellow turban, yellow gown and black apron with the row of flat-irons across the bosom." Once she had her sister's likeness in hand, Way promised, she would return the favor. The portrait exchange would have served as a surrogate visit, supplementing the sisters' letters and providing each with what Way termed an "ocular demonstration" of the other's unfolding life. And like their letters, the portraits would have idealized that "demonstration," tempering the vicissitudes of fortune and the depredations of age with the literary and pictorial conventions of sentiment. As professionals whose work routinely naturalized those conventions, Way and Champlain were explicit about the role of idealization, even artifice, in representation. Champlain's self-portrait was no exception. Way instructed her sister: "You may flatter [your appear-

---

8. On miniature prices, see Reider, "Gifting and Fetishization;" Verplanck, "The Social Meanings of Portrait Miniatures," 195–223, 201–3; Mona Leithiser Dearborn, *Anson Dickinson: The Celebrated Miniature Painter* (Hartford Conn.: Connecticut Historical Society, 1983), 155–68; MacMullen, *Sisters*, 24, 92.

ance] as much as you like provided you don't flatter away all the likeness . . . just keep probability in view." Although unfinished, the portrait seems to do just that. Forty-seven years old at the time that she began her self-portrait, Way Champlain depicted herself poised in an indeterminate spot between youth and old age. Unlined, full, and firm, her painted face resists our attempts to fix her age, much less the contours of her life history. It defies biography, belying the passage of time itself.

Betsey Way Champlain never sent the portrait to her sister. In any event, by 1818, Mary Way's failing eyesight would have made it difficult to see her sister's face reduced onto an ivory the size of a small child's hand. Still, the painting contributed to the Way-Champlain family bonds. Along with the sisters' voluminous correspondence, it was passed mother to daughter over three generations, helping to create family tradition and consolidate family identity.[9]

Elizabeth Freeman's portrait was painted by the daughter-in-law of a former employer whose entire family claimed her as close kin. Freeman's name among the Sedgwicks, "Mumbet," was a double diminutive, collapsing "Mammy," "Mother," and "Mah" (variously) into "Bett." "Mumbet" was more than a nickname. It enshrined Freeman as an ersatz mother to the youngest Sedgwick children, especially Catharine. Her father, Theodore, an ardent Federalist, built a 30-year career in politics and public service; stints in the Massachusetts House and Senate, the U.S. House and Senate, and a seat on Massachusetts's supreme court pulled him away from home for at least six months every year. Her mother, Pamela Dwight Sedgwick, suffered from poor health and crippling depression that confined her to bed for months at a time. Catharine recalled that her parents' physical and emotional absences left Freeman to serve as the "main pillar of our household." Accordingly, the little girl gave the servant something like the love reserved for a mother. Indeed, near the end of Freeman's life, Catharine praised her as "'Mother'—my nurse—my faithful friend—she who first received me into her arms" and a "necessary link in the family chain." She remembered how as a child she "clung" to Freeman with "instinctive love and faith." She described herself as Freeman's "particular treasure."[10]

9. See Eliza Champlain to Betsey Way Champlain, January, 1818, *Sisters,* 98. Way's business and her faltering eyesight encouraged her to dictate letters through Eliza when the young woman was visiting. The history of the correspondence is described in *Sisters,* 477–78, n. 2.

10. Kelley, ed., *Autobiography,* 68; 125–26; Sedgwick, "Mumbet."

The family ties outlived the servant. Freeman's gravestone, purchased and inscribed by the Sedgwicks, memorialized her as their "Good Mother." Freeman's grave is in the section of the Stockbridge, Massachusetts, cemetery reserved for the Sedgwicks. And several years after Freeman's death, when Henry Dwight Sedgwick, one of Catharine's brothers, wrote an abolitionist lecture around his memories of and deep love for "Mah Bett," he confessed to his audience that knew her "as familiarly as I knew either of my parents."[11] I will return later to the peculiar family relations that obtained between Elizabeth Freeman and two generations of Sedgwicks. But for now, it is enough to observe that contemporary writers and scholars endorse the Sedgwick family story. For the most part, the portrait serves as a rare life portrait of an African-American woman and as an illustration for a text-based recounting of Freeman's 1783 lawsuit. Where the painting is discussed, it signifies an unproblematic gesture of familial affection.[12] Like the tombstone, then, the ivory miniature substantiates Freeman's special place in the Sedgwick clan, blurring multiple boundaries between real and fictive kin.

Although the painting surely signals Freeman's special relationship with her former employers, it may also have deepened the ties between those who were born Sedgwicks and those who married them. It isn't clear for whom the portrait was painted. But it is easy to imagine Susan Ridley Sedgwick painting it as a gift for Catharine, her beloved sister-in-law, or Theodore Sedgwick II, her husband. Whoever the recipient, the painting surely belonged to the Sedgwicks and not the Freemans, for it was donated to the Massachusetts Historical Society in 1884 by Maria Banyer Sedgwick, the artist's daughter.

*　*　*

Whatever these images confirm about the peripheral position of female artists in the early republic or about the familial resonance of ivory portrait miniatures, placed alongside each other they provoke new questions about the picto-

11. The tombstone inscription is quoted in Kelley, ed., *Autobiography,* 71, n. 33. *Practicability,* 18. Authorities disagree over who delivered the lecture; some attribute it to Henry Dwight Sedgwick, others to Theodore Sedgwick II. I have here followed the lead of Sedgwick specialists.

12. For example, Sidney Kaplan, *The Black Presence in the Era of the American Revolution, 1770–1800* (Washington, D.C.: New York Graphic Society in association with the Smithsonian Institution Press, 1973), describes the image as "lovingly painted in watercolors," 217. For similar references, see Jon Swan, "The Slave Who Sued for Freedom," *American Heritage* (March 1990): 51–55.

rial representation of race. The contrast in the sitters' lives is recapitulated in the stark contrast of painted flesh—one black, the other ivory.

It is hard not to notice Freeman's blackness. To achieve it, Sedgwick had to violate the fundamental conventions that governed portraiture in general and ivory miniatures in particular. The gentle delineation of features that characterize ivory miniatures is replaced by bold definition. Thick, heavy lines articulate Freeman's brows, nose and mouth, drawing attention to her most "African" features. Her solid form is without grace. Asymmetrical breasts hang heavy, unsupported by muscle or stay. Fabric strains around the girth of laboring arms. Delicate touches—the ruffled cap, the gold beads—suggest both feminine sensibility and genteel aspiration. But these small, fine details are overpowered by both the scale and shape of Freeman's form. And then, of course, there is her skin. Sedgwick layered washes of a single color, probably Cologne Brown, to outline Freeman's features and to model the planes of her face. She filled in the background with the same color, ignoring pictorial conventions that demanded an unobtrusive background. Like drapery and clothing, background was typically used to flatter the sitter's coloring. Instead, Sedgwick framed Freeman's face with the bold white of her cap and chemise and the clear blue of her dress. The effect is flat, graphic, and black. Brow, nose, lips, breasts, and skin: Susan Ridley Sedgwick represented Elizabeth Freeman as a catalogue of racial signifiers. [13]

It would be a mistake to confine our discussion of race to this one very rare image. The fashion for *ivory* miniatures, which spurred the renaissance in miniature painting in mid-eighteenth-century England and its emergence in late-eighteenth Anglo-America, coincided with the transatlantic elabora-

13. Ivory miniatures depicting African-descended people are exceedingly rare. But for examples of a different strategy for representing people of color, see the portraits of Haitian-born hairdresser Pierre Toussaint, his wife, Juliette Toussaint, and his niece Euphemia Toussaint, all painted by Anthony Meucci around 1825. Now part of the collection at the New-York Historical Society, they can be viewed online (www.nyhistory.org). On racialized aesthetics and the representation of race in the long eighteenth century more generally, see Gwendolyn DuBois Shaw, *Portraits of a People: Picturing African Americans in the Nineteenth Century* (Andover, Mass.: Addison Gallery of American Art, Phillips Academy; Seattle, Wash.: In association with the University of Washington Press, 2006); David Bindman, *Ape to Apollo: Aesthetics and the Idea of Race in the Eighteenth Century* (London: Reaktion Books, 2002); Marcus Wood, *Blind Memory: Visual Representations of Slavery in England & America, 1780–1865* (London: Routledge, 2000); Albert Boime, *The Art of Exclusion: Representing Blacks in the Nineteenth Century* (Washington D.C.: Smithsonian Institution Press, 1990).

Fig. 3. John Hoskins, miniature portrait of a man, perhaps Sir John Wildman. Watercolor on vellum, 1647. Photo © Victoria and Albert Museum, London, Eng.

tion of racial ideologies and identities. Just as ivory miniatures played a role in the simultaneous expansion of polite society and the rise of the affectional family, so too did they play a role in the construction and representation of whiteness. English portrait miniatures, which emerged in the Tudor courts and spread to the gentry and middling classes by the seventeenth century, were originally watercolor-on-vellum or, less frequently, oil-on-copper (fig. 3). The densely colored paintings fused gentility with the constellation of associations that would characterize the genre for more than two hundred years: intensely private images that might become public at the owner's discretion; tiny subjects who draw the viewer forward, into an intimacy born of proximity; the suggestion that possession of the picture signaled possession of the sitter. By the beginning of the eighteenth century, however, the miniature was in decline. Its popularity was restored first by the substitution of ivory for vellum and then by the adoption of a subdued palette that exploited the color, translucence, and texture of ivory.[14]

These shifts were neither obvious nor easy. Ivory did not accommodate watercolor. Before the would-be miniaturist wrestled with the standard technical questions about creating a convincing representation, she first had to manage to get the paint to adhere to the support. This demanded the painstaking preparation of each component of the painting. The slippery sheet of ivory had to be degreased, bleached, and ground with pumice powder. The paint—pigment, water, and binder (gum arabic and sometimes sugar candy)—had to be mixed in precise proportions; as late as the 1820s, after the introduction of high-quality commercially manufactured paint cakes, some miniaturists still

14. See John Murdoch, Jim Murrell, Patrick J. Noon, and Roy Strong, *The English Miniature* (New Haven: Yale University Press, 1981), 85–157.

opted to regrind the pigments to obtain the desired "fineness of texture." Even with properly prepared support and paints, applying watercolor to ivory was notoriously difficult. The painter first lightly traced the outline of the sitter on the ivory. Less assured artists were encouraged to draw the outline to scale on a sheet of paper which could then be placed beneath the ivory where, as one instructor observed, the support's "transparency will enable you to trace it very distinctly." Next, the painter colored in the shadowed areas of the face and background with a relatively dark "dead color" before washing solid colors onto the background and sitter's body, moving gradually from darker to lighter colors. To control the intensity of color, novice painters were encouraged to turn the picture upside down when they painted in the face's "general" color, which provided its foundation. By beginning with the chin and working down toward the forehead, the brush would become "exhausted" and "naturally make the forehead the lightest part" of the face.

Draperies and flesh required different paint mixtures and different application methods. Except for the flimsiest empire dresses, clothing required opaque colors that were "floated" onto the ivory by laying the picture "horizontally," to allow the paint to "become perfectly flat from its fluidity." The features and planes of the face were added to the ivory (now turned upright) through layers of cross-hatching and stippling. The paint used for flesh was as translucent as the painter could manage to mix it, for sheer layers of delicate color allowed the translucent ivory to glow through the paint. The face's highlights were rendered by leaving the ivory bare or by gently removing paint with the tip of a lancet. By exposing the support in this way, the painter conferred upon the sitter a complexion that was literally ivory.[15]

By the end of the eighteenth century, American miniaturists, following a style established some thirty years earlier by English artists, had learned to

15. My account of the process draws on T. S. Cummins [sic], "Practical Directions for Miniature Painting," printed in William Dunlap's 1834 *Rise and Progress of the Arts of Design in the United States* (New York: Dover Publications, 1969) vol. 2, part 1, 10–13. Significantly, Dunlap himself struggled with the technical aspects of miniature painting; he managed to work as a miniaturist for years before Edward Malbone showed him how to prepare the ivory. Dunlap, "Autobiography of the Author," in *Rise and Progress of the Arts of Design*, vol. 1, 269–70. For further discussions of the technical difficulties presented by ivory miniatures, see Murdoch, et al., *English Miniature,* 16–19; 163–95; Frank, *Love and Loss,* 1–13, 155–230; Carol Aiken in Johnson, *American Portrait Miniatures,* 13–26; Harry B. Wehle and Thomas C. Bolton, *American Miniatures, 1730–1850* (New York: Doubleday, 1927).

Fig. 4 (left). Richard Cosway, miniature portrait of an unidentified woman. Water-color on ivory, 1798. Photo © Victoria and Albert Museum, London.

Fig. 5 (right). Edward Greene Malbone, Mrs. Richard Sullivan (Sarah Russell) (1786–1831). Watercolor on ivory, 1804. Yale University Art Gallery, New Haven, Conn., Lelia A. And John Hill Morgan, B.A. 189. LL.B. 1896, M.A. (Hon.) 1929, collection.

exploit watercolor and ivory alike to create gently colored portraits of lumi-nous ladies and gentlemen (figs. 4 and 5).[16] This distinctly English style of miniature portrait (epitomized on one side of the Atlantic by Richard Cosway and on the other by Edward Greene Malbone) was well suited for the aesthetic ideal of the late eighteenth and early nineteenth centuries, with its emphasis on restrained colors and elegant forms. But ivories also resonated with an Anglo-American social aesthetic that fused gentility, sensibility, and white-ness. On both sides of the Atlantic, artists and patrons prized ivories because they were luminous, transparent, delicate, and softly harmonious—politically-freighted terms that located both artifacts and sitters squarely within the cult of sensibility.[17]

16. See Murdoch, et al., *English Miniature*, 16–19; 163–95; Frank, *Love and Loss*, 1–13, 155–230; Johnson, *American Portrait Miniatures*, 13–26; *American Miniatures*.

17. For a complementary discussion of racialized portraiture in eighteenth-century Britain, see Angela Rosenthal, "*Visceral* Culture: Blushing and the Legibility of Whiteness in Eigh-teenth-Century British Portraiture," *Art History* 27:4 (September 2004): 563–92. The literature on sensibility is too large and complex to be cited here in any detail. But on sensibility among

Scholars have begun to explore the ways in which the transatlantic culture of sensibility was bound up not only with class and gender but with race: sensibility was simultaneously confirmed by the visible register of emotion on pale skin, challenged by the cruel traffic in black bodies, and complicated by centuries of colonial encounter and conquest. The feeling and discernment that characterized men and women of sense may have originated in their hearts and minds. But those same qualities were most immediately apprehended on their bodies—in their posture and gait, through their expressive repertoire, and on their skin. Indeed, precisely because European skin registered "every passion by greater or less suffusions of colour," in Thomas Jefferson's words, it revealed an individual's character.[18] Like a scrim, white skin's opacity was an illusion; its fundamental transparency was revealed to sensible observers by the rise of feeling and the play of color.

This combination of mutability and transparency was predicated on and validated by scientific explanations of human character and variety. Broadly speaking, Anglo-Americans had two vocabularies for making sense of skin color, one based on ancient ideas about the humors, the other on anatomical science. Humoral theory posited that complexion, which included temperament and mental and physical capacity along with skin color, resulted from the interaction of climate and body. Because complexion was the product of ongoing, dynamic interaction, it was also mutable; it responded to changes in age, geography, and living conditions. Anatomical theory, on the other hand, fixed skin color within the body; scholars variously associated skin color with the topmost layer of the epidermis or with a thin membrane lying immediately beneath it. As literary historian Roxann Wheeler has recently demonstrated, humoral and anatomical models persisted side by side and in combination well into the nineteenth century. Taken together, they worked against the straight-

eighteenth-century and early nineteenth-century Anglo-American elites, see esp. Sarah Knott, *Sensibility and the American Revolution* (Chapel Hill, N.C.: University of North Carolina Press, 2009); David S. Shields, *Civil Tongues and Polite Letters in British America* (Chapel Hill, N.C.: University of North Carolina Press, 1997); and Jay Fliegelman, *Declaring Independence: Jefferson, Natural Language, and the Culture of Performance* (Stanford, Calif.: Stanford University Press, 1993).

18. Thomas Jefferson, *Notes on the State of Virginia, with an Appendix* (New York: T.B. Jansen & Co., G. Jansen & Co., 1801), 205. On the political and cultural significance of transparent skin as an index of individual sentiment and character, see Fliegelman, *Declaring Independence*, 192–95.

forward reduction of skin color to race.[19] Notwithstanding the significance of emergent racial ideologies, eighteenth- and early nineteenth-century natural scientists viewed "white" skin as more than the opposite of black.

In fact, even American commentators who were explicitly preoccupied with the elaboration of race along a black-white axis agreed that European whiteness was not a single color but a compendium of them. Samuel Stanhope Smith, president of Princeton University and author of the influential *Essay on the Causes of the Variety of Complexion*, argued that the climate accounted not only for, say, differences between Europeans and Asians. It also accounted for color differences among Europeans. As he explained, "white may be regarded as the colourless state of skin, and all the shades of the dark colours as different stains inserted into its substance." But Europeans were not white *per se*: "In Britain and Germany they are fair, brown in France and in Turkey, swarthy in Portugal and Spain." And in Anglo-America, Smith detected a "certain paleness of countenance." Generally speaking, the "American complexion does not exhibit so clear a red and white as the British, or the German. And there is a tinge of sallowness spread over it which indicated the tendency of the climate to generate bile." Complexions differed among classes as well as nations. Smith observed that "the poor and laboring part of the community in every country are usually more dark in their complexion;" exposure and privation left these unfortunates bereft of "the delicate tints of colour" that marked the higher classes. Happily, in the United States, republican society and the widespread distribution of property eliminated these class-based differences in complexion, except between field and house slaves.[20]

Even those who were not persuaded that climate alone determined skin

19. Roxann Wheeler, *The Complexion of Race: Categories of Difference in Eighteenth-Century British Culture* (Philadelphia: University of Pennsylvania Press, 2000), especially chapter 1, 2–48.

20. Samuel Stanhope Smith, *An Essay on the Causes of the Variety of Complexion and Figure in the Human Species,* second edition (New Brunswick, N.J.: J. Simpson & Co. and Williams and Whiting, NY, 1810), 49, 66, 67–68, 162, 168. Scholarly discussions of Smith include Bruce Dain, *A Hideous Monster of the Mind: Race Theory in the Early Republic* (Cambridge, Mass.: Harvard University Press, 2002), 41–49, Knott, *Sensibility and the American Revolution*, 207–14; Wheeler, *Complexion of Race*, 251–53; Scott Juengel, "Countenancing History: Mary Wollstonecraft, Samuel Stanhope Smith, and Enlightenment Racial Science," *ELH* 68 (2001): 897–927; Winthrop Jordan, *White Over Black: American Attitudes Toward the Negro, 1550–1815* (Chapel Hill, N.C.: University of North Carolina Press for the Institute of Early American History and Culture, 1968), 486–88.

color accepted the mutability and variety of European skin. An 1814 essay refuting Smith observed that "the infants of Europeans, when newly born, are almost as remote from their parental fairness of complexion, as the infants of Africans are from their hereditary blackness." Nature "bleached" the skin, "complet[ing] the European complexion" "through the agency of the *cutaneous absorbents*" which removed the "superfluous matter which obstructs its transparency, and sullies its fairness."[21] And armchair physiognomists were encouraged to read skin color along with facial structure as a register of character. An 1809 essay on physiognomy, for example, insisted that "whoever has reflected on the principles of our nature, well knows, that fluids as they circulate through the organized matter with which our bodies are composed, tinge the very outsides of the channels through which they flow, with their predominant colour." The skin's transparency, along with the "incessant return of those same fluids to the same places" created the complexion and revealed an individual's "passions." These varieties of mood and character registered in "hues as varied as their motions . . . some are red, others of a leaden cast; some are yellow, others green and even black."[22] Whatever they had to say about the significance of black skin, American theorists agreed with Oliver Goldsmith on the significance of white skin. In Goldsmith's words, "Of all the colours by which mankind is diversified, it is easy to perceive that ours is not only the most beautiful to the eye, but the most advantageous. The fair complexion seems, if I may so express it, as a transparent covering to the soul; all the variations of the passions, every expression of joy or sorrow, flows to the cheek, and, without language marks the mind."[23]

It was this delicately colored transparency, celebrated in polite culture and *belle lettres* and validated by natural science, that ivory miniatures promised to capture. Betsey Way Champlain herself alluded to these significations in "On Flattery" (1819), a 155-line poem that describes (among other things) her negotiations with two comically demanding patrons. These aging, dissolute members of New London's gentry are determined to influence the portraits they have commissioned from her. The couple is especially anxious about the depiction of their skin, for their advanced years, along with their vices, are

21. "Complexion in the Human Species," *Port-Folio*, July 1814, 30.
22. "Familiar Letters on Physiognomy," *The Visitor*, 1809, vol. 1, p. 148.
23. Oliver Goldsmith, *An History of the Earth, and Animated Nature*, 4 vols. (Philadelphia: Matthew Carey, 1795), v. 1, 375.

imprinted on their complexions. The wife is freckled, tan, and coarse. Her husband sports an oozing sore on his chin. Appearance portends behavior. During their sittings, a stream of bickering reveals a marriage based upon years of bad faith, worse temper, and boundless stupidity. Exposed before the artist's eye, they refuse to accept accountability for their faces or, by extension, their lives. Instead, the sitters insist that their current appearances are temporary aberrations, the result of an ill-advised "blouzing" or a maid's carelessness with a cap pin. By turns, they implore and command Way Champlain to see them—and thereby make them—what they wish to be. "Lend a flush," the woman wheedles, "And let your goodness show me what I was." All business-like pomposity, the man tells Betsey to "omit" the evidence of his maidservant's "careless mishap." Casting herself as the beleaguered innocent, the poet-painter has no choice but to comply. As she explains, "they the cash detain, were nothing feigned."[24] Whatever their moral shortcomings, the wealthy couple understood what was at stake in an ivory miniature and they were willing to wield the power of patronage to secure it.

Because of the cultural resonance of complexion, and because it ranked high on the list of things that patrons hoped to secure when they commissioned an ivory miniature, the depiction of skin was the subject of enormous technical discussion and instruction among Anglo-American artists. After all, it was easier to see transparency than to make it. Accordingly, manuals that sought to instruct amateurs and professionals alike in the art of the water-colored ivory devoted pages and pages to the exact mix and application of colors necessary to conjure luminous "white" flesh.

The first step was to learn to observe with a precision that escaped even sensitive viewers, for as Peter Cooper explained, when "observing the colour of the human face, the uneducated eye sees nothing more than the general or local colour, making no nice distinctions between shadows, 'demi tints,' 'pearls,' or 'grey tints.'"[25] Once the artist learned to recognize the components of complexion, he or she could begin to notice that they shifted with a sitter's mood.

24. Elizabeth Way Champlain, "On Flattery," in *Sisters*, 40–42. On skin and representations of skin as communicative surfaces, see Mechthild Fend, "Bodily and pictorial surfaces: skin in French art and medicine, 1790–1860," *Art History* 28:3 (June 2005): 311–39; Susan Sidlauskas, "Painting Skin: John Singer Sargent's *Madame X*," *American Art* 15:3 (Fall 2001): 8–33.

25. P[eter] F. Cooper, *The Art of Making and Colouring Ivorytypes, Photographs, Talbotypes, and Miniature Paintng on Ivory, &c. By PF Cooper, Miniature, Portrait, Pastil, and Equestrian Painter, and Photographer* (Philadelphia: Published by author, 1863), 28.

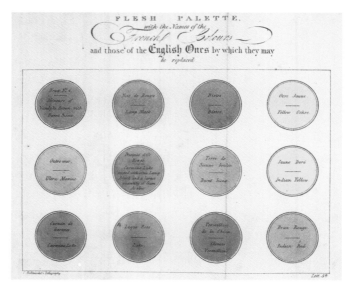

Fig. 6. "Flesh Palette," from L[éon Larue] Mansion, *Letters upon the art of miniature painting* (London: R. Ackermann, 1822). Courtesy, The Winterthur Library: Printed Book and Periodical Collection, Winterthur, Del.

As one manual explained, the excitement of the first sitting would render a subject flushed; the subsequent return of composure revealed the "ordinary complexion"; the effort required by an extended sitting changed the complexion yet again. Realizing this, the painter could make an informed decision about how to represent the subject: "The natural complexion, somewhat heightened, may be the best colour to be applied to the picture."[26]

Painting that complexion, heightened or otherwise, demanded that a painter identify and replicate the multiple shades that comprised it. This was no simple process (figs. 6 and 7). In an 1821 manual, J. Dougall warned that "the colours of carnations . . . or of those parts of the human body which appear uncovered . . . are so various that no rules can be laid down." Instead, he advanced a set of "broad principles" about the colors of men, women, and children.[27] But other writers were far more explicit, listing the various combinations of paint required by particular features. The key lay in the careful combination of

26. John Dougall, *The Cabinet of the Arts; Being a New and Universal Drawing Book,* second edition (London: Ackermann, 1821), 226.
27. Ibid., 268.

Fig. 7. Edward Greene Malbone, Mrs. Richard Sullivan (Sarah Russell) (1786–1831), detail. Watercolor on ivory. Yale University Art Gallery, Lelia A. And John Hill Morgan, B.A. 189. LL.B. 1896, M.A. (Hon.) 1929, collection.

minute bits of different colors. As one writer explained, even though Venetian red, mixed with a little Indian yellow offered "the nearest approach to the general colour of "flesh," it could not begin to capture the tonal complexity of the white face.[28] And so a 1788 manual specified that "Vermillion and Carmine" be applied with "strongest Touches at the Corners of the Eyes, next the Nose, under the Nose, the Ears and Under the Chin." The shadows of temples and neck were to be "blueish Teints with Indigo" and the parts of the face that "rise and come forward to the Sight" should be in "Yellow Teints are composed of Oker and Vermillion." Finally, the artist should "dot . . . over the Shadows with green Teints."[29] Another writer preferred Indian red and indigo for the dead color with ultramarine blue and "the madder lakes" to add a finer touch to the flesh. Then the "lights and shades" of the complexion could be created out of "light red, pink madder, well ground vermillion, and raw terra de sienna."[30] A *Course of Lectures on Drawing, Painting, and Engraving* stipulated the order for applying shadow tints: Begin with those that are a mixture of "carmine, gamboge, and Indian Ink" before preceding the "blue and grey tints," which were to be inserted "at the edges of the first shadows"; add the reddish shadows last. Then, at a second sitting, a "general colour" (either carmine and gamboge or Venetian red and gamboge) could be painted to "cover . . . the whole face," except of course for the highlighted areas, which required yet another sitting, color scheme, and application pattern.[31] Even John Dougall, the champion

28. Cooper, *Art*, 26.

29. John Russell, *Elements of Painting with Crayons* (Dublin, 1773), 70–75.

30. Mr. Hayter, *Introduction to Perspective, Drawing, and Painting* (London: Black, Parry, & Co., 1815), 180–81.

31. W. M. Craig, *A Course of Lectures on Drawing, Painting, and Engraving, Considered as Branches of Elegant Education* (London: Longman, Hurst, Rees, Orme, and Brown, 1821), 350–55.

of "broad principle," took pains to stipulate the precise combinations of colors demanded by the lights and shadows of the "carnations" by dividing skin into color zones of nose, chin, forehead, hands, fingertips, and joints. He also included detailed instructions for the whites of the eyes, the balls of the eyes, the eyelid, and the lips.[32] Painting white flesh was more than a paint-by-numbers proposition, but it also demanded a level of premeditation and precision that no aspiring artist could afford to ignore.

Tracing the connections between these kinds of instructions and the literally thousands of extant ivories painted by metropolitan and provincial artists in late eighteenth- and early nineteenth-century America is no easy task. Letters written among Betsey Champlain, her sister Mary Way, and her daughter, Eliza Way Champlain, also a miniaturist, allow us to see snatches of their attempts to acquire the color theory and technique necessary to paint whiteness, and thereby realize the style prescribed in art manuals and hailed by critics and connoisseurs. Throughout the correspondence, Betsey Champlain used her sister and later her daughter to supply high quality ivory and particular colors that were not to be had in New London. But she also relied upon them to share information that only more accomplished painters might provide, information available only in New York City. And most of what they passed along pertained to the vexing issue of color in general and a sitter's flesh in particular.

Several years after moving to New York to further her career, for example, Mary Way wrote her sister a lengthy letter, cataloguing her own considerable improvements and summarizing the learning that had made them possible. She relayed the wisdom of "connoisseurs" like William Joseph Williams, John Jarvis, Joseph Wood and quoted liberally from a book that Wood loaned her, John Payne's *Art of Painting in Miniature, on Ivory*. In effect, she offered her sister a crash course on the techniques and conventions of the ivory miniature. Way explained that "transparent colours only must be used for the flesh, and for draperies, opaque or body colours, as they set off each other [making] the flesh tints appear to more advantage." The color of that flesh depended upon the "force, strength, and disposition, or situation of the colours, in point of light, that are placed near it." And though faces required a "thousand different tints" too tedious to recount, Betsey should remember that "the most natural

32. Dougall, *Cabinet*, 268–70.

shades for the face are purples, blues, and greys, especially for a delicate complexion. These, however, should be warm'd, more or less . . . with red browns and yellows, such as burnt umber, burnt terra sienna, . . . or gamboge mixed with a little carmine." In order to see these tints clearly, lighting was critical: Arrange one high light that "strikes with most force upon the temple" creating a "delicate shade tint" along the cheekbone under the eye. As Way pointed out in a later letter, a painter who mastered these techniques could dispense with tricks like backing the support with foil or a daube of white paint to increase the luminosity. Ivory, she pronounced, was "handsomer, without [them], then any mortal complexion."[33]

Letters scattered over the next decade reveal Betsey Champlain working to improve her depiction of sitters' faces by focusing on their complexions. In 1824, after struggling with six recent front faces, she realized that she had "never fixed my room properly for the purpose." "Better late than never," she hung blinds and shutters that "shut or open at pleasure." One shutter was fitted with a door "divided into two—the upper to admit as much light upon the patient as will produce this rich gold shade I have before mentioned." It was, after all, easier to paint a luminous face when the sitter was lit to create the desired glow. In her refurbished room, Champlain reported, "you see before you what you are to copy, without laying more upon Fancy than she is able to bear or crowding her delicate stomach with too solid food for her digestive properties."[34]

Champlain also emulated fine paintings to hone her color perception and brush skills. She was particularly moved by one patron's snuffbox, which was decorated with the "likeness of a French king who is said to have reign'd in the 16th century." Fascinated by the way that the crimson turban "left a rich reflection upon forehead and ear," she badgered the client and his friends until she learned the name of the New York City merchant who sold the marvel. She then asked her daughter to visit the store immediately "and see if there is any you think will answer as a modle for a painter," preferably a "front face, dark and richly shaded" or a "female, with ringlets."[35] Five years later, she obtained

33. See Mary Way to Betsey Way Champlain, c. 1814, *Sisters*, 27–30; Mary Way to Eliza Champlain, Dec. 1816, *Sisters*, 59.

34. Betsey Way Champlain to Eliza Champlain, 16 Nov. 1824, *Sisters*, 322–23.

35. Betsey Way Champlain to Eliza Champlain, 1822, *Sisters*, 264.

Fig. 8. Elizabeth Way Champlain, unfinished portrait of an unidentified sitter. Watercolor on ivory, n.d. Courtesy of Ramsay MacMullen.

a far better "modle" by copying a miniature painted by Nathaniel Rogers. The result was the "highest style of shading, and looks as if it would speak." The thrill was in the colors: "A white merino shawl, shaded to resemble black, and pencil colour'd ermine, the white draper very dingy." The face was "drawn upon the deepest yellow ivory that can can [sic] be," which was exploited for the "harmonizing tints between the light and shade" and the highlights, which Champlain left "naked . . . natural as life." Her son William confirmed that the deeply shaded background set off the face of the sitter; the contrast between the two "gives life, ay being, to the peice [sic]."[36]

Most of Betsey Champlain's work is lost. Her paintings survive only in the shadow form of letters, making it difficult to see exactly how and when she refined her technique over the course of her career. Nevertheless, she brought at least some of these lessons to bear on an unfinished portrait of an unidentified sitter (fig. 8). The young woman's dotted dress graces her body, it doesn't do battle with it. The unfinished lace collar draws our eyes up to the sitter's face which is crowned by a heavy, black turban. As Mary Way's authorities promised, the dark, flat black of the turban intensifies the delicate stippled tints that Champlain had begun to apply to contour the young woman's face. A deep, brownish vermillion shades the nose while a fainter version defines chin and jaw. A mixture of yellowish red brings the blush to her cheeks. Minuscule

36. Betsey Way Champlain to Eliza Champlain, January 1825, *Sisters*, 327; William Champlain to Eliza Champlain, 13 February 1825, *Sisters*, 328.

blue and gray dots mark the shadows around the eyes and beneath the mouth. It is precisely this delicately fashioned transparency that we see in the subtle reds, browns, yellows and pinks of Champlain's unfinished self-portrait. Race was thus inscribed not only in the shocking blackness of Elizabeth Freeman's likeness, but in the painstakingly crafted whiteness of Betsey Champlain's.

*   *   *

Seeing the racial ideology and the racialized aesthetic at work in both paintings, we can return to the familial contexts in which these images, and thousands like them, were produced, circulated, and viewed. We can situate the representations at the intersection of race, family, and sentiment. Elizabeth Freeman's portrait and the stories that swirl around it serve as a forceful reminder that Federal Era New England was neither absolutely white nor absolutely free.[37] It directs our attention to the ambiguous boundaries that separated the various legal categories of dependency—economic and familial—that obtained in the Early Republic. Elizabeth Freeman was a slave and a wage earner but she was also a family member. The will she dictated shortly before her death in 1829 enumerates her own family. A daughter, a granddaughter, and four great-grandchildren survived her to inherit an estate that included real property, furniture, clothing and jewelry. Of the possessions she bequeathed to her daughter Elizabeth, two had special significance: a "short gown that was my mother's" and a black silk gown that was "rec'd of my father." Passed across the generations, the clothing registered Freeman's identity as a daughter and mother. It tethered Freeman's daughter, also named Elizabeth, to a family that stretched back to include grandparents. With the legal transmission of her property, Elizabeth Freeman claimed the lineal family that slavery had denied her.[38]

At the same time that Freeman was preserving and extending a lineal family, she was also a member of the Sedgwick family. To incorporate Freeman into their family imaginary, the Sedgwicks discursively severed her from

37. John Wood Sweet, *Bodies Politic: Negotiating Race in the American North, 1730–1830* (Baltimore: Johns Hopkins University Press, 2003); Joanne Pope Melish, *Disowning Slavery: Gradual Emancipation and "Race" in New England, 1780–1860* (Ithaca, N.Y.: Cornell University Press, 1998). Barbara Ryan situates Elizabeth Freeman and Catharine Maria Sedgwick's fiction in the context of racialized service and dependence in *Love, Wages, and Slavery: The Literature of Servitude in the United States* (Urbana, Ill.: University of Illinois Press, 2006), chapter 1.

38. Last Will and Testament of Elizabeth Freeman, Oct. 18, 1829, Sheffield Historical Society, Sheffield, Mass. Located at www.mumbet.com, accessed Feb. 1, 2007.

her own. Neither Henry Dwight Sedgwick nor Catharine Maria Sedgwick acknowledged Freeman's regard for her father and mother, whose memories she preserved in the clothing they had given her. Henry's published account of Freeman's life acknowledged that she was once married, her husband a casualty of the Revolutionary War. He likewise mentioned her surviving child and her "large family of grand-children and great-grand-children." Although his abolitionist lecture mentioned Freeman's descendents, it did not dwell on the damage that their mother's enslavement must have inflicted on the family. Instead, he memorialized Freeman as a servant "who knew her station and perfectly observed its decorum" with none of the "submissive or subdued character" that so often resulted from slavery. Catharine Maria Sedgwick, who never mentioned Freeman's husband, acknowledged her surviving family only to dismiss them as "riotous and ruinous descendants" given to "reckless consumption." Such remarks recapitulate predictable stereotypes about African-Americans' suitability for domestic service and their irresponsibility, fiscal and otherwise. But they also register a plaintive enviousness. "Mumbet" may have been the "main pillar" of the Sedgwick household (in Catharine's terms); she may also have been a servant "whose fidelity to her employers was such as has never been surpassed" (in Henry's).[39] Yet the fact remains that Freeman left that household and those employers in 1808, choosing to support her own household and serve her own family. Memoirs and fantasies notwithstanding, Elizabeth Freeman's priorities diverged from those of the Sedgwicks.

What, then, were the conditions under which Susan Ridley Sedgwick painted Elizabeth Freeman in 1811? Did Freeman even sit for the portrait? How was the miniature displayed, and to whom? Who claimed ownership of the likeness, of "Mumbet"? Here, it is suggestive to consider the possibility that the painting was a gift, given from one Sedgwick to another. That symbolic exchange would have recalled a literal one. As children, Elizabeth Freeman and her sister were gifts, given by their owner, Pieter Hogeboom, to his daughter, Annetje, to celebrate her wedding.[40] Freeman entered the household of Captain John Ashley, the man she would later sue for freedom, as dowry, as a gift exchanged between white kin to symbolize status, obligation,

---

39. *Practicability,* 16, 18; Sedgwick, *Autobiography,* 69; Sedgwick, "Mumbet" mss.
40. "Africans and the End of Slavery in Massachusetts," on-line exhibition, Massachusetts Historical Society (http://www.masshist.org/endofslavery/?queryID=54), accessed Oct. 15, 2007.

and love. Withal, it is hard not to read Freeman's portrait as a stunning act of appropriation, in which the possession signaled by an ivory miniature stood in for the possession of an African-American woman, a former slave, a "mother." This appropriation depended upon the strikingly racialized representation of "Mumbet." But it also depended upon a set of historically specific social relations, upon the murky distinctions between "slave," "servant," and "family" that survived the abolition of slavery in Massachusetts for several decades.

Betsey Way Champlain's self-portrait allows us to glimpse the tangle of race, family, and sentiment from a different perspective. It is governed by an aesthetic that is as deeply racialized as the conventions governing the likeness of Elizabeth Freeman. The delicately stippled complexion reminds us that as both an ideology of race and a system of visual signifiers, nineteenth-century "whiteness" emerged not only in a distinctly American opposition to "blackness" (or, for that matter, "redness") but also out of transatlantic discourses on aesthetics, gentility, and natural science. Considered alongside thousands of similar miniatures produced in the Early Republic, Champlain's painting suggests that the visual codes of whiteness were elaborated and disseminated not only in "public," in the realm of politics and work but also in "private," in the bosom of the affectionate family.[41]

Betsey Way Champlain's self-portrait should also caution us against underestimating the complexity of those family affections. Like so many other nineteenth-century ivory miniatures, the painting was undertaken as a gift. Although it never reached its intended recipient, Mary Way, it was eventu-

41. This perspective significantly revises the standard historical accounts of race in North America, which associate nineteenth-century whiteness with masculinity, commerce, and politics. Women, and the family more generally, enter the equation only when abolitionist and feminist agitators together raise the specter of race and slavery in the private sphere. The classic accounts are David Roediger, *Wages of Whiteness: Race and the Making of the American Working Class* (New York: Verso, 1991); Noel Ignatiev, *How the Irish Became White* (London: Routledge, 1995); Karen Sanchez-Eppler, *Touching Liberty: Abolition, Feminism, and the Politics of the Body* (Berkeley, Calif.: University of California Press, 1993); Jean Fagan Yellin, *Women and Sisters: The Anti-Slavery Feminists in American Culture* (New Haven: Yale University Press, 1989); and Louise Michele Newman, *White Women's Rights: The Racial Origins of Feminism in the United States* (New York: Oxford University Press, 1999). Scholars considering the visual representation of race and racial identity look to the Civil War to structure their inquiries. In their telling, the nineteenth-century imaginary juxtaposed black/slave/South against white/free/North. See, for example, Mary Niall Mitchell's "'Roseboom and Pure White,' Or So It Seemed," *American Quarterly*, (Sept. 2002): 369–410.

ally passed to the artist's daughter, Eliza Way Champlain, who in turn gave the painting to her daughter. Rather than reinforcing familial bonds within a single generation, it reinforced them across several generations. In the end, the painting realized its purpose: it became a symbol of family, a symbol of love. But it was also a symbol of unrealized aspiration. Betsey Way Champlain could never have scraped up the cash to commission such a painting. Most of the time, she barely managed to make her rent. It was only her skill, her labor, that made the gift possible. Just as the image flattered her likeness—"keeping probability in view" while erasing the marks of time and care—it flattered her rank and her income. Her gift surely recalled the gifts that circulated among her neighbors and friends, from the miniatures that she herself had painted for her patrons to bestow upon others to the exquisite portrait painted by Nathaniel Rogers that she used as a "modle" for her own masterpiece. The sisters' planned exchange recalled exchanges witnessed from a distance, a distance defined by fortune and by gender. On ivory, if not in life, Betsey Way Champlain could claim more than gentility; she could claim the security that went with it. Like the portrait of Elizabeth Freeman, Betsey Way Champlain's self-portrait testifies to power of love, to the persistence of family mythologies, to the magic of portraiture. And like the portrait of Elizabeth Freeman, Betsey Way Champlain's portrait reminds us that love—like the gifts that concretize it—is always a creature of history and history's contradictions.

Hares Haeredem: The Spectator
Through Samuel Dexter's Spectacles

KATHERINE STEBBINS MCCAFFREY

IN THE YEAR 1792, sixty-six-year-old Samuel Dexter sat for a portrait of a type quite familiar to colonial historians: in it, Dexter surrounded himself with the objects he considered emblematic of his life (fig. 1). Though he seems to slouch some and his gaze is somewhat bewildered or bemused, Dexter looks pleased to affiliate himself for posterity with his library—proud of what his books said *to* him, as well as what they said *about* him. But Dexter's portrait has a secret, as many from the period do. The dark eyes and vague gaze whisper something that upon reflection should seem obvious: this is a devoted reader who is losing his sight. Absent from the portrait, as from numerous eighteenth-century portraits save those of Benjamin Franklin, are the gold spectacles that Samuel Dexter acquired sometime in the 1780s to try to improve his failing vision and maintain his identity as a reader.[1]

Today, Samuel Dexter's gold spectacles invite historians to see reading practices and readers' identities as a hall of mirrors (fig. 2). In their final resting place, the Massachusetts Historical Society, Dexter's spectacles and their accompanying spectacle case seem to present a picture-perfect narrative of eighteenth-century spectatorship and its technologies, for the case bears the inscription *"Hares haeredem, velut unda supervenit undam,"* which is an abridged extract from the Roman poet Horace's *Epistles* that the Englishman Joseph Addison chose as an epigraph in the Saturday, July 7, 1711, issue of *The Spectator,* the enormously influential and enduring serial written and edited by Addison and his friend, Richard Steele.[2] Like the dazzling materials used

1. Lauren B. Hewes, *Portraits in the Collection of the American Antiquarian Society* (Worcester, Mass.: American Antiquarian Society, 2004), 145–47; on the portraits of Benjamin Franklin wearing glasses, see Charles Coleman Sellers, *Benjamin Franklin in Portraiture* (New Haven: Yale University Press, 1963), 68–69, 71, 73, 329.

2. There are many books and articles that address *The Spectator* and its relationship to eighteenth-century American and British culture and society, in addition to recent work on coffeehouses as historical sites and literary venues, and of course Habermas's seminal work on the public sphere [Jürgen Habermas, *The Structural Transformation of the Public Sphere: An Inquiry into a Category of Bourgeois Society* (Cambridge, Mass.: The MIT Press, 1991)]. Most helpful to

Fig. 1. John Johnston. *Samuel Dexter* (1726–1810). Oil on canvas, 1791.
Courtesy, American Antiquarian Society, Worcester, Mass.

to make the artifact itself, the literal connection between Spectator and spectacles threatens to overwhelm all other interpretations and qualifications. It
plays to current assumptions that spectacles and texts have long enjoyed a cozy

me have been: Erin Mackie, *Market à la Mode: Fashion, Commodity, and Gender in the Tatler and
Spectator Papers* (Baltimore: Johns Hopkins University Press, 1997); Brian Cowan, *The Social
Life of Coffee: The Emergence of the British Coffeehouse* (New Haven: Yale University Press, 2005);
David S. Shields, *Civil Tongues & Polite Letters in British America* (Chapel Hill, N.C.: Published
for the Institute of Early American History and Culture, Williamsburg, Virginia by University
of North Carolina Press, 1997); and Michael Warner, *The Letters of the Republic: Publication and
the Public Sphere in Eighteenth-Century America* (Cambridge, Mass.: Harvard University Press,
1990).

Fig. 2. Gold temple spectacles, ca. 1785, and gold-plated spectacle case, ca. 1810 belonging to the Dexter family. Courtesy of the Massachusetts Historical Society, Boston, Mass.

relationship.[3] This kind of thinking ignores the fact that words had a long history before spectacles came into the picture. For about five thousand years after the initial emergence of written language, no one spent any time or energy associating spectacles with literacy or knowledge, because spectacles were not invented until the end of thirteenth century.[4] From that point on, representations of spectacles and the messages encoded in styles of spectacles often entered into highly contested cultural discourses, dialogues enabled to greater or lesser degrees by the actual circulation of spectacles. During the emergence and aftermath of the Enlightenment in England, for example, sophisticated and scientifically produced English spectacles like Dexter's were traded across the Atlantic and often sold as fashionable items linked to a rapidly expanding

3. Alberto Manguel, *A History of Reading* (New York: Penguin, 1996), "The Book Fool," esp. 296.

4. For general information about the history of spectacles, see the collectors' website, www. antiquespectacles.com; Richard Corson, *Fashions in Eyeglasses from the Fourteenth Century to the Present Day* (London: Peter Owen, 1967; second revised edition, 1980); Frank W. Law, *The Worshipful Company of Spectacle Makers: A History* (London: The Company, 1978); Alan Macfarlane and Gerry Martin, *Glass: A World History* (Chicago: University of Chicago Press, 2002); and Edward Tenner, *Our Own Devices: How Technology Remakes Humanity* (New York: Vintage, 2003). See also, Manguel, *A History of Reading.*

world of consumer goods. As spectacles spread throughout the colonies, they redrew the line that divided things seen from things unseen and increasingly forced the question of what constituted a necessity or a luxury.[5] Glitteringly refined, Dexter's spectacles seem to have been built to cross this line—built, that is, not just to facilitate but to *flaunt* access to some configuration of the public sphere, the social space represented for Jürgen Habermas by, among other things, papers like *The Spectator.*[6]

Look beyond surface reflections, however, and it becomes clear that the Dexter spectacles and case tell a story with a wider circuit. The spectacles do capture Samuel Dexter's struggle in his last years to liberate himself from material expressions of pride or avarice; all the while he remained dependent upon a device that both enabled the virtuous habits he wished to cultivate while it simultaneously expressed the vices he hoped to weed out. But, as it turns out, Dexter's son Samuel is the one who bought and inscribed the case for the spectacles that he inherited, and who in his last years seemed to turn his back on the excesses of his youth in order to follow the general outline of his father's lights. *Hares Haeredum,* Horace wrote. "Heir follows heir." Heritage. Legacy. These are all problems of visible remains. For two generations, then, these spectacles corrected vision, negotiated print cultures, and testified to early Americans' conflicted attempts to style themselves as serious, rational readers. This larger tension between the virtue of learning and the vice of fashion resonated in the particular circumstances of the Dexter men, for whom the spectacles came to serve as a memorial to a multigenerational struggle to balance religious faith against secular success.

* * *

Born in 1726, the elder Samuel Dexter had a long career as a reader (and writer), and one that tells a familiar story of a Republic of Letters built on the

5. On the political economy of fashion see Linzy Brekke, "The 'Scourge of Fashion': Political Economy and the Politics of Consumption in the Early Republic," *Early American Studies,* 3, No. 1 (Spring 2005): 111–39. On the problem of vision, glasses, and fashion, see Katherine Stebbins McCaffrey, *Reading Glasses: American Spectacles in the Age of Franklin* (Ph.D. diss. Boston University, 2007), 297–98.

6. See Habermas, *The Structural Transformation of the Public Sphere,* Chapters 2 and 3; Shields, *Civil Tongues & Polite Letters in British America;* and Warner, *The Letters of the Republic.* Richard Bushman, *The Refinement of America: Persons, Houses, Cities* (New York: Knopf, 1992), especially Chapters 2 and 3, which deal in part with the presentation of the self through the exchange of letters and the regulation of the body.

Puritan faith in literacy and an expanding commercial reliance on numeracy in the Anglo-Atlantic world. After being trained up to follow in his father Samuel's footsteps through Harvard and into the ministry, Dexter had shocked his parents by proving perhaps too much inclined toward scholarship—on the strength of his own reason and reading, and fueled by a contrary nature, he soon questioned Christianity's claims to divine authority, abandoned Calvinism as a doctrine that "did violence to the moral attributes of God," and departed Harvard to apprentice himself to the Boston merchant Samuel Barrett.[7] Within fifteen years he had married, started his own shop, fathered five children (of which four lived), and made so much money selling Britain's baubles to his fellow colonists that, a year later, he retired.[8] In 1762, flush with pride in his speedy success, Samuel Dexter left his mercantile business for a position in the Massachusetts legislature, only to find himself openly at odds with the other patriots on how to conduct the Revolution. In a dramatic move, and perhaps one driven by his descent into an especially dark period, Dexter chose to extract himself from his commercial and political networks, removing to the relative wilds of Woodstock, Connecticut.[9] Restored to health by strict dedication to none but "his family and a very few friends,"[10] "the management of . . . private concerns,"[11] and his extensive library, which was remembered as "the wonder of all the villagers," he eventually came to embrace and enjoy the area, which made him feel "as if we were out of the world."[12]

7. [Samuel Dexter, son], "Biographical Notice of the Hon. Samuel Dexter," *The Farmer's Museum,* Vol. 16, No. 45 (August 27, 1810). This is the same notice that appears in *Monthly Analogy and Boston Review,* IX (July 1810): 3–4, as well as other magazines of the time. The quote regarding the father's attitude toward Calvinism and the reaction of his parents comes from this source, and thus should be understood as from the perspective of Samuel's son. Orrando Perry Dexter, et al., *Dexter Geneaology, 1642–1904; Being a history of the descendents of Richard Dexter of Malden, Massachusetts, from the notes of John Haven Dexter and original researches* (New York: J. J. Little, 1904), 53–58 [Hereafter *Dexter Genealogy*].

8. *Dexter Genealogy,* 53–58; Carlton Albert Staples, *Samuel Dexter, 1726–1810: A Paper Read Before the Dedham Historical Society, February 3, 1892* (Dedham, Mass., 1892), 6–11; William Pencak, "Dexter, Samuel," *American National Biography Online* (http://www.anb.org/articles/01/01-00217.html); Clarence Winthrop Bowen, *The History of Woodstock, Connecticut* (Norwood, Mass.: The Plimpton Press, 1926), Chapter 14.

9. Bowen, *History of Woodstock,* 185. Staples, *Samuel Dexter,* 8–9.

10. [Samuel Dexter, son], "Biographical Notice of the Hon. Samuel Dexter," *The Farmer's Museum,* 16:45 (August 27, 1810).

11. Samuel Dexter, Commonplace-book, 1763–1809, P-201, 1 reel (microfilm), Ms. SBd-219, Massachusetts Historical Society, p. 94. (Hereafter referred to as Commonplace-book.)

12. Staples, *Samuel Dexter,* 9. Jane Kamensky has traced some of the Dexter family's history

Once smallpox drove the Dexter family from Woodstock at the close of the Revolution and his wife died of cancer, Samuel lived a less settled life, and one focused on earnest preparations for his own demise.[13] In the spring of 1785, he sold his family's Dedham property, then moved to Marlboro, then Roxbury, then Weston, and, finally, he spent the last decade of his life in Mendon, Massachusetts. [14] All the while he grew ever more engrossed in the "large and choice library" that he had insisted on carting with him to each new place. It "attracted much attention at the time of its removal," one writer recalled, "but he was greatly devoted to the use of it in his retirement."[15] Sometime between leaving Woodstock and arriving at Mendon, Dexter came by his golden spectacles, either in response to the normal aging of his eyes, or possibly after hitting his head above the eye in an accident in January of 1788 as he was preparing to depart for church. All those books, and all those miles. Imagine for a moment what it would be like to be Samuel Dexter as he watched those letters gradually blur before his eyes.[16] Although he lived in a kind of self-exile after 1775, he never left the universe of ideas preserved on the page, and, in the end, that was the home he most cared about. To be expelled from the pantheon of patriots was one thing, to be banished from books quite another. To maintain his independence as a reader, and to unlock the door to his domain, Dexter had to have those spectacles.[17]

In theory, Samuel Dexter could have had spectacles made by someone con-

---

in her book, *The Exchange Artist: A Tale of High-Flying Speculation and America's First Banking Collapse* (New York: Viking, 2008). Many thanks to Dr. Kamensky for allowing me to read an early draft of Chapter One.

13. Commonplace-book, 231, 234–235.

14. *Dexter Genealogy,* 53–54.

15. Bowen, *History of Woodstock,* 189.

16. Dexter makes reference in his Commonplace-book (p. 251) to hitting his head above the eye in an accident in January of 1788 as he prepares to depart for church. By January of 1802, he is complaining of ophthalmia and fears "total blindness" (p. 308) but it is very difficult to say whether the one followed from the other. "Ophthalmia" referred very generally to eye problems, ranging from errors of refraction and accommodation to infectious diseases, in the eighteenth and early nineteenth centuries. David Fleishman, an expert collector, has dated the spectacles at 1785, and they could have easily been bought before Dexter starts mentioning these eye problems in the commonplace-book. In theory, he could have bought them as early as before the beginning of the Revolution, in 1774 or 1775, when he was in his late fifties; styles like his were available from the 1750s onward.

17. Readers with spectacles means older people no longer require the assistance of younger people; see Tenner, *Our Own Devices,* 217.

nected to his brother, John, a Marlboro goldsmith.[18] But it is unlikely given that Americans did not seriously attempt to copy and improve upon the English style of spectacles until the fledgling optical industry opened up shop in Philadelphia around the turn of the century.[19] Another possible source could have been someone like his brother Ebenezer, a physician, for on a handful of occasions physicians dispensed spectacles in the colonies during the eighteenth century.[20] But Ebenezer had died before the war, and, in any case, Samuel's generation did not usually look to the emergent medical community for this kind of cure. Instead, people sought spectacles on the advice of family, friends, and even acquaintances; purchased pamphlets like those written by the English spectacle makers James Ayscough, Benjamin Martin, and George Adams; or—as in Dexter's specific case—consulted popular reference works like William Buchan's *Domestic Medicine*.[21]

Primed by earlier reading in Buchan, Dexter would have done his best to select appropriate lenses from the range of powers stocked by a merchant. He probably procured the spectacles through a watchmaker like J. Deverell, who advertised "an elegant pair of Gold Temple Spectacles" for sale in Boston in 1785, or a merchant like Amos Atwell, who had opened a shop in 1791 that sold "Fresh Goods," including spectacles, directly across from Samuel's oldest son Andrew's store in Providence, Rhode Island.[22] Merchants like these had

18. *Dexter Genealogy*, 36, 59.

19. See Deborah Jean Warner, "Optics in Philadelphia During the Nineteenth Century," *Proceedings of the American Philosophical Society*, Vol. 129, No. 3 (September 1985): 291–99.

20. See T. H. Breen, *The Marketplace of Revolution: How Consumer Politics Shaped American Independence* (New York: Oxford University Press, 2004), 144, 146; and John Van Solingen v. Benjamin d'Harriette, July 14, 1730, in Richard B. Morris, ed., *Select Cases of the Mayor's Court of New York City, 1674–1784* (Washington, D.C.: American Historical Association, 1935), 554–60.

21. See, for example, Benjamin Franklin to Jane Mecom, London, July 17, 1771, ALS, American Philosophical Society, Philadelphia, Penn. The major works by members of the Worshipful Company of Spectacle Makers that circulated in the colonies were: Benjamin Martin, *An Essay on Visual Glasses (Vulgarly Called Spectacles)* (London: Printed for the Author, 1756); James Ayscough, *A Short Account of the Eye and the Nature of Vision, Chiefly Designed to Illustrate the Use and Advantage of Spectacles* (London: E. Say, 1752); and George Adams, *An Essay on Vision, Briefly Explaining the Fabric of the Eye and the Nature of Vision. . .* , second edition (London: Printed for the Author, by R. Hindmarsh, 1792). See also William Buchan, *Domestic medicine: or, A treatise on the prevention and cure of diseases, by regimen and simple medicines*, Twentieth edition (Waterford [N.Y.]: Printed by and for James Lyon & Co., 1797).

22. "Spectacles" (Advertisement for J. Deverell, watchmaker) *The Massachusetts Centinel*, September, 3, 1785. "Fresh Goods" (Advertisement for Amos Atwell and Son) *The United States Chronicle*, June 6, 1791. Kamensky discusses Andrew's business in Chapter One of *The Exchange Artist*.

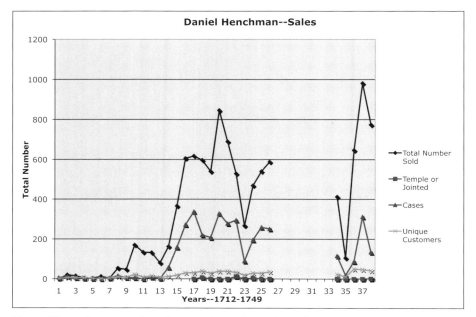

Fig. 3. Chart showing sales of spectacles and number of customers buying spectacles in Daniel Henchman's Boston bookshop, 1712–1749. Based on the Daniel Henchman account and day books. Microfilm at the American Antiquarian Society.

been importing spectacles, mainly from London, on a regular basis going back to the 1710s. Starting in the 1720s, the Boston bookseller Daniel Henchman's account and day books suggest that the sale of spectacles started to take off. Between 1713 and 1748, his sales climbed from twenty to 981 pairs, while the population of Boston doubled (fig. 3). All the while he sold more spectacles to traders from outlying towns.[23] After the French and Indian War, advertisements show a growing variety of styles of spectacles available from an increasing number of outlets on the coast, and even beyond the coast, in smaller towns throughout many of the colonies, especially in the north and mid-Atlantic

23. Refer to the Daniel Henchman Papers, microfilm collection at the American Antiquarian Society for examples of this. Henchman's customers are discussed in Chapter 2 of *Reading Glasses,* and digested in Appendices 1, 2, and 3. See Stebbins McCaffrey, *Reading Glasses,* 383–94. These calculations are based on population estimates for 1710, 1720, 1730, 1742, and 1760, as listed in Lawrence W. Kennedy, *Planning the City Upon a Hill: Boston Since 1630* (Amherst, Mass.: The University of Massachusetts Press, 1992). Alan McBrayer to David Fleishman, Katherine Stebbins McCaffrey, Laura Brandt, and Charles Letocha, June 20, 2007, email correspondence in the possession of the author.

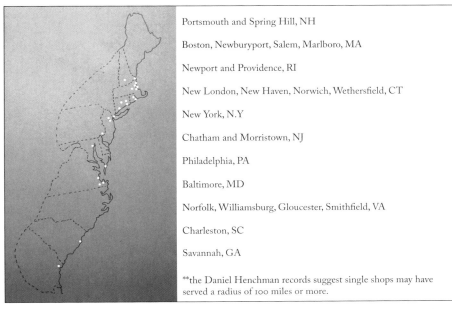

Portsmouth and Spring Hill, NH

Boston, Newburyport, Salem, Marlboro, MA

Newport and Providence, RI

New London, New Haven, Norwich, Wethersfield, CT

New York, N.Y

Chatham and Morristown, NJ

Philadelphia, PA

Baltimore, MD

Norfolk, Williamsburg, Gloucester, Smithfield, VA

Charleston, SC

Savannah, GA

**the Daniel Henchman records suggest single shops may have served a radius of 100 miles or more.

Fig. 4. Map showing cities and towns with one or more shops selling spectacles from the 1760s to the 1780s. From top to bottom, the cities and towns are: Portsmouth and Spring Hill, N.H.; Boston, Newburyport, Salem, Marlboro, Mass.; Newport and Providence, R.I.; New London, New Haven, Norwich, Wethersfield, Conn.; New York, N.Y.; Chatham and Morristown, N.J.; Philadelphia, Penn.; Baltimore, Md.; Norfolk, Williamsburg, Gloucester, Smithfield, Va.; Charleston, S.C.; and Savannah, Ga. The Daniel Henchman records suggest single shops may have served customers within a radius of 100 miles or more. Based on advertisements collected in three electronic sources—Digital Evans, Past Portal (Colonial Williamsburg), and the digital edition of the *Pennsylvania Gazette*—and checked against the Prime file at Winterthur Museum, Winterthur, Del. Map by author.

(fig. 4). These spectacles went home, alone or in sets of half or one dozen, in the pockets of the elites, artisans, many of middling status, and their mothers, fathers, friends, nurses, and maids.[24]

Owners, like the spectacles themselves, varied, but they nearly all shared at least one thing: old age. Advertisers offered correction for short sight as well as long, but the vast majority of buyers bought convex spectacles for correcting the defects that develop as the eye ages, a trend also suggested by the near

24. Again, refer to advertisements in the colonial papers from the era, as well as the Daniel Henchman accounts, both digested in Stebbins McCaffrey, *Reading Glasses*, Chapter 2, and 383–94.

total absence of concave spectacles from the period in extant collections.[25] For
most of Dexter's lifetime, buying spectacles meant taking up what are referred
to today as reading glasses, and few in that day missed the connotations of
physical and mental decline that came with their use. Stories celebrating those
who managed to live into the eighth decade or beyond without the need for
spectacles perennially registered a resigned attitude toward spectacles, and the
continual wish that perhaps another cure for aged eyes might someday be
discovered.[26] Glimpses of one's bespectacled face in a mirror surely whispered:
remember death.

Not that Samuel Dexter needed reminding. By the time he got his spectacles, Dexter's focus had already shifted from earthly matters to spiritual questions. Thanks to his spectacles, Samuel penned letters and his mother's obituary, but mainly he spent his time writing for himself: he produced unknown
quantities of manuscript pages, which he periodically burned in fits of shame;
a thirty-seven-page will with two lengthy postscripts and two even lengthier
codicils; his three-hundred-and-thirty-page-plus commonplace book, which
he took time, before dying, to edit with pen as well as penknife; and one surviving palimpsest probing the validity of Trinitarian versus Unitarian doctrines.
All betrayed his renewed interest in living a Christian life, and all put his spectacles to the kind of use they were designed to encourage: hands-on reading of
many texts in succession, lengthened hours of writing and revising, more time
spent attending to every detail on the page.[27]

25. I have found concave lenses to be very rare in the material record for this period, even
though they were highly advertised at the time. They do not show up until the mid-nineteenth
century or later in collections such as those at the Rokeby Museum, Ferrisburg, Vt.; the New
Hampshire Historical Society, Concord, N.H.; the Connecticut Historical Society, Hartford,
Conn.; the Maine Historical Society, Portland, Me.; the Massachusetts Historical Society; and
the private collection held by the Stout family of Ipswich, Mass. Instead, single lens perspective
glasses seem to have been used by myopes. See also Daniel Henchman Papers. Microfilm collection at the American Antiquarian Society, in particular, the purchases of Rev. Thomas Foxcroft,
on August, 15, 1748; August 9, 1732; and December 5, 1732.

26. An early example of this would be *The Most Wonderful Relation of Master John Macklain*
([London]: Printed for T. Vere & W. Giberson, 1657), title page, 2–5, 8–9, 12. A later example
of this would be James Calder, "Information to Old People," *New York Magazine*, Vol 2 (1797):
568.

27. Commonplace-book, 4, 114, on p. 270–71 he writes "There seems to be no end of burning
old wills, and executing new ones"—dated Weston, June 14, 1792; he describes his mother's will
on p. 296–99. The obituary is copied in *Dexter Genealogy,* 42–43, and appeared in *The Columbian Centinel,* June 21, 1797. The palimpsest is listed as a commonplace-book, and it is housed

The single piece Samuel Dexter produced for broad public consumption during his bespectacled period was a sixty-page anonymous pamphlet in which Dexter used a close reading of the marginal translations included in the King James Bible to argue God did not damn Esau for failing to be a "second-sighted man."[28] This argument also conveniently absolved Dexter of what he came to consider the cardinal sin of his life: his rejection of the opportunity to continue his father's ministry in favor of the pursuit of worldly wealth and status. To atone for the folly of his youth, Dexter made plans for a funeral sermon that, by his own strict instruction, would make no mention of him—the deceased—at all. Instead, it would be a meditation on a passage from Paul's second letter to the Corinthians, chapter four, verse eighteen: "The things which are seen are temporal; but the things which are not seen are eternal."[29] Decrying the ambition of those who sought to "lay up treasures on earth" and in "their vicious lives appear to be *totally* regardless of the doctrine of future existence"—in other words, condemning his younger self—Dexter urged the minister to tell "his hearers to imagine they hear ONE FROM THE INVISIBLE WORLD asserting this great truth, that 'things which are *eternal,*' are infinitely more important than 'things which are *temporal*.'"[30]

Only Dexter was not, as he imagined himself to be, growing more virtuously immune to the lure of earth's treasures in his waning years. The Dexter that claimed to care nothing for the visible, material world is the same Dexter who simultaneously eschewed the many more modest choices of spectacles available in favor of the most expensive, most up-to-date, most formidable and flashy spectacles that could be had. Costing as much as four times what the same design would fetch in silver, and ten times as much as the steel version,[31]

in a folder with the Ward-Perry-Dexter Papers, 1733–1927, Ms N-1727, Massachusetts Historical Society.

28. "Philotheorus" (Samuel Dexter) *Thoughts on Several Passages of Scripture. . . .* (Worcester, Mass.: Isaiah Thomas, 1791), 7–8, 10, 14–18, 45.

29. Samuel Dexter's will is listed in the Worcester County Probate Records for 1810, Vol. 39, beginning on page 391; these are available on microfilm at the Massachusetts State Archives, see page 399 [Hereafter Will]. The sermon is Samuel Kendal, *A Discourse Delivered at Mendon, June 14, 1810* (Boston, Mass.: John Eliot, 1810).

30. Will, 399; Kendal, *A Discourse Delivered at Mendon.*

31. This general sense of the cost of the spectacles is based on the John McAllister account books: Account and day books, John McAllister, Philadelphia optician, Downs Special Collections, Winterthur Library, Winterthur, Del. Prices are listed in the appendices of Stebbins McCaffrey, *Reading Glasses,* 391–97, especially 397.

Fig. 5. Unknown. Leather spectacles attributed to Esak Hopkins. United States, ca. 1770. RHi X4 276. Iron, glass, leather, and silk ribbon. Personal Gear. Museum Collection. 1921.1.47. Courtesy, the Rhode Island Historical Society.

Dexter's spectacles were in the newer style, called temple spectacles. Developed in the mid-eighteenth century by the Worshipful Company of Spectacle Makers, temple spectacles eventually replaced the considerably more fragile and inconvenient armless designs made of horn, fishbone, wood, or thin strands of metal that had circulated for four hundred years (figs. 5 and 6).[32] The London spectacle guild had parlayed its late seventeenth-century connections with members of the Royal Society and its eighteenth-century connections to the crown into dominance of the vision aid market, both at home and in the American colonies.[33] The company capitalized on immigrant labor from

32. See, for example, the early spectacles shown in Corson, *Fashions in Eyeglasses.*

33. Spectacles were sold under a wide variety of signs in many shops that didn't specialize in them, but the spectacle makers had early on regularized their signage, advertising, and trade cards. E. G. R. Taylor, *Mathematical Practitioners of Tudor & Stuart England* (Cambridge, Eng.: Cambridge University Press, 1970), especially pages 248–49, 256–59, 262–63, 276–77, 280–91, 294–95, and 302–3; Corson, *Fashions,* 47; Law, *A History,* Chapter 3. Only a handful of cards are left from that earliest period, in the collection of the British Museum, and they are often reproduced in secondary sources, such as Corson, *Fashions,* 47. When compared to the print ads and descriptions of signage in Taylor, they suggest a strong degree of uniformity among spectacle makers. See also D. J. Bryden and D. L. Simms, "Archimedes as an Advertising Symbol," in

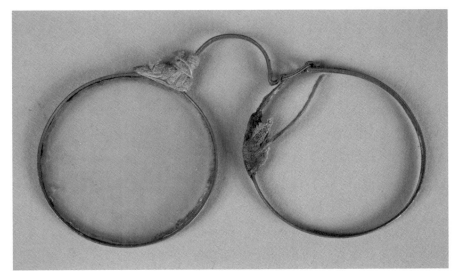

Fig. 6. Wire-rimmed spectacles, owner unknown, 18th century. Gift of Mrs. Carl W. Noren, Connecticut Historical Society Collections. Courtesy, the Connecticut Historical Society, Hartford, Conn.

Italy and the fortune in raw materials, including gold and silver extracted in distant realms by slave or indigenous labor, which increasingly flowed through Atlantic trade networks and into English hands.[34] The spectacle makers advertised their wares as part of a spectrum of fashionable aids intended to enhance

<hr />

Technology and Culture, 34, No. 2 (April 1993): 387–91; as well as Bryden and Simms, "Archimedes and the Opticians of London," in *Bulletin of the Scientific Instrument Society,* 35 (1992): 11–14. , D. J. Bryden and D. L. Simms, "Spectacles improved to perfection and approved of by the Royal Society," *Annals of Science,* 30 (1993): 1–32. See also, Adams, *An Essay on Vision;* as well as E. G. R. Taylor, *The Mathematical Practitioners of Hanoverian England, 1714–1840* (Cambridge, Eng.: For the Institute of Navigation at the University Press, 1966).

34. Laura Rigal, "Electric Books of 1747," *Common-place,* 1, No. 2 (January 2001). For more on mining in Brazil, see also Kathleen J. Higgins, *"Licentious Liberty" in a Brazilian Gold-Mining Region: Slavery, Gender, and Social Control in Eighteenth-Century Sabara, Minas Gerais* (University Park, Penn.: Penn State University Press, 1999). On the importance of situating materials in their historical eras (and the revelations that frequently follow), see Robert Friedel, *A Material World* (Washington DC: Smithsonian, 1988). Many thanks to John Mayer for calling my attention to this excellent work. Richard Bushman, "The Complexity of Silver," in *New England Silversmithing, 1620–1815,* Jeannine Falino and Gerald W. R. Ward, editors (Boston: Colonial Society of Massachusetts, 2001); Silvio Bedini, *Thinkers and Tinkers: Early American Men of Science* (New York: Charles Scribner's Sons, 1975), 299.

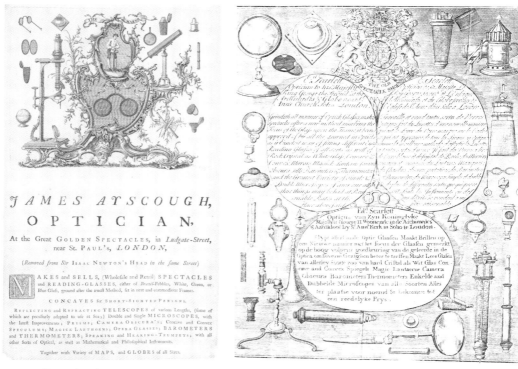

Fig. 7 (left). Edward Scarlett Trade Card (mid-eighteenth century). Courtesy of the Science & Society Picture Library, a division of the National Museum of Science and Industry, London, England.

Fig. 8 (right). James Ayscough Trade Card (ca. 1750). Courtesy of the Science & Society Picture Library, a division of the National Museum of Science and Industry, London, England.

scientific inquiry and promote aesthetic development (figs. 7 and 8).[35] In the colonies, the emergence of temple spectacles coincided with a shift in where spectacles were commonly sold, from being offered in bookstores, post offices, and print shops to being offered as one more item in the general avalanche of English goods from any number of merchants.[36] During periods of non-importation, some Americans branded spectacles necessities by labeling them cutlery, and long after the Revolution many sellers categorized them as hard-

35. See, for example, the advertisements copied in Law, *A History,* as well as Ayscough, *A Short Essay on Vision,* and especially the pamphlets of Benjamin Martin, all cited in note 21.

36. See especially Appendix 1 in Stebbins McCaffrey, *Reading Glasses,* 383–90 to track this trend.

ware, as Amos Atwell did.[37] Yet, no matter what Revolutionary-era Americans like Samuel Dexter told themselves, when they purchased these types of spectacles, they bought into a vast commercial and imperial network heavily dependent upon vision to perpetuate and secure its hierarchies.

In refashioning spectacles at mid-century to be more reliable and refined, the Worshipful Company had also made them, in a way, less polite. Temple spectacles might be durable and practical, but they were much less discreet than the designs that had preceded them. This may well have been part of the reasoning—another part being the bald admission of age and decay—behind why Samuel Dexter decided not to include them in his portrait.[38] As props, books were well established as sending a positive message of improvement to the viewer, but until the second quarter of the nineteenth century, Americans declined to allow the spectacles the same status.[39] Although spectacles always represented an investment in the word—and in Samuel Dexter's case, a significant investment—they remained too forceful a reminder of the lure of the material world and the discomfiting power of the gaze. As beautiful as the spectacles were, they showcased the level to which refinement depended on calculated display.[40] The older Samuel Dexter got, the more distressed he became by his own visibility, and the more completely he sought to escape or repress it. In the same year that he sat for his portrait, for example, Dexter decried at length his decision to mark the height of his success in the 1760s by commissioning a fake coat of arms for his family. As an old man, he "concealed [the herald]...in a trunk, in my closet, and, probably, its end will be to be burned,"

37. Annapolis, Md., "Annapolis (in Maryland) June 22, 1769. We, the Subscribers . . . [to] prevent the Use of foreign Luxuries and Superfluities . . ." (Annapolis, Md.1769), 2; similarly, in "An Inventory of Goods on hand taken 20th August 1770," the Merchant Firm of Briggs & Blow of Williamsburg listed "16 pair spectacles, 10 pair Temple, 5 Plain Irons" under their account of cutlery. See "Prentis Store Historical Report Block 18–1 Building 5 Lot 46," Colonial Williamsburg Digital History Center Archive, available at http://www.pastportal.com/, accessed August 4, 2005. The original papers are available in the William and Mary College Archives, Williamsburg, Va.

38. Hewes, *Portraits in the Collection of the American Antiquarian Society*, 145–47.

39. Except for Benjamin Franklin, spectacle-wearers uniformly declined to be shown in their spectacles in formal portraits until the nineteenth century. This statement is based in part on my survey of the portraits in collections of the Connecticut Historical Society, Hartford, Conn., but reviews of collections of portraits by Gilbert Stuart, John Singleton Copley, and Charles Willson Peale all confirm this trend.

40. Bushman, *The Refinement of America,* 45, and Chapter 3.

along with a handful of "literary vanities. . . . I despise it," Dexter went on in his commonplace book, "and myself for having procured it."[41] No surprise, then, that even though he depicted himself as a reader, Dexter would decline to capture his unusually expensive temple spectacles in his portrait. Gold temple spectacles signaled exactly the kind of fashionable inflation of self-importance that Dexter wanted to consign to his past.

As much as he may have wished it, in truth Samuel Dexter's funeral message did not come in the form of an immaterial voice from beyond. It, too, had a material manifestation—six hundred copies prepaid by Dexter and issued from the press of John Eliot "on good paper, with a fair type," just as Dexter himself had directed. The spectacles and the sermon, and many of his final preparations, betrayed the fact that as Dexter tried to make choices informed by his deepening spiritual convictions, he nonetheless grew increasingly concerned about how he looked to posterity. Witness not only the burned manuscripts and the heavily edited commonplace book, but also his final request for "a plain coffin of pine board, blacked, without a cloth covering, and without any kind of inscription, or other ornament." In his will he forbade "any gentlemen, termed persons of distinction and figure, to be my pall-holders," thereby excluding many of his friends. Instead he preferred to purchase the services of "twelve men of sober life, who have families in poor circumstances, of or near the town, or parish to which I last belonged" for the sum of "five dollars and a pamphlet." Similarly, he requested that "any poor persons" who had watched over him be paid "thirty-seven cents and five mills" for each night at his bedside. Setting aside rings as parting gifts for friends, he worried aloud that they would be considered an old-fashioned gesture. "As I have not of late years mixed with the fashionable world, I know not but some other memorial of friendship, respect, or affect has been substituted in the place of rings," he wrote. "My executors are to conform to custom in this respect." Without question, the generous will continued to dispense his remaining fortune as Dexter had done, or was suspected of having done, in life, with over five thousand dollars famously set aside to fund the study of scriptures at Harvard. Yet even as he cautioned his relatives against "showy and ostentatious" expressions of mourning, believing "great evil grows of the practice," Dexter admitted that it was possible to go so far in the other direction that one risked being "censur-

41. Commonplace-book, 276.

able for [one's] singularity."[42] In other words, it was beginning to dawn on Samuel Dexter that in his rush to encourage righteous simplicity, he might be promoting something like conspicuous non-consumption.

Samuel Dexter's spectacles, and his faith, helped him read and write to a ripe old age. In January of 1802, he complained of "ophthalmia"—a term applied to many eye ailments in that day—and feared "total blindness." On his eighty-third birthday in March of 1809, he penned again his yearly expression of "holy gratitude . . . for any mitigation of my bodily pains & infirmities" that God saw fit to bestow.[43] At the time of his death the following summer, Dexter's spectacles passed to his youngest son and namesake, Samuel, presumably in the unlisted jumble of personal effects and household goods divided by his sons and sons-in-law according to the instructions left in the otherwise voluminous will, some of which was reproduced against his wishes along with his funeral sermon.[44] Sometime in the handful of years between Samuel the father's departure from the earthly realm in 1810 and Samuel the son's abrupt death during a scarlet fever epidemic in 1816, Samuel the son had the gold-plated case made.[45] The youngest of Dexter's children, born in 1761 at the height of his father's mercantile career, Samuel had decamped to Woodstock with his parents in 1775 only to return to Cambridge in the fall of 1777 to enter Harvard. He finished at the top of his class, went on to study and practice law, dabbled in banking, and served as Secretary of War in his close friend John Adams's administration, as well as briefly as Thomas Jefferson's Secretary of the Treasury.[46]

That the elder Samuel carried his prize spectacles about without a case could not have been numbered among his unusual habits. According to the Henchman accounts, purchasers usually bought spectacles without cases.[47] By 1810,

42. Will, 404, 406; Kendal, *A Discourse*, 23; Staples, *Samuel Dexter*, 17.

43. Commonplace-book, 302, 332.

44. Will, 404, 406; Kendal, *A Discourse*, 4–5.

45. Lucius M. Sargent, *Reminiscences of Samuel Dexter, Originally written for the Boston Evening Transcript, by Sigma* (Boston: Henry Dutton & Son, 1857), 71.

46. The US Treasury has a brief general biography of Samuel Dexter available on its website. See http://www.treas.gov/education/history/secretaries/sdexter.shtml. For insight into Samuel Dexter Junior's career, see Kamensky, *The Exchange Artist*, Chapter One.

47. Stebbins McCaffrey, *Reading Glasses*, Appendix 2, 391–93.

Fig. 9 (left). Temple spectacles (ca. 1800). Marked with a "30" (to denote the power of the lens, probably by reference to age) on the outer left temple piece. Photograph by the author. Courtesy, Rokeby Museum, Ferrisburgh, Vt.

Fig. 10 (right). Temple spectacles (ca. 1810). Photograph by the author. Courtesy, Rokeby Museum, Ferrisburgh, Vt.

however, there was an emerging sense that every pair of spectacles deserved its own protective container (figs. 9 and 10). In addition, both and either could be marked with not only makers' marks and buyers' or sellers' addresses, but also personal names or initials and a rudimentary system for denoting powers of vision.[48] While spectacles began the eighteenth century as an unreliable tool for reading, spectacles in the first quarter of the nineteenth century demanded more directly than ever to be *read*, literally and figuratively, as an increasingly substantial public declaration of private property, individual bodily ability, and basic belief in the value of literacy and numeracy.

For Samuel the younger, the case presented an unusual literary opportunity (fig. 11). On it and through it he renewed and revised the themes of visibility and invisibility, heritage and legacy that so consistently absorbed his father's attention. Like the obituary that appeared in magazines and newspapers during the summer of 1810, which Samuel the son is suspected to have authored, the engraved case provided a comment upon his father's generosity and personal style.[49] More than that: it functioned as a piece of revisionist history, not unlike his father's faux coat of arms. For example, though Samuel Sr. was certainly familiar with the works of Horace, he did not record owning any

48. See for example the early Robinson family spectacles in the collections of the Rokeby Museum, Ferrisburgh, Vt., and also the Isaiah Thomas spectacles in the collection of the New Hampshire Historical Society, Concord, N.H.

49. [Dexter], "Biographical Notice."

Fig. 11. Gold-plated spectacle case belonging to the Dexter family, ca. 1810. Courtesy of the Massachusetts Historical Society.

editions of Horace in his library inventory, nor did he comment at length upon Horace in the pages that remain in his commonplace book. He did, coincidentally, make a bare mention of Horace when he had injured his head above his eye back in 1788, but whether his son had any idea of this is extremely hard to say.[50] Son Samuel emulated and enjoyed Horace more extensively, at Harvard and through his correspondence with his friend John Adams, who owned and quoted freely from several editions.[51] And while the father Samuel almost certainly used his spectacles to peruse his multivolume set of *The Spectator,* like many, many others did in the eighteenth century—one does not have to look far to find spectacle buyers leaving Daniel Henchman's bookstore with copies of *The Spectator* in tow[52]—in fact Samuel Sr. never sat, as it might seem, gazing at his case, with words extracted from *The Spectator* branded across the reflection of his bespectacled face.

Son Samuel read both Horace and *The Spectator,* and responded by linking them, through the case, with his father's life and the glasses left in his care. This was not an obvious connection to make, in part because Mr. Spectator

50. Samuel Dexter catalogued his library in his Commonplace-book, 8–20. He most likely added to this list, started early in the book, as he acquired books, just as he made notes when he lent them (for example, to his son Samuel, see p. 15). Dexter makes note of his 9-volume set of *The Spectator* on p. 18, and to Horace on p. 251.

51. For John Adams's use of Horace, including in his letters with Dexter, see Dorothy M. Robathan, "John Adams and the Classics," *The New England Quarterly,* Vol. 19, No. 1 (March 1946): 91–98.

52. Daniel Henchman records John Dennie, a frequent purchaser of spectacles as far back as April 9, 1720, as buying "1 set of Spectators" on September 24, 1722, for example.

and the denizens of the coffeehouses did not conspicuously or uniformly mark themselves by wearing actual spectacles. Isaac Bickerstaff, the lead persona in Steele's *Tatler* wore old-style nose spectacles.[53] But in *The Spectator,* though Mr. Spectator boasted "I have, methinks, a more than ordinary Penetration in Seeing," Addison and Steele chose to forgo depicting actual spectacles in favor of portraying the act of social observation as akin to the *sense* of wearing spectacles. In some later engravings of coffeehouses, temple spectacles functioned as a conduit for information, a frame for scenes, and as a mask that created the kind of urban anonymity upon which Mr. Spectator thrived.[54] And in both serials, they repeated one conceit, that in public spaces people made snap judgments based on nothing but "the Intimations Men gather from our Aspect," because "A Man, they say, wears the Picture of his Mind in his Countenance." Moreover, Mr. Spectator went on, "one Man's Eyes are Spectacles to [those] who look at him to read his Heart."[55]

This posture had social dimensions, but for Samuel the son, it had very personal dimensions as well. It mimicked the stance that his father took in relation to him as he set out for Harvard. From the start, his father's advice had a clear theme: literacy, and the growing role it played in making a living. Samuel the son's studies would not be for the sake of pure intellectual or spiritual development, they would have to prepare him to support himself. In a way, his father argued in a letter, this education was his inheritance, invested.[56] At Harvard, son Samuel mounted a mini-rebellion just as his father once had, immersing himself in epic poetry and publishing a long poem extolling "The Progress of Science."[57] He quickly found himself more inclined to read things from a secular perspective, and without the guilty conscience that plagued his father. He also wasted no time in fretting over the volatility of the new economy, as his father once had. Instead, he tried to make circumstances work

53. *The Tatler,* No. 103, December 6, 1709; Donald F. Bond, ed., *The Tatler* (Oxford: Clarendon Press, 1987), 364. See also *The Tatler,* No. 88, November 1, 1709; Bond, *The Tatler,* 273ff. *The Tatler,* No. 64, September 6, 1709; Bond, *The Tatler,* 110ff. *The Tatler,* No. 176, May 23–25, 1710; Bond, *The Tatler,* 321ff. *The Tatler,* No. 93, November 12, 1709; Bond, *The Tatler,* 303–04.

54. Quoted in, among other places, Michael G. Ketcham, *Transparent Designs* (Athens, Ga.: University of Georgia Press, 1985), 12. For examples and a discussion of coffeehouse engravings, see Stebbins McCaffrey, *Reading Glasses,* 187–92.

55. *The Spectator* No. 206, Friday, October 26, 1711 (Steele); Bond, *The Spectator,* Vol. 2, 307. See also *The Tatler,* No. 145, March 11–14, 1709–10; Bond, *The Tatler,* 165.

56. Commonplace-book, 166–72.

57. See Sargent, *Reminiscences,* Chapters 4 and 5.

to his advantage, and as the fortunes of his sometimes quite public speculative enterprises abruptly rose and fell in the early Republic, Dexter moved quickly on to the next big thing with scarcely a backward glance.[58]

The spectacle case suggests Samuel did not miss some of the ironies in how he ended up using his inheritance, such as it was. In his letter, Horace reminded his friend Florus, "Experience shows you, as your riches swell / Your wants increase. . . . With heirs following heirs like waves at sea, / And no such thing as perpetuity," Horace asked, "What good are farmsteads, granaries, pasture-grounds / That stretch long leagues beyond Calabria's bounds, / If Death, unbribed by riches, mows down all / With his unsparing sickle, great and small?" Instead of obsessing about accumulating a fine estate to pass on to his descendents, Horace vowed in the letter that *he* would not "fear what my next heir may think" if the descendent found "There's less than he expected left behind."[59] As Michael Ketcham has argued, various essays in *The Spectator* also addressed this issue, tracing the dissolution of traditional forms of society, which were often figured in inheritance. But rather than bemoaning the sad state of affairs, *The Spectator*'s writers set to replacing the old modes of exchange with new stories that reconciled people to the social and economic flux around them, while demonstrating, as Erin Mackie has pointed out, how to remain upstanding consumers on such unsteady terrain.[60]

That meant that for Joseph Addison, Horace's dark view of material acquisition provided the impetus to ponder the deepest questions of existence. As Mr. Spectator wandered the fields and forests of his friend Sir Roger Coverley's estate, he looked beyond the land to think about Horace's view of heredity in an entirely different way. Why, he wondered, did "the Soul, which is capable of such immense Perfections, and of receiving new Improvements to all Eternity, . . . fall away into nothing almost as soon as it is created"? Turning to the extract, Mr. Spectator concluded that, since "Man can never have taken his full measure . . . before he is hurried off the Stage, . . . he does not seem born to enjoy Life, but to deliver it down to others." Thus, he argued, men should look "on this World as only a Nursery for the next," in which, he reasoned, ". . . The several Generations of rational Creatures, which rise up and disappear

---

58. This is the case made in Kamensky, *The Exchange Artist,* Chapter One.

59. Horace, *The satires, epistles and art of poetry of Horace,* translated into English verse by John Conington (London: Bell, 1888).

60. Ketcham, *Transparent Designs,* 1–3.

in such quick Successions, are only to receive their first Rudiments of Existence. . . . Afterwards," he concluded, souls are "to be transplanted into a more friendly Climate, where they may spread and flourish to all Eternity."[61]

Dexter's spectacle case offered a tangible way to experience the lesson encapsulated in this quote. The Dexter spectacles were made of solid gold, instead of the more common silver or steel bows, which meant that they wouldn't tarnish or rust. Their brilliance lasts for what, to humans, seems like forever.[62] How could such a precious and lasting thing have persuaded Samuel Dexter to put aside earthly riches? It could if Dexter looked *through* those spectacles, not *at* them. If he looked through them to read the *gold-plated* case in his hand or on his desk, he would be materially reminded of Addison's vision of the earth as heaven's hothouse, or Horace's vision of the deeply illusory quality of material possessions—the lesson that, as Shakespeare famously put it, "All that glisters is not gold."[63] If looking through the gold spectacles to view the plated case did not remind Dexter the younger to focus his vision, as his father had come to, on lasting, invisible, heavenly goals, then at the very minimum, it suggested to him that he was capable of learning to sense when he was in the presence of things of *real* value versus things bearing only a *surface shine.* But to make the material motto work, Dexter would have to *keep reading the text*—and not let his eyes refocus on his own image, that of the smartly ornamented spectator reflected in the case.

In this way, Dexter molded his father's meditations concerning the invisible, spiritual world into a very visible secular object lesson. And perhaps by 1810 he believed he had begun to learn it—after all, Dexter had the case made right around the time he took his final major office, that of the first president of the Massachusetts State Temperance Society. In a similar maneuver, three weeks before his illness and subsequent death, he happened to produce a manuscript titled "Thoughts on the Immortality of the Soul." In it, the younger Dexter argued for the existence of the invisible world on the basis that scientists had shown that "the inability of a blind man to discover colors . . . does not disprove their existence." This prompted one eulogist to applaud his "far reaching and comprehensive view, beyond the ken of ordinary optics," just as the "gigantic

61. *The Spectator* No. 111, Saturday, July 7, 1711 (Addison); Bond, *The Spectator,* Vol. 1, 456–59.
62. See Hans-Gert Bachmann, et al., *Gold: The Noble Mineral* (East Hampton, Conn.: Lapis International, 2003).
63. The quote is from Shakespeare's *The Merchant of Venice,* Act 2, Scene 7.

telescopes of Herschell and Rosse . . . surpass all others, in their powers of celestial investigation."[64] For Samuel the son and his contemporaries, temple spectacles belonged more firmly to the realm of science, the logic of which could be substituted for traditional religious reflections.

At least once the case and its message attracted attention. Years after Samuel the son's death in 1816, one of his contemporaries recalled it, writing that "Mr. Dexter . . . had great pleasure, in treasuring up the memorials of those, who were the natural guardians of his earlier years. I recollect, that he had preserved a pair of spectacles, which had belonged to his father, and for which he had caused a case to be prepared, bearing for its inscription—*Hares Haeredem velut unda supervenit undam.*" By then, however, the context had shifted again. Instead of pondering the quote's original sources, the *Epistles* or *The Spectator,* the words reminded him, he wrote, of a letter of Daniel Webster's, in which Webster "expressed much anxiety to find a pair of steel spectacles, which his father had worn, the last ten years of his life; he feared they were lost, but [after] devot[ing] a day to hunting for them, he found them." The lesson, Dexter's friend wrote, was that it was not "an unusual thing, for great men to enjoy a peculiar satisfaction, in looking through the eyes of their fathers."[65] As much as those who inherited the revolution talked about seeing through their father's eyes, though, descriptions suggest that the younger Samuel Dexter did not use the spectacles all that much before he died at the age of fifty-five.[66]

Thus, in matters of spectatorship, the Dexter spectacles and case did not function as simple lens and mirror. They mark the intersection of broader trends in the dissemination and use of spectacles with one family's own shifting understanding of salvation and birthright. They are fine specimens of eighteenth- and nineteenth-century vision aids, and they capture the contradictions and complications that marked the understanding of the visual world at

64. Sargent, *Reminiscences,* 36–38; See also Samuel Dexter, "Thoughts on the Immortality of the Soul," MS 724, Houghton Library, Harvard University, Cambridge, Mass.

65. Sargent, *Reminiscences,* 71.

66. Sargent, *Reminiscences,* 20–23. Jane Kamensky notes that during the end of the Adams administration, Dexter the younger was skewered by Democratic-Republican newspapers with the accusation that he seemed like a "doddering grandmother"; because old women were often depicted in drawings as sporting spectacles, it is possible this was a coded reference to his own use of vision aids, however, it seems slim in comparison with other descriptions that make no mention of the use of spectacles, even in his office. Kamensky, *The Exchange Artist,* 47.

that moment in history. But gaze on them from another viewpoint, and their shapes quickly shift into something altogether different.

Throughout the eighteenth century, users thought and spoke of spectacles as a second pair of eyes.[67] For late eighteenth-century users, the new style of temple spectacles also acted as something of a shroud. Those wishing to convey intimacy or sincerity frequently felt compelled to draw back the curtain, as it were, by taking off or at least propping up their spectacles to reveal the actual, undistorted eyes behind.[68] This image of the confusion of body and accessory was taken up in *The Spectator,* as it neared the end of its run. In the Saturday, October 18, 1712 issue, Addison reproduced a letter that referenced the fifth chapter of Paul's second letter to the Corinthians, arguing,

> *. . . this Veil of Flesh parts the visible and invisible World: But when we put off these Bodies, . . . new and surprising Wonders present themselves to our Views; when these material Spectacles are taken off, the Soul, with its own naked Eyes, sees what was invisible before. . . . Death opens our Eyes, enlarges our Prospect, presents us with a new and more glorious World, which we can never see while we are shut up in the Flesh.[69]*

"And," the writer concluded, *"methinks this is enough to cure us of our Fondness for these Bodies"* and *"make us willing to part with this Veil, as to take the Film off of our Eyes, which hinders our Sight."[70]*

When Samuel Dexter Sr. died in 1810, he was only too happy to cast off the veil and join the invisible world. So much so that, in addition to the notes about bequests, gifts, inheritances, coffins, services, sermons, and mourning, he added to his will one last set of instructions, which, as it turns out, were followed to the letter.[71] After burying his wife and then his mother, Samuel Sr. began to think about the family's vault. He grew more disgusted by the thought of bones "cast about" by cemetery workers, "disturbed and thrown together to make room for other bodies. . . It is my ardent wish to meet my relations, who have been and may be laid in my tomb, in a better world," he wrote, but "I do not think it proper to rescind the resolution I have made" to be buried instead at "the spot hereby assigned for the place of my interment,"

---

67. See, for example John McAllister to Thomas Jefferson, Philadelphia, December 1, 1806.

68. Cynthia Wall, "The English Auction: Narratives of Dismantlings," *Eighteenth-Century Studies* 31, No. 1 (1997): 1–25, especially page 8.

69. Ibid.

70. Ibid.

71. See Dexter's Will; Bowen, *History of Woodstock,* 187–89; Staples, *Samuel Dexter,* 11–13; *Dexter Genealogy,* 55–57.

which he had "fixed upon . . . before I left Woodstock," the single place where he had felt least bound by earthly concerns.[72] That spot was about three and a half acres that had once been part of his farm. On his burial day, just as he wished, his poor but virtuous pall-bearers lowered his simple coffin into the center of the lot, and when the service was done, they covered it over and left it completely unmarked. The family then transferred the land to the local minister so that it might be used for "mowing, pasturage, and tillage for ever." Though late nineteenth- century historians noted the site "has not been left vacant according to his directions," they uniformly agreed that Samuel Dexter Sr. had succeeding in erasing all evidence of his earthly remains.[73] This suggests that, in the end, the younger Samuel may have meant for the spectacle case to act as nothing more than a small sepulcher, as a place to bury the spectacles, a valuable vestige of his father. In the absence of a tomb or marker, he may well have focused his grief on this portable site, turning Addison's epigraph into his father's epitaph.

After his own death in 1816, observers noted that the younger Samuel Dexter lived and died by another of Horace's quotes, from *Ars Poetica*: "—*Si vis me flere, dolendum est / Primum, ipsi tibi.*" "If you wish me to weep, you must first feel grief." He knew, they noted, how to use his allegedly "cold and repulsive" manner to draw figurative blood and literal tears in the courtroom. Observers marveled at the younger Samuel Dexter's way with words, and they also noted young Samuel's ability to make abstruse concepts simple and compelling.[74] No surprise, then, that interred together in their final resting place, the Massachusetts Historical Society, the Dexter spectacles and case seem to present a picture-perfect narrative of spectatorship and its technologies. But cast off the first impression. Release the clasp and cast open the casket carefully prepared by the son. Draw out the eyes that sustained his father's lights; unfold the arms that embraced his father's mind. Place these relics side by side, and consider them from many angles. Recognize their genealogy, as well as what they have bequeathed to the present. Return the spectacles, finally, to their dark velvet bed. As Horace's words swing into sight, watch the Dexters disappear.

---

72. Will, 403–4.

73. Will, 402–3; Staples, *Samuel Dexter*, 10; Sargent, *Reminiscences*, 14–15.

74. Sargent, *Reminiscences*, 8, 41. See also Joseph Story, *A Sketch of the Life of Samuel Dexter* (Boston: John Eliot, 1816).

Fig. 1. Nathaniel Emmons. *Samuel Sewall*. Oil on canvas, 1728. Courtesy of the Massachusetts Historical Society. Boston, Mass.

"Often concerned in funerals:"
Ritual, Material Culture, and the Large Funeral in the Age of Samuel Sewall

STEVEN C. BULLOCK

WAIT STILL WINTHROP'S corpse lay silently at home for a week in November 1717, while family members buzzed with activity. They approached the governor, his predecessor, the lieutenant governor, and members of the colony's council to walk alongside the body as it moved to the burying ground. They bought hundreds of pounds worth of rings, gloves, and clothing—as well as 32 new halberds and 16 new drumheads for the regiment that would accompany the procession. And they ordered the painting of almost fifty black lions on escutcheons bearing the family coat of arms.[1]

The splendid ceremony they organized was fully worthy of the Winthrop family that had produced Wait Still's grandfather, the first governor of Massachusetts, as well as his father and brother, both governors of Connecticut. Like these eminent ancestors, Wait Still's trip to the grave had a military escort and attracted substantial public interest. Besides the regiment, the eminent bearers, and the deceased's horse bearing the black lion, the procession, a newspaper noted, included "the Chief Gentlemen and Inhabitants both of Town and Country." The Boston diarist Samuel Sewall, who served as one of the bearers, recorded that "the Streets were crowded with people."[2]

But Wait Still's ceremony differed from his ancestors'. Most notably, unlike

---

1. "A Memorandum of persons invited to Wait Winthrop's Funeral, Nov. 14, 1717, with the distribution of Mourning Emblems," *The Winthrop Papers*, 6 vols, in *Collections of the Massachusetts Historical Society*, 6th ser., (Boston, 1892), 5:354–56. All information below about the presents given at the Winthrop funeral comes from this list, which is hereafter cited as "Winthrop List." The editors suggest that the "Memorandum" is "somewhat confused and probably imperfect." (II, 356) They do not reveal if the heading given the document, which is not in the Massachusetts Historical Society collections, appears in the original. The purpose of the list was probably more to plan for distributing gifts rather than deciding who would attend. New England funerals in this period did not rely upon invitations and were open to all who wished to attend.

2. *Boston News-Letter*, November 18, 1717; Samuel Sewall, *The Diary of Samuel Sewall, 1674–1729*, ed. M. Halsey Thomas, 2 vols. [paginated continuously.] (New York: Farrar, Straus and Giroux,1973), II, 867 (November 14, 1717). Hereafter cited as Sewall, *Diary*.

his grandfather's 1649 and his father's 1676 ceremonies, his 1717 funeral offered participants extensive gifts. A long (and probably incomplete) list records that the family distributed gloves, scarves, rings, and escutcheons to at least 41 individuals or families, 70 officials, 12 council members, and the entire 100-person lower house of the legislature. As a bearer (as well as part of the council), Sewall received each of these gifts. We can presume that the pious layperson went home with a prayer on his lips; we can be sure that he returned with a ring on his finger, gloves on his hands, and yards of material over his shoulders.[3]

With the possible exception of the weekly church service (which in these years increasingly featured funeral sermons), funerals were eighteenth-century New England's most common, most substantial, and most highly developed public ceremony. They were also, for the region's wealthy elites, its most expensive. Rich families spent freely on the material goods they displayed and gave away at funerals. In a year when all of Boston paid £1700 to the province for poll and property tax, the Winthrops' ceremony cost almost £600, more than the tax payments from any other locality in the colony—and more than twice as much as all Maine put together.[4]

Contemporaries would have called the 1717 Winthrop ceremony a "large funeral," a burial for well-to-do New Englanders that included extensive gifts, expanded use of mourning attire and funeral decorations, and a substantial number of participants. The large funeral of Winthrop's time was bigger, more visible, and more elegant than earlier ceremonies, so different that contemporaries worried about the strain of these new demands. The "expence of funerals of late years . . . is become very extravagant," Massachusetts legislators complained in 1721, leading to "the impoverishment of many families."[5] Yet despite such anxieties, and the legislative action it inspired, the large funeral remained popular until the Revolutionary era.

This paper examines the origin and significance of the large funeral. During the early years of the eighteenth century, it argues, New Englanders such as Samuel Sewall, whose diary provides the major source for this study, adapted the seventeenth-century Calvinist funeral ceremony to the needs of eigh-

3. Winthrop List.

4. *The Acts and Resolves, Public and Private, of the Province of Massachusetts Bay*, vol. 2 (Boston, 1874), 80–84. See also Alvin Rabushka, *Taxation in Colonial America: 1607–1775* (Princeton, N.J: Princeton University Press. 2008), 462.

5. *Acts and Resolves*, II, 229–30.

teenth-century elites, dressing up its older structures with genteel material culture. The enormous expense of Wait Still Winthrop's 1717 funeral at first seems
distant from the simple, almost wordless ritual established in the 1630s under
Winthrop's grandfather. But a closer look suggests that the large funeral elaborated upon rather than broke free from that structure, a process that created a
more complex version of the earlier system rather than making it completely
different. By offering room for expanding material culture, the Puritan funeral
allowed wealthy New England families in the eighteenth century to employ
the emerging vocabulary of gentility, an increasing emphasis upon carefully
restrained self-presentation that provided a means of expanding material culture that could express both the honor and taste of the family. The large funeral
dramatized the older burial service, making it more theatrical, more expressive,
and more genteel.

This reshaping can be seen more clearly by looking at three major issues:
what people brought to the funeral; what happened there; and what people
brought from it. After examining mourning, ceremonies, and gifts, the discussion concludes by briefly suggesting how the seemingly motley elements of the
large funeral disintegrated in the age of the American Revolution.

These changes have often been noticed, but they are seldom explained convincingly. A long series of works beginning with Alice Morse Earle in the
late nineteenth century describe the great increase in material goods at early
New England funerals. David Stannard suggests that more expansive funerals
resulted from inward-turning tribalism, while Laurie Hochstetler has made
the case that they carried an increasingly explicit religious content that distinguished them from earlier Puritan practice. But such discussions tend to mine
Sewall's diary and other sources for examples rather reading them closely for a
range of practices and their meanings. More important, these arguments have
obscured the eighteenth-century funeral's connection with its predecessors—
and given even less attention to the significance of genteel values, and to the
later, more revolutionary, changes that swept away the entire structure by the
end of the century.[6]

6. Among the large literature, see Alice Morse Earle, *Customs and Fashions in Old New England* (London, 1893), 373–75; David E. Stannard, *The Puritan Way of Death: A Study in Religion,
Culture, and Social Change* (New York: Oxford University Press, 1977); Gordon E. Geddes, *Welcome Joy: Death in Puritan New England* (Ann Arbor, Mich.: UMI Research Press, 1981); Laurie
Hochstetler, *Sacred rites: Religious rituals and the transformation of American Puritanism* (Unpub-

Fig. 2. *A Neighbor's Tears*. Boston, 1710. Courtesy of the Massachusetts Historical Society.

As these studies note, the examination of early eighteenth-century funerals must rest upon the diary of Samuel Sewall, an untiring participant in and observer of New England life and particularly of funerals. His extensive diary, the fullest diary of a mainland English colonial before the mid-eighteenth century, notes that, in the forty-five years before his 1730 death (the longest unbroken stretch of his diary), he attended more than 500 funerals, an average of one funeral a month. He served as a bearer 140 times, about once every four months. Sewall did not consider these ceremonies burdensome social obligations. He filled his diary with lovingly recorded specifics about the funerals he attended—and even many he had not. As he remarked to his fellow bearers at a ceremony almost exactly ten years before Winthrop's death, "we were often concern'd in Funerals."[7]

Sewall offers an insider's understanding of this world. By 1717, he had long

---

lished Ph.D. dissertation, University of Virginia, 2007), 207–60. There is also a large literature on gravestones, a topic that I do not discuss here. See, for example, James Deetz, *In Small Things Forgotten: An Archaeology of Early American Life* (Garden City, NY: Anchor Press, 1977), 89–124; Peter Benes, ed., *Puritan Gravestone Art*, 2 vols. (Boston: Boston University, 1976, 1978); Dickran and Ann Tashjian, *Memorials for Children of Change: The Art of Early New England Stonecarving* (Middletown, Conn.: Wesleyan University Press, 1974).

7. Sewall, *Diary*, I, 582 (December 12, 1707). These figures are calculated from an examination of all funerals noted in Sewall's diary.

been close to nearly all the centers of power within New England, as a Harvard graduate and former tutor, a member of the council, and a respected jurist, as well as a deacon of Old South Church and a close friend of many of the colony's ministers, including Cotton Mather. With the death of Winthrop in 1717, he became (at the age of 65) the chief justice of the colony's highest court. Just as important, Sewall was also deeply interested in the larger issues that were at the heart of the changes within funerals. He was first a staunch defender of the region's traditions—calling Winthrop a "a very pious. . . New-England Man" was high praise indeed. But Sewall also lived in the larger cultural and material world made possible by increased commerce and communication. Sewall himself had helped to create that expansion, as both a merchant and someone who had managed what was at the time the only press in all New England. Used with a range of evidence from the period, Sewall's diary allows a close look at the changes and the continuities within funerals and their material culture, a series of changes that reveal the ways that Sewall and his contemporaries struggled to preserve their connections with the community within a world that operated on a new scale and according to new standards.[8]

I.

Samuel Sewall found the months surrounding Wait Still Winthrop's death particularly difficult. His wife had died three weeks before—an event that "fill'd our House with a flood of Tears." Other family members and close associates followed. By December, he noted that he had served as bearer for half of the people who had served in that role for his wife only two months ago. He told a correspondent that he felt "the Breakers . . . passing over me, Wave after Wave, Wave after Wave, in a most formidable Succession."[9]

Other people recognized Sewall's situation—and shared it. In the church service the next day, Sewall's son, a minister, was almost unable to read the note that Sewall had posted asking for prayer. "Our Ruffled Mind can scarcely

---

8. The standard biographies of Sewall are T. B. Strandness, *Samuel Sewall: A Puritan Portrait* (East Lansing, Mich.: Michigan State University Press, 1967); and Ola Elizabeth Winslow, *Samuel Sewall of Boston* (New York: Macmillan, 1964).

9. Samuel Sewall to Rev. Thomas Cotton (London), August 28, 1717, II, 79; Samuel Sewall to Gurdon Saltonstall, January 15, 1717/8, II, 81, *Letter-Book of Samuel Sewall (1686–1729)*, 2 vols., in *Collections of the Massachusetts Historical Society*, 6th ser., 1–2 (1886–88); Sewall, *Diary*, II, 874 (December 16, 1717).

Think, for Tears," mourned a poet writing about Sewall's wife's death before describing the widower as being "in Sorrow almost Drown'd."[10]

Sewall and his contemporaries, who often referred to death as "dissolution," a dissolving, or breaking apart, understood the agonies created by the death of a loved one. But they also knew of its dangers, especially because the New England tradition had given these difficulties much thought. The first generation of settlers crafted a set of practices that sought to avoid the problems created by excessive grief. The large funeral of the early eighteenth century took shape within the context of expectations and expressions that were deeply rooted in these early experiences. The difficulty was figuring out how to take this restrictive set of burial customs and make it more expressive of the differentiated social world in which they operated. Earlier funerary activities had often been accompanied by mourning cloth, and eighteenth-century ceremonies expanded this usage. By 1717, however, these black textiles no longer seemed adequate to express the significance of Hannah Sewall and Wait Still Winthrop. The new large funeral attempted to adapt Puritan practices to a world that required more substantial and more visible expressions.

New England's earliest settlers modeled their funeral practices upon the innovations of Continental Calvinists that had been brought to the British Isles. In each of these locations, reform was driven by distaste for the Catholic culture of death, with its belief in purgatory, prayer to and for the dead, and extensive and often emotional religious rituals. These practices "are no way beneficiall to the dead, and have proved many wayes hurtfull to the living," declared the Westminster Assembly of the 1640s, the influential conference of British reformers. The Assembly's "Directory of Worship" recapitulated the central elements of this larger Reformed tradition. It ordered that the body be taken directly to the burying ground and "immediately interred, without any Ceremony." Such burial was a communal activity, not a religious rite. Ministers could encourage Christians to think about their religious "duty," but otherwise had no specific role.[11]

---

10. Sewall, *Diary*, II, 864 (October 20, 1717); John Danforth, *Greatness & goodness elegized, in a poem, upon the much lamented decease of the honourable & vertuous Madam Hannah Sewall, late consort of the Honourable Judge Sewall . . .* [Boston, 1717].

11. Westminster Assembly of Divines, *A Directory for the Publique Worship of God, Throughout the Three Kingdoms of England, Scotland, and Ireland* (London, 1644), 35. See also the attack on Anglican funeral services for the same reasons by John Canne, *A Necessity of Separation from the*

New England Puritans, however, did not need the advice of the "Assembly of Divines." They had already independently adopted the restrained practices of Reformation Geneva. According to an erstwhile Bostonian who had made his way back to England in 1641 (two years before the Westminster meetings began), "nothing is read, nor any Funeral Sermon made" at burial. Instead the neighbors "carry the dead solemnly to his grave, and there stand by him while he is buried."[12] The lack of other testimonies about these early occasions may indicate how successfully Puritan leaders reduced the importance of funerals. The tradition continued into the eighteenth century. Although Cotton Mather might resolve decades later in 1711 to be "exemplary in the Religion of the Funeral," he carefully identified his goal not as proclaiming God's word or extending spiritual counsel but exhibiting a more individual "holy Behaviour."[13]

In reshaping funerals, New England reformers from John Winthrop to Mather sought to prevent sorrow from undermining the foundations of spiritual life. Such concerns were widely shared even in Sewall's day. "Stop your Pursuing Griefs for her," exhorted a poem published upon the passing of one of Sewall's daughters in 1710. "Our loss," it noted, was "her profit," allowing her to enter a world of "triumphant hallelujahs."[14] Sewall himself had made the point more eloquently three years before, commenting to a Minster after a burial that "our Condolance for the departure of our friend, was join'd with Congratulations for her being gon to her Rest and Reward."[15]

Although Puritans denied the religious significance of burial, they recognized its social significance. The Westminster Assembly explicitly noted that funerals could recognize the deceased's "rank and condition." The first generation of New England settlers acted in the same way. For the 1649 ceremonies after the death of Governor John Winthrop (Wait Still's grandfather), the

---

Church of England Proved by the Nonconformists' Principles, ed. Charles Stovel (London, 1849; originally pub. Amsterdam, 1634), 112–13.

12. Thomas Lechford, *Plain Dealing or News from New England*, ed. J. Hammond Trumbull (Boston: J. K. Wiggin & W. P. Lunt, 1867; originally pub. London, 1642), 87–88.

13. Cotton Mather, *Diary of Cotton Mather*, 2 vols. (New York: F. Ungar Pub. Co., 1957), II, 96 (August 17, 1711).

14. John Danforth, *Profit and loss: an elegy upon the decease of Mrs. Mary Gerrish . . .* [Boston, 1710].

15. Sewall, *Diary*, I, 582 (December 12, 1707).

government provided a barrel and a half of powder for military salutes, more than had been allotted to the harbormaster for the entire previous year.[16]

Such expanded ceremonies for civic and religious leaders were not just a concession to social propriety. Puritan ministers argued that more extensive mourning was even commendable in such cases—a view expressed in the 1683 funeral sermon given for Sewall's father-in-law, a man who had served as treasurer for the colony in some of its most difficult financial straits. The eminent minister Samuel Willard began by warning conventionally against wallowing in grief. But, he went on to say, the death of a church member who held public office concerned more than family and friends. It was a "publick loss": "It is we and not [the dead] that are indangered and endamaged by it." "We may therefore," Willard suggested, "weep for our selves." Sewall told a London correspondent that he felt the same sense of loss when Winthrop and other colleagues died in 1717: "We stand in aw to think what God may be about to do with us when he is removing so many of our Principal Pillars in the Civil Order."[17]

The attention given to community loss in Puritan consideration of mourning as well as the provisions for social differentiation provided the justifications for the extensive freight of material goods added by the founders of the large funeral. The opening wedge of this expansion of objects came in the use of mourning, the cloth that grieving families (and sometimes sympathetic community members) used to embody their intense feelings of loss that was also referred to as mourning. "You have put me into Mourning by telling me of the Death of my Unkles," Sewall noted to a London correspondent in 1696, showing the close correlation between the uses of the term mourning as both the loss itself and its expression in clothing.[18]

Mourning cloth was primarily used by the families of the deceased. They were the first (and often the only) people who wore it. When his father died in 1700 while Sewall was riding circuit as a judge, his wife "provided Mourning" for the children, leaving one of their sons at home during the funeral "because

16. Nathaniel B. Shurtleff, *Records of the Governor and Company of the Massachusetts Bay in New England, 1628–1686*, 5 vols. (Boston: W. White, 1853–54), II, 239; III, 162.

17. Samuel Willard, *The High Esteem Which God hath of the Death of his Saints* (Boston, 1683), 14–15. Samuel Sewall to Rev. Thomas Cotton (London), August 28, 1717, Sewall, *Letter-Book*, 2:79.

18. Samuel Sewall to John Storke, October 30, 1717; Samuel Sewall to John Storke, July 31, 1696, Sewall, *Letter-Book*, 2:76; 1:164.

. . . [she] lik'd not his cloaths."[19] The death of a daughter in 1724 similarly led Sewall to supply (presumably with better results) all his remaining children with new suits.[20] Interestingly, he gives little attention to the use of such clothing by widows, a central preoccupation of the nineteenth-century versions of the practice. He offers only his observation of the widow of late governor Joseph Dudley at church in early 1721 (ten months after the funeral). She had, he noted, "her Mourning a little turned up, that one might see her face."[21]

Although mourning cloth was already a traditional part of funerals, its use grew substantially around the turn of the eighteenth century.[22] The family of the very wealthy Andrew Belcher, who died two weeks before Winthrop in 1717, had suits made for some fifty people, including his first cousins and all his former apprentices.[23] The funeral of Governor William Burnett twelve years later included not just "His Excellency's whole Family," but also "divers others . . . put into Mourning."[24] Elite New Englanders even began to don mourning to commemorate public figures. "Going into Mourning for publick persons is a new thing" in Boston, Sewall told a merchant in 1694 who had sent some mourning clothing commemorating the death of Queen Mary the previous year.[25] The practice soon became more common. Sewall went into mourning for the Lieutenant Governor six years later.[26] By 1738, the governor and the council, as well as other "Gentlemen," dressed in mourning for a ceremony commemorating the death of Queen Caroline.[27]

19. Sewall, *Diary*, I, 431 (May 25, 1700).

20. Samuel Sewall, Jr., Note Book, (August 16, 1724) as quoted in "Introduction," Samuel Sewall, *Diary of Samuel Sewall, 1674–1729,* 3 vols., in *Collections of the Massachusetts Historical Society,* 5th ser., 5–7 (1878–82), 1:xix. This edition of Sewall's diary, with a variety of material not found in the later edition, is hereafter cited as Sewall, *Diary* (MHS ed.).

21. Sewall, *Diary*, II, 974 (February 16, 1720/1).

22. See "The Interment of William Lovelace, New York, 1671," *The American Historical Review*, 9 (1904): 522–24, for the extensive use of mourning in an elaborate earlier funeral.

23. John Cotton to Rowland Cotton, November 7, 1717, Miscellaneous Bound Collection, Massachusetts Historical Society, Boston, Mass. (hereafter MHS).

24. *The New-England Weekly Journal*, September 15, 1729.

25. Samuel Sewall to Thomas Burbank of Rumsey, July 22, 1695, *Letter-Book*, 1:154. Sewall had earlier that year noted mourning for the Queen in England by merchants as well as courtiers. I, 329, 331 (March 29, April 30, 1695).

26. Sewall, *Diary*, I, 451 (July 27, 1701).

27. Benjamin Walker, Jr., Diary, MHS, March 23, 1737/8; *Boston Evening Post*, March 20, 27, 1738. See also the diary of Benjamin Lynde, Jr., March 23, 1738, in *The Diaries of Benjamin Lynde and of Benjamin Lynde, Jr.* (Boston, 1880), 153. I am grateful to Sally Hill of the New England Historic Genealogical Society for generously sharing her transcriptions of the Walker diary.

Mourning cloth could be used beyond the body as well. It provided decoration in a wide range of places. Mourning cloths covered the pulpit upon the deaths of Sir Edmund Andros's wife in 1688 and of Queen Caroline in 1738.[28] Sewall in other places notes a "Mourning Coach," "Horses in Mourning," and "Mourning Guns" in the harbor. He even owned a "Mourning Rapir," adding to its effect upon one occasion by also tying "a black Ribband into my little cane."[29] Wherever it was used, mourning cloth followed a distinctive visual strategy that made objects both more separate and less distinct. Covering objects (and people) with black cloth disconnected them from everyday experience, suspending normal functions. Mourning also made objects less defined, pushing them further into the background by hiding sharp edges and individual colors.

Early eighteenth-century New Englanders spent freely on such mourning. King's Chapel covered not only their pulpit and their desk, but also their communion table when King George I died in 1727.[30] Wait Still Winthrop's family ten years earlier had bought about 140 yards of black cloth for that ceremony.

But even the most extensive use of mourning cloth did not seem sufficient by then. Boston was six times larger than at the death of Wait Still's grandfather—New England as a whole ten times as large—and its residents, critics charged, were engaged in "Extravagant Consumption of foreign Commoditys."[31] In such a setting, families wanting to show the proper degree of mourning required larger, more theatrical display. In response they not only placed greater numbers of people in mourning; they also provided an equivalent amount of decoration, and offered more gifts from the family to people in attendance. These changes ensured that spectators would not dwarf the core group of family, that they and the coffin would be visible, and that the people in attendance would receive a token from the family.

Sewall and his contemporaries referred to a burial on this scale as a "great" or a "large funeral." The diarist described the commemoration of two of his nephews in 1728 as "A very large Funeral, with abundance of Boys walking

28. Sewall, *Diary*, I, 160 (February 10, 1687/8); *Boston Evening Post*, March 27, 1738.

29. Sewall, *Diary*, I, 387 (February 14, 1697/8); II, 618 (May 2, 1709).

30. Henry Wilder Foote, *Annals of King's Chapel from the puritan age of New England to the present*, 2 vols. (Boston: Little, Brown, and Co., 1882, 1896), I, 350.

31. [Thomas Paine], *A discourse, shewing, that the real first cause of the straits and difficulties of this province of Massachusetts Bay, is it's extravagancy* (Boston, 1721), 3.

regularly, And a great concourse of Spectators."[32] The 1715 ceremony for the wife of Cambridge's minister was "a great Funeral," and "would probably have been much greater" if it had not rained.[33] As the accounts make clear, the terms seem to have referred primarily to the number of people in attendance, but they also provided a useful way of denoting such ceremonies.[34]

Funeral activities on this scale required considerable investment in time, attention, and money. They often consumed a substantial proportion of the wealth left by the deceased—often, a 1750s account suggested, one-fourth of the entire estate.[35] Wait Still Winthrop's family spent slightly less, one-fifth of his substantial wealth, when he died in 1717, buying, among other things, nine dozen buttons, over 100 yards of ribbon, and several hundred yards of material. As a bearer, Sewall received a scarf, a ring, and a pair of gloves.[36] The family of Winthrop's brother, Fitz-John, had paid out almost exactly the same sum when he died in 1707.[37] Twenty years later, the Anglican King's Chapel allotted a smaller sum upon the death of their rector, but they still spent £169 to have him "honourably Interred"—almost two-thirds of his salary for the entire year.[38] And though the colony spent £1100 upon the burial of Governor William Burnet in 1729, some of his supporters still felt that he had been treated shabbily.[39]

The huge sums spent on large funerals marked a dramatic shift in their gifts and decorations, helping to create ceremonies that could attract, as in the 1723 burial of Increase Mather, "a vast number of [both] Followers and Spectators."[40] But even the new objects added in the large funeral did not end the older Puritan practices. A look at burial customs in the age of Sewall suggests that their essentials remained relatively unchanged.

32. Sewall, *Diary*, II, 307 (January 8, 1727/8).

33. Sewall, *Diary*, II, 794–95 (July 30, 1715).

34. Benjamin Walker Jr. regularly uses the term in his diary. See, e.g., December 26, 1729, January 1, 1729/30, June 6, 1733.

35. "Of the Extravagance of our Funerals," *The Independent Reflector*, 29, June 14, 1753, 116.

36. Winthrop List; Sewall, *Diary*, II, 867 (November 14, 1717). Because of the declining value of Massachusetts currency, the expenditures in the paragraph cannot be compared precisely.

37. *Winthrop Papers*, 3:412–13.

38. Foote, *Annals of King's Chapel*, I, 360–61, 355, 336; *New-England Weekly Journal*, March 11, 1728.

39. *Journal of the Honourable House of Representatives, of his Majesty's Province of the Massachusetts-Bay, in New England: Begun and Held at Salem, in the County of Essex, on Wednesday, the Twenty-eighth Day of May . . . 1729* (Boston, 1729), 81–83, 109. William Winslow to [David Ayrewell?], September 22, 1729, Miscellaneous Bound Manuscripts, MHS.

40. Sewall, *Diary*, II, 1008 (August 29, 1723).

II.

Almost twenty years before the death of Wait Still Winthrop, Sewall was invited to the funeral of a very different man. While Sewall idolized Winthrop as "very pious," he considered John Ive "debauched, atheistical." Recalling his "notoriously difficult life," Sewall found himself "Sick of going." But he had been invited—perhaps asked to serve as a bearer—and he knew Ive's parents, so it was hard to stay away. Only an unexpected visit from Increase Mather as he was about to leave kept him from attending.[41]

Sewall did not discount the funeral's religious significance. But his accounts again and again emphasize not prayers or pious reflections but the most public element of the ceremony, the procession. Sewall's attraction to funerals was part of his intense desire for human connection that fed his desire to record his activities for over half a century. The perspective was not simply Sewall's. It points to what may be the heart of New England's funerals. By refusing to make the burial spiritual, the Puritans made it social. A close look at Sewall's diary (and other contemporary evidence) suggests the elements of these cere- monies and helps explain why Puritan practices continued into the eighteenth century.

Cotton Mather found the slow pace of funerals frustrating. Although they probably lasted only about two hours, he complained for years about his time being "thrown away Unprofitably." The minister was particularly upset about the first part of the funeral, when the family and funeral goers gathered in the house before the trip to the grave, the burial, and the return. In 1684, he noted the tedium of "sitting in a Room full of People . . . where they take not much Liberty for Talk." Although he attempted to turn the experience to spiritual profit, the situation continued to rankle. He warned families in a 1713 sermon that people would attend more funerals if they did not "make us Mispend our Time." Four years later, he resolved to petition the city selectmen about "the loss of Time."[42]

<hr>

41. Sewall, *Diary*, I, 396 (July 18, 1698). See the letters of Sewall to John Ive (Sr.), June 10, October 28, November 4, 1698 in *Letter-Book of Samuel Sewall*, 1, 201, 204, 206–7. For the com- ment on Winthrop, see Sewall, *Diary*, II, 716 (May 27, 1713).

42. Cotton Mather, *Diary of Cotton Mather*, 2 vols. (New York: F. Ungar Pub. Co., 1957), I, 83 (February 9, 1683/4); II, 461 (June 28, 1717); [Cotton Mather], *A Christian Funeral* (Boston, 1713), 21. For some indication of the length of a funeral, see Sewall, *Diary*, I, 560–61 (January 24, 1706/7).

Funerals frustrated the impatient minister in part because Puritan practices did not give him control over its activities. Mather was forced to accept the instructions of distressed families who lacked his extensive experience. Yet, as a Congregationalist minister, he was expected to attend funerals regularly not only for his own parishioners but also for community leaders of all sorts. And Sewall's diary suggests that clergymen in Boston did have a significant part in this early stage of the ceremony. Their prayer at its opening seems to have been the only time that words were required. Sewall's complaints about a 1708 Anglican service in Boston included its failure to include "Prayer at the House."[43] But even an opening prayer was not even fully accepted by all Congregationalist churches. Cotton Mather noted in 1726 that it was expected in "many," but not all, New England localities.[44]

The time at the house of mourning also made another activity possible. As a 1706 poem suggests, it was "usual" to prepare elegies and other pieces upon the death of learned and prominent figures—and to attach them to what was called the hearse, meaning broadly any object that held or decorated the coffin. "It seems there were some Verses; but none pinned on the Herse," Sewall noted in 1685 when the Rev. Thomas Shepherd was buried.[45] Sewall's mention of these elegies leaves open the possibility that they may have been read aloud at the house of mourning. Such a practice, however, seems unlikely, since the enthusiastic versifier Sewall presumably would have noted at least one such performance. These pieces could sometimes be printed later. Sewall himself published two such commemorative works and Cotton Mather found the "dreadful Elegies, or Epitaphs (or What-shall's-call-em!)" written for Fitz-John Winthrop so appalling that he later composed one of his own for the printed version of his funeral sermon.[46]

The time at the house of mourning seems to have counted as preparation rather than the ceremony proper. Sewall described one clerical prayer as coming "before the Funeral,"[47] suggesting that the procession itself marked the

43. Sewall, *Diary*, I, 601 (August 28, 1708). For other examples of prayer, see I, 74 (August 19, 1685); I, 565 (April 23, 1707).

44. Cotton Mather, *Ratio disciplinae fratrum Nov-Anglorum. A faithful account of the discipline professed and practised; in the churches of New-England* (Boston, 1726), 117.

45. Sewall, *Diary*, I, 66 (June 9, 1685).

46. Cotton Mather to John Winthrop, December 16, 1707 in "The Mather Papers," *Collections of the Massachusetts Historical Society*, 4th ser., 8 (Boston, 1868): 407.

47. Sewall, *Diary*, I, 565 (April 23, 1707).

Fig. 3 (left). John Charmion. *AE. M. S. Eximij Pietate, Eruditione, Prudentia Viri D. Ebenezrae Pembertoni.* [Boston, 1717]. Courtesy of the Massachusetts Historical Society. Fig. 4 (right). John Charmion. *Sacred to the Lasting Memory of the Reverend, Mr. Ebenezer Pemberton.* [Boston, 1717]. Courtesy of the Massachusetts Historical Society.

official start of the ceremony. Gloves, scarves, and escutcheons, when they were provided, must have been handed out at this point in the ceremony.[48]

Judging by the amount of attention he devotes to it, the procession that followed the time at the house seems to Sewall the most important element of the entire funeral. While he only rarely notes events at the house of mourning, he invariably includes the trip to the burying ground, and especially the

48. This is stated more clearly in two later sources: *Connecticut Courant*, December 26, 1774, datelined Boston, December 22, italicized in original; Samuel Stearns, *The American Oracle* (New York, 1791), 243.

pallbearers. The office of what he unfailingly refers to as simply the "bearers" was purely honorific. It required no particular physical prowess. "Porters" or "underbearers" carried the coffin itself, which in turn held up the pall covering it.[49] But Sewall was not interested in practical matters. While he fails to provide the name of a single one porter, he identifies hundreds of bearers, carefully recording their names whenever he attended a funeral—and sometimes making a list when he was not there. When he did not immediately recall or could not learn a name, he left blanks to be filled in later. He even listed the bearers according to their position around the coffin.[50]

The bearers held such significance because they formed the most visible representation of the family's relationship with the community. Since family members could not serve in the role and clergy served only upon the death of other ministers, the position required outsiders who could honorably uphold not only the pall but the family's reputation. Neighborhood, church, social, and political connections all played a part in this complex calculus. The Winthrop family, of course, had access to the highest levels of colonial society. Wait Still's bearers included both the present and the immediate past governors and lieutenant governors, as well as Sewall and another man who was similarly both a judge and a member of the council.

Few other families could attract such lofty figures. The bearers at the 1707 funeral of the widow of Deacon Jacob Eliot suggest the options open to a less significant family. Sewall, who would be placed in the least honorable position at the chief justice's coffin, took the foremost spot at the widow's. Across from him walked another council member. The son-in-law of a former governor took up another place. Sewall's role in the ceremony also was connected to his position as a deacon of Old South, a post held by the widow's late husband and perhaps all three of the remaining bearers.[51]

Leaders of significant organizations could expect to have the members march before the coffin. As with Winthrop, military companies appeared "in arms" for governors or high-ranking civil and military officials. Fellows and

49. Sewall, *Diary*, I, 667 (August 11, 1711). See Jeremiah Bumstead, Diaries, 1722–1733, American Antiquarian Society, August 23, 1723.

50. Sewall, *Diary*, II, 1045–6 (April 14, 1726), clarifies some of the system that Sewall used. For an example of room left for unknown names, see the entry for January 27, 1710/1 (II, 652). The practice may suggest that Sewall may have filled in unknown names later in other places.

51. Sewall, *Diary*, I, 582 (December 12, 1707).

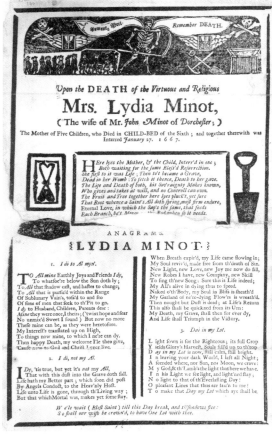

Fig. 5. *Upon the Death of the Virtuous and Religious Mrs. Lydia Minot.* Cambridge, 1667. Courtesy of the Massachusetts Historical Society.

students walked first when Harvard presidents died—and parishioners led the procession upon the death of their ministers.[52]

Except in such unusual circumstances, however, the bearers and the coffin they surrounded served as the procession's start and focal point. The rest of the procession was generally prescribed less carefully. One or sometimes two principal mourners directly followed the coffin, generally the closest relative of the deceased, whether parents, children, or spouse. In the tragic case of a prominent figure who fell ill the day before his wedding in 1711 and then died, what Sewall called "the most compleat. . . disappointment I have been acquainted with," his intended served as the principal mourner.[53] Widows were generally "led" by a male escort.[54] Other family members followed, designated simply as the "mourners."[55] Sewall notes that he was part of a group of a half-dozen at the funeral of his grandson in 1703.[56] Civic leaders in attendance sometimes were

52. For examples, see Sewall, *Diary*, II, 945 (April 8, 1720), II, 1016–17 (May 6, 1724); see also I, 572 (September 15, 1707). For Mather's funeral, see II, 1059–60 (February 19, 1727/8).

53. Sewall, *Diary*, II, 667 (August 3, 7, 1711).

54. Sewall, *Diary*, II, 891 (March 26, 1718).

55. Sewall, *Diary*, II, 623 (August 6, 1709).

56. Sewall, *Diary*, I, 493 (December 14, 1703); see also I, 439 (December 5, 1700).

given a special place behind the family. At a 1709 funeral, Sewall recorded that he marched with another member of the Council; the president of Harvard and a third councilor walked directly behind.

Following the family came the other attendees, "those who," Cotton Mather, suggested, "out of Respect and Good Will *Accompany* the Bereaved."[57] Men and women were grouped. Ministers and (when they did not march separately) magistrates walked beside the women or the mourners. Sewall went alongside the family with the governor in a 1718 funeral.[58] A decade earlier, Sewall had noted that "at first I walk'd next the women" with one minister before "Mr. Cotton Mather came up and went with me."[59]

This shifting about suggests that the demeanor of the participants was not strictly regulated. A passing horseman who talked with a pallbearer might bring a rebuke from a minister, but Sewall considered it normal to hold conversations along the way.[60] At another funeral a week after walking (and talking) with Cotton Mather in 1708, Sewall had a more troubling encounter with his own minister, Ebenezer Pemberton. Pemberton was deeply angry with Mather for writing a contentious letter to the governor and he complained "very warmly" on the way to the gravesite.[61]

After writing so extensively about the funeral procession, Sewall has little to say about its ending point, what contemporaries called the burying ground. After arrival the company watched as the body was placed into the tomb or into the grave before being covered over. Sewall noted that this requirement complicated the 1707 funeral of Samuel Torry in 1707, since the group had to wait "a pretty while before any appeared to fill the Grave."[62] In "some towns," Cotton Mather noted, a minister made a "short Speech."[63] Sewall implies that this does not seem to be the case in Boston. The few remarks he made at his mother's 1701 funeral in Newbury began by asking the attendees to "Forbear

---

57. [Cotton Mather], *A Christian Funeral: A brief Essay, On that Case, What should be the Behaviour of a Christian at a Funeral?* (Boston, 1713), 6.

58. Sewall, *Diary*, II, 891 (March 26, 1718).

59. Sewall, *Diary*, I, 585–86 (January 23, 1707/8); for the same experience, see I, 586–87 (January 31, 1707/8).

60. Sewall, *Diary*, I, 267 (September 23, 1690).

61. Sewall, *Diary*, I, 586–587 (January 31, 1707/8).

62. Sewall, *Diary*, I, 565 (April 23, 1707).

63. Cotton Mather, *Ratio disciplinae*, 117.

a little."[64] Several years later, he noted the oddity of a Quaker funeral where "one spake much at the Grave."[65]

The actions (and perhaps the words) at the burying ground concluded the primary part of the ceremony. Mourners and bearers seem to have been invited back to the house of mourning, as Sewall implies when he explains about a 1726 funeral where he had served as a bearer: "I went not back to the House 'twas so near night."[66] His diary entry notes his direct observations of the procession at Cotton Mather's funeral two years later, but only a second-hand report of a conversation that took place "when the Mourners return'd to the House."[67]

Beyond such interchanges, the activities within the house of mourning remain unclear. Sewall's diary makes no mention of the alcohol that appears regularly in funeral bills—and that Massachusetts legislators in 1742 considered so problematic that they prohibited distribution of wine and rum at ceremonies. A 1713 Cotton Mather sermon similarly condemns people who solemnly marched as mourners and then stumbled drunk in the streets.[68] Although Sewall must have witnessed similar behavior, he never notes either drinking or eating. He once speaks of "a table spread," but his entry may suggest that this was odd because food was available before the trip to the gravesite.[69]

Sewall sometimes also notes a concluding ministerial prayer after the return to the house of mourning. Since all three of these entries occur between 1724 and 1726, this practice may have been something new (and, given the lack of evidence after Sewall's death in 1730, perhaps even short-lived). Sewall first remarks on such a prayer at family funerals in 1724 and 1725.[70] A more detailed entry the following year suggests such prayer may have been offered directly after the return to the house and may even have been primarily for the family. Having heard that the Rev. Thomas Foxcroft of Boston's First Church was going to pray, Sewall notes that he "stay'd and all the Bearers, and enjoy'd the Benefit of that excellent Prayer."[71]

64. Sewall, *Diary*, I, 444 (January 15, 1700/1).

65. Sewall, *Diary*, I, 511–12 (July 24, 1704).

66. Sewall, *Diary*, II, 1044 (March 25, 1726).

67. Sewall, *Diary*, II, 1060 (February 19, 1727/8). See also I, 560–61 (January 24, 1706/7); II, 631 (January 10, 1709/10).

68. [Mather], *A Christian Funeral*, 21–22.

69. Sewall, *Diary*, I, 565 (April 23, 1707).

70. Sewall, *Diary*, I, 1021 (August 18, 1724); II, 1038 (October 17, 1725).

71. Sewall, *Diary*, II, 1044 (April 4, 1726).

Despite an occasional impressive prayer, the funerals that Sewall attended were, to an extraordinary extent, a sequence of actions rather than a series of words. Ministers prayed (and sometimes spoke), and family members must have called together the procession, but they seem to have done so, in classic Puritan fashion, without a settled ritual of carefully prescribed and shaped phrases. Neither Sewall nor Cotton Mather, the period's most prolific giver of funeral sermons, note any specific phrase that might have been used at the ceremonies other than Biblical phrases referring to the "House of Mourning" and the "long home" of the grave. Nor were funerals opportunities for impressive improvisation. Other than the few times Sewall noted satisfying ministerial prayers or his own speech at his mother's grave, he does not think it worth recording anything said formally at a burial service. Even funeral sermons, which became increasingly common in Sewall's lifetime, were kept distinct from the ceremony itself. Following Puritan tradition, they were given as part of the regular church calendar, whether at Sunday worship or (in Boston) at the Thursday lecture.

New England funerals lacked an accepted ritual because Puritans rejected the use of ritual reading and their conception of the funeral left no other group with the power to impose one. Puritans had stripped wedding services (as well as funerals) from the purview of the church, but matrimony remained under civil authority. By contrast, government had little interest in controlling funerals beyond overseeing the use of bells and the managing of burying grounds. New England burial ceremonies were regulated by custom as mediated through the families of the deceased.

But these absences did not make the New England funeral irrelevant. Freed from religious and civil authority, burials became powerful expressions of social inclusion and solidarity. The ceaseless participation in the lives of community members that Sewall shared with ministers and other leaders helped establish both the experience and the ethic of common concern and common destiny. Sewall found it difficult to exclude even the debauched Ive from this community. Widespread participation in communal mourning furthermore helped to build and maintain social capital, becoming a key element in the extraordinary solidarity that helped Boston and other Massachusetts localities first meet challenges to its charter and then throw off British authority. Perhaps not surprisingly, as a central community ritual, funerals (both real and mock) often became a means of gathering and mobilizing people for revolutionary resistance.[72]

The central communal role of funerals in New England helped to make its ceremonies distinct in ways that went beyond the region's adherence to Puritan standards. New England's funeral was not invented on its own—out of whole cloth, as it were. The same sorts of objects appear elsewhere. New England was different, taking English precedents that were varied and often localized, and adhering to them more systematically than either the mother country or other British colonial regions. Elsewhere in America, funerals put on by the well-to-do were more uncommon and more private. New England's early development (with the largest English city in America during the early eighteenth century and the only one with a substantial intellectual life) and its relative religious unity and social cohesion gave the large funeral a presence it failed to develop elsewhere.

Even outsiders recognized the weight of these expectations. The great English hymn-writer Isaac Watts quizzed Boston minister Benjamin Colman in 1740 as to why New Englanders complained about the need for paper money when they "use so much of the metals of gold and silver in funeral rings." Colman was forced to admit that "Boston has always been too expensive in funerals." A New Yorker was more harsh in the 1750s; he considered the "needless and exorbitant" expense of Boston's funerals "a romantic Affectation . . . carried to an enormous Profuseness."[73]

By the time of the Revolution, the large funeral was on its way toward becoming a victim of its own success. The large funeral had earlier succeeded in incorporating older Puritan practices so well that even Sewall, ever watchful for deviations from cherished New England ways, found the ceremonies uncontroversial. The large funeral also accomplished its other goal, of creating a larger and more widely visible expression of social position. The elements of this expansion can be seen in an examination of the gifts that, more than anything else, distinguished the large funeral from its predecessors.

72. Ann F. Withington, *Toward a More Perfect Union: Virtue and the Formation of American Republics* (New York: Oxford University Press, 1991), 92–184.

73. Isaac Watts to Benjamin Colman, October 12, 1739, in Charles C. Smith, "Letters of Dr. Watts," *Proceedings of the Massachusetts Historical Society*, 2d ser., 9 (1894–95): 369; Colman to Watts, January 16, 1740, in Thomas Milner, *The Life, Times, and Correspondence of the Rev. Isaac Watts* (London, 1845), 654; "Of the Extravagance of our Funerals," *The Independent Reflector*, 29, June 14, 1753, 117.

III.

Wait Still Winthrop's funeral in November 1717 required extensive preparation. His son John had to arrive from New London. And, even though invitations were not normal practice, bearers and other notables still had to be notified. But objects presented just as many problems as people. The suit worn by Winthrop's servant Mingo in the procession presumably had to be specially made in the eight days between death and burial, as well as the clothing for the horse that he led. Even more important, the family also needed to arrange for the most extensive use of goods, the gifts to be given for funeral participants.[74]

To aid them in this task, the Winthrop family prepared a substantial list of the gifts to be given to participants. The list, the only one surviving from colonial New England, reveals the level of effort required for a large funeral. Besides the half-dozen bearers, the numerous civil and military officials, and the immediate family who made up the primary elements of the start of the procession, the Winthrops listed some 65 people also expected to march. All of them, from the governor as the most prominent bearer to the postmaster who walked farther back, received at least one item from a repertoire of gifts that included scarves, escutcheons, rings, and gloves. Choosing the proper combination required careful consideration. Members of the council, the upper house of legislature, received scarves and gloves; members of the assembly, only gloves. Paul Dudley (the former governor's son) and Francis Wainwright (the former governor's son-in-law) both received gloves, scarf, and rings. Yet Mrs. Dudley received gloves and a ring, while Mrs. Wainwright, who had been born a Dudley, was given only gloves.[75]

Although the list documents gifts being given on a scale that would have been almost unthinkable in New England only a few years before, the choices made by the Winthrop family were not unusual within their own context. They might even have used as their model the funeral for one of Winthrop's fellow council members, a ceremony performed on the same day that Winthrop died. Although the Winthrop burial procession seems to have attracted more observers, the Belcher family gave out even more gifts. Such presents were the signature element of the large funeral, the characteristic that, more than

74. Winthrop List.

75. Winthrop List. The connections between the Dudleys and the Wainrights is noted in Sewall, *Diary* (MHS ed.), 3:14n.

anything else, defined the new practices of the early eighteenth century. Sewall noted this shift in lists that he kept of the gifts he received while acting as a bearer. In the years between 1697 and 1704 and between 1707 and 1713, he served in 66 ceremonies and received at least one gift in each.[76]

Funeral presents were central to these ceremonies—so important that both Sewall and the Winthrops kept track of them—because they helped convey a rich range of meaning. The gifts given at funerals were first objects in themselves; each gift held particular significances and had separate histories within the ceremonies. But gifts also operated together to shape the funeral both culturally and socially. Besides helping to make these ceremonies more genteel, they also served as a means of both drawing people to the funeral and bringing them closer together.

Sewall first mentions funeral scarves in 1686 and then does not note one again until five years later. By the time he began keeping a list of the gifts he received as a bearer in 1697, families had already begun giving them regularly. Sewall received scarves at 61 of the 66 ceremonies noted in the lists, making them the most common gift on the list.[77] Scarves were so popular in part because of their continuity with mourning wear. Both used large amounts of cloth to distinguish wearers from people in everyday clothing. Donning a scarf was even more distinctive because it immediately identified a participant in a ceremony. When Sewall returned to Boston from a Salem court session in November 1711, he noted a friend wearing a scarf, and immediately asked "what funeral."[78]

Scarves made particularly dramatic statements. Worn over the shoulder as what might today be considered a sash, they consisted of three to four yards of fine fabric. They seem to have been given only to the central figures in the ceremony, to family members first and then to a select group of people who played key roles in the funeral, such as pallbearers, ministers, and government officials. Wearing a glossy fabric that almost covered the torso clearly distinguished these central figures from the rest of the funeral procession. The Winthrop family gave scarves to the council but not the much larger assembly; to the three highest officers of the regiment but not the others. The family also

76. Sewall, *Diary* (MHS ed.), 1:469–70; 2:10–11.
77. Sewall, *Diary* (MHS ed.), 1:469–70; 2:10–11.
78. Sewall, *Diary*, II, 671 (November 15, 16, 1711).

seems to have determined that only men would receive scarves, even though Sewall often notes them being given to women as well.[79]

The Winthrops may have made this distinction between men and women because the expense of giving away more than fifty scarves would have been substantial. Other New Englanders certainly felt the strain. Less than four years later, the Massachusetts legislature, calling scarves "very extravagant," banned their use. The 1721 prohibition proved successful. Scarves, the first funeral gift to become widely popular, also became the only one to be completely abandoned. "A-la-mode and lutestring scarfs were our mourning twenty years ago," recalled a Boston minister in 1740, but "we reformed to rings which were about half the expense."[80]

The escutcheon, the second major gift used in the large funeral, played a more limited role in the ceremony. Bearing the shield from a family's coat of arms painted on cloth and stretched on a frame, escutcheons appeared less often than scarves and other gifts. They were offered only by prominent families. Sewall notes only 17 in his entire diary, with the first coming in 1707 with the death of Fitz-John Winthrop, former governor of Connecticut and elder brother of Wait Still. The family of the latter distributed about 25 escutcheons, paying 12 shillings for eight of them in silk.[81] Sewall also notes them at ceremonies for Harvard President John Leverett and former governor Joseph Dudley.[82] Like the more common scarf, escutcheons were closely connected to other funeral elements. They were often used to decorate the pulpit, the pall (or coffin itself), the hearse, the coach, or even the horses pulling it. Unlike mourning clothing and scarves, however, escutcheons could also be used outside the funeral. Escutcheons bearing royal symbols were placed on courthouse walls in 1690s Maryland and printed on paper money in Connecticut forty years later.[83]

Rings, the third funeral gift, were even more common outside the funeral.

79. Sewall, *Diary*, I, 612 (December 22, 1708); II, 870 (November 22, 1717). Winthrop List.

80. *The Acts and Resolves, Public and Private, of the Province of Massachusetts Bay . . .* (Boston, 1874), II, 229–230; Benjamin Colman to Isaac Watts, January 16, 1740, in Thomas Milner, *The Life, Times, and Correspondence of the Rev. Isaac Watts* (London, 1845), 654.

81. Winthrop List.

82. Sewall, *Diary*, I, 581 (December 4, 1707), II, 945 (April 8, 1720), 1016–17 (May 6, 1724).

83. *Proceedings and Acts of the General Assembly, April 1684–June 1692*, Archives of Maryland (Baltimore, 1894), XIII, 290; Jonathan Belcher to Richard Waldon, April 25, 1737, Jonathan Belcher Letter-Books, MHS, V, 179.

Fig. 6. Mourning ring. 1766. Courtesy, Historic New England, Boston, Mass.

They could be used as an honorable gift in many situations. Sewall sent one to Increase Mather in 1717 "as a Token of Thankfullness and Respect," just as he had for many years before presented a ring bearing a suitable inscription to the governor at the start of the New Year. This honorific role made them logical choices as funeral gifts as well. Rings were often given within the ceremony, presumably before the procession, although Sewall notes a 1687 ceremony where they were distributed "at the House after coming from the Grave."[84] But the separate standing of the gift meant that even rings commemorating death could be separated from the funeral itself. This seems to have been the more common usage in the years before the large funeral. They were often specified as gifts in the will or given to family members and close friends outside the confines of the ceremony. Sewall sent one to his father after the death of his daughter in 1690 and when another of his daughters died in 1696, Sewall gave gloves to the bearers at the ceremony, but handed out the rings individually outside it.[85] As with other gifts, the number of rings rose over time. Sewall gave five in 1696. The Winthrops gave ten times as many and one observer suggested that Peter Faneuil gave out hundreds when his uncle died in 1738.[86]

Gloves were the last major gifts to be adopted as part of the large funeral. Seventeenth-century ceremonies had included them only irregularly and on a small scale. One-sixth of the funerals on Sewall's 1697–1704 list provided them. Soon, however, they became even more common than scarves. Only one of those funerals in Sewall's 1707–1713 list failed to include them. Gloves offered an array of advantages to families planning funeral ceremonies. They were already worn not only in mourning suits, but as a ubiquitous part of elite clothing, making them a convenient emblem of elite standing. Seventeenth-century portraits often portrayed sitters with gloves for this very reason. At

84. Sewall, *Diary*, I, 153 (November 11, 1687). See also I, 396 (July 18, 1698).
85. Sewall, *Diary*, I, 364–65 (December 25, 1696).
86. Winthrop List; John Boydell to John Yeamans, March 8, 1737/8, D. S. Greenough Collection, MHS.

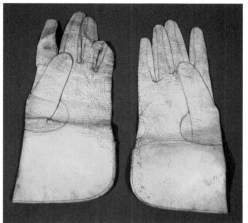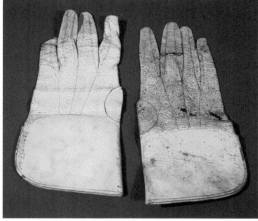

Fig. 7. Gloves given at a Connecticut Funeral, 1765. Courtesy, Connecticut Historical Society, Hartford, Conn.

Fig. 8. *John Winthrop.* Oil on canvas, ca. 1630–91. Courtesy, American Antiquarian Society, Worcester, Mass.

the same time, however, gloves were also relatively cheap and easily available in mercantile stocks. When Sewall served as an executor in 1724, the price of each pair of gloves he bought was only one-quarter that of the rings (which in turn were half the price of scarves).

As relatively inexpensive items, gloves could be given freely. As the large funeral developed, it became normal practice to distribute gloves to everyone who participated in the ceremony, not just the central figures. "All had gloves men women boys & girls," noted another Boston diarist of a 1728 ceremony.[87] As executor, Sewall provided twelve dozen for a ceremony in 1724, a number common by then among relatively well-to-do New Englanders. Another of Sewall's ministerial friends, Benjamin Colman, bought the same number when his daughter died in 1735. But the wealthier (or the showier) could offer even more. The 1717 ceremony for Sewall's (and Winthrop's) fellow council member Andrew Belcher included 1,000. Although gloves were sometimes sent to a select few before the funeral or posted afterward to people who could not attend, gloves on a large scale could only have been given at the ceremonies themselves.

As this survey suggests, the repertoire of gifts within the large funeral was not definitively fixed until the 1720s. Scarves were central to turn-of-the-century ceremonies; rings and gloves became more popular later. Once the 1721 ban on scarves took effect, however, no other object emerged afterwards. Even hatbands, a staple of English funerals, never became part of the New England ceremony.[88] Funeral gifts afterwards changed only by expansion. The largest New England ceremony on record came soon after Sewall's death in 1730. Peter Faneuil's extraordinary funeral for his uncle eight years later included "hundreds of Gold Rings" and gloves for the 1100 people in attendance. Another source puts the number of gloves even higher at 336 dozen, a total of more than 4000 pairs.[89]

While each gift, from showy scarves to widely-distributed pairs of gloves, had particular significances and uses by themselves, they also worked together to shape some of the important characteristics of the ceremony. The rise of funeral presents helped to make the ceremonies of well-to-do New England-

87. Walker, Diary, July 2, 1728.
88. The only use of hatbands that I have found is in the funeral of Rev. Samuel Myles of the Anglican King's Chapel in 1728. Walker, Diary, March 8, 1727/8.
89. John Boydell to John Yeamans, March 8, 1737/8, D. S. Greenough Collection, MHS.

ers both less separated from everyday life, and, in the process, more polished. Earlier funerals, symbolized by the scarf, had used a distinct set of practices, almost a separate vocabulary. Ministers and other learned men had often been celebrated by Latin poems or complex anagrams and acrostics pinned on the pall. Processions for civic leaders sometimes included carrying the different pieces of their armor.[90] The new large funeral, however, moved away from these activities in favor of practices that were closer to everyday life. Gloves and rings formed part of ordinary experience, and part of the growing commerce that made consumer goods increasingly available throughout the Atlantic world. This commercial expansion allowed families to gather large quantities of goods for funerals more easily and more cheaply.

But the new vernacular funeral involved more than taking advantage of new economic opportunities. It also allowed New England elites to communicate to a broader audience. In this, as in much else, the large funeral formed a part of the emerging culture of gentility. Both relied upon carefully considered and controlled gestures that could be easily understood and that used expensive material goods as part of their fundamental vocabulary. Just as important, both gentility and the large funeral conveyed similar messages, not only about the taste, honor, and standing of its practitioners, but also about the desire to connect with, and refine, the broader community in which they operated.

Presents shaped the large funeral socially as well as culturally, drawing people, ordering them more clearly, and bringing them closer to the family. Gifts first helped attract people to the ceremonies. This was particularly true for ministers who attended funerals as part of their professional duty and considered rings and gloves part of their payment for their service. One of the clergymen who participated in the procession for council member Andrew Belcher in December 1717 noted to his father that he wished that another minister had attended "so he might have carryed home, a scarf for his wife."[91] Even the

90. Nathaniel B. Shurtleff, *Genealogical Memoir of the Family of Elder Thomas Leverett, of Boston* (Boston, 1850), 12n. On poems on the hearse, see Stannard, *Puritan Way of Death*, 203; [Cotton Mather], *An Elegy on the Much-to-be-deplored Death of That Never-to-be-forgotten Person, the Reverend Mr. Nathaniel Collins . . .* (Boston, 1685), front matter, n.p.

91. John Cotton to Rowland Cotton, November 7, 1717, Miscellaneous Bound Manuscripts, MHS. Cotton notes six ministers before adding an "&c." The ministers from Old South, Belcher's (and Sewall's) church, are not listed. Sewall's account enumerates the bearers but does not mention the ministers. Sewall, *Diary*, II, 866 (November 6, 1717).

wealthy Sewall felt the pull. Although he was glad that Increase Mather's visit had kept him from attending the funeral of the immoral Ive, he could not help noting in his diary that he had therefore "lost a Ring."[92]

The large processions encouraged by extensive presents in turn helped validate the standing of well-to-do families. Sewall wrote of "very thin" as well as large funerals.[93] "Few there," he reported another time, "their little Room not full,"[94] fittingly failing even to note the name of deceased. As he and his contemporaries well knew, participation could be expected only from the family and its ministers. Families who sought a more substantial ceremony felt obliged to provide for larger numbers, particularly through elaborate and expensive goods that increased the sense of the special character of the ceremony.

Presents also helped shape these larger processions. Along with mourning clothing and other decorations, gifts shaped large numbers of people into an ordered array, differentiating bearers from mourners, ministers, and magistrates from the other marchers, who were in turn distinguished from onlookers by gloves. Gifts not given to everyone generally went first to people who held such special position in the procession. At the 1720 funeral of former governor Joseph Dudley, council members and ministers both received scarves. Dudley's son wore a mourning cloak while leading the widow. Such careful attention to goods made the elements of the procession clearer to the enormous numbers of observers that Sewall noted as looking "out of windows" and standing "on Fences and Trees, like Pigeons."[95]

Even as presents created new meanings for the funeral, helping it become more genteel, attract more participants, and create a more orderly procession, these gifts also reinforced the social goals of the Puritan ceremony. Presents created a complex interchange between families and their communities that helped bind them together. Rather than being simply signs of self-regard, presents allowed families to show respect to other funeral participants, to reach out, and to signal their desire for connection with the larger community. Cotton Mather refers to "the Civilities (of a Glove, or a Ring, or a Scarf,) given me at a Funeral," tellingly describing them as signs of respectful social interac-

92. Sewall, *Diary*, I, 396 (July 18, 1698).
93. Sewall, *Diary*, II, 741 (October 27, 1713).
94. Sewall, *Diary*, I, 600 (August 23, 1708).
95. Sewall, *Diary*, II, 945 (April 8, 1720).

tions. In accepting these gifts, he and others committed themselves to enter the communion created by the ceremony.[96] Anthropologists argue that gifts always come with strings attached; they entail an obligation to continue the relationship and to reciprocate later. In this context, the family's gifts were less about alienating goods than creating connections, a continuation of the essentially social role of the Puritan burial service that persisted despite the sometimes dazzling decorations added in the age of Sewall. Gifts shored up society—or, to use what may be a more apt metaphor, they helped repair the social fabric in moments when it seemed in danger of coming unraveled.[97]

By the time Sewall died in 1730, the large funeral had become virtually universal among well-to-do New Englanders. Participants and observers alike expected these ceremonies to include substantial numbers of gifts, extensive use of other objects, and full attendance. The practice of glove-giving pioneered in the large funeral had become virtually obligatory even for poorer people. But the triumph of the large funeral proved short-lived. Although it continued to expand in both size and expense in the short run, the large funeral eventually came to seem unmanageable and unsatisfying.

The large funeral continued to grow after 1730, as larger quantities of gifts and mourning display in turn spurred other families to outdo their predecessors. Governor Jonathan Belcher, who asked Sewall to serve as a bearer when his father died in 1717, sponsored an even more impressive ceremony when he lost his wife in 1736. A newspaper account judged that "the most grand and showy Funeral ever solemnized in these Parts, came far short of This in Expence and Magnificence." ". . . [I]t would be endless," the report noted, "to mention all the Tokens of Respect and Honour shewn to the Memory of the deceased." But only two years later Peter Faneuil created an even more magnificent ceremony for his uncle.[98]

This tendency toward expansion helped make the large funeral insupportable. This great expense may have come to seem even greater because funeral gifts, while important in the ceremony, seldom seem to have been considered

96. Mather, *Diary*, II, 96 (August 17, 1711).

97. Marcel Mauss, *The Gift: Forms and Functions of Exchange in Archaic Societies,* trans. Ian Cunnison (New York: Norton, 1967), is the classic study. See also Mark Osteen, ed., *The Question of the Gift: Essays Across Disciplines* (London: Routledge, 2002); Lewis Hyde, *The Gift: Imagination and the Erotic Life of Property* (New York: Random House, 1979).

98. *Boston Evening Post,* October 18, 1736.

significant afterwards. Judging from their survival in current collections, rings were the most likely gift to be saved. Yet the examples of two ministers suggests a less reverent attitude. The cosmopolitan Benjamin Colman used them to buy British books. The collected piles of gloves and rings assembled over the years by another minister became a means of raising cash. Scarves by design were made long enough to turn into a shirt. Gloves were presumably worn for, and worn out by, everyday use. No colonial-era scarf and only a single, fully documented pair of gloves from a funeral seems to survive.[99]

Even by the 1720s and 1730s, many New Englanders complained that funerals had become too extravagant. Massachusetts legislators took up the issue of funerals again in 1742. Having successfully banned scarves two decades earlier, they now prohibited almost all gifts beyond gloves for a few ministers. But New Englanders largely ignored the measure. Major change only came as a result of a broader public movement that began in the 1760s and became part of the resistance movement against British policies. These reformers called for more restrained funerals that they termed "the new mode." These new standards had become common by the late 1780s.

The transformation reshaped each of the main elements of both the large funeral established by Sewall and his contemporaries and the Puritan ceremonies they had sought to preserve. Mourning clothing itself was perhaps the least changed. Although it seems to have been used less often by people beyond the family, well-to-do women increasingly made it part of the changing world of fashion. Grief also gained new significance. Rather than being distrusted, as it had been in Puritan times, it came to symbolize admirable sensibility, portrayed in the popular genre of mourning art with its central image of a woman grieving by a grave.[100] Funeral ceremonies also underwent substantial changes. Even Congregationalists, having lost much of their cen-

99. Henry Newman to Benjamin Colman, May 31, 1722, Henry Newman, New England Letter-Book, February 2, 1721/22–September 13, 1723, Society for the Promotion of Christian Knowledge Manuscripts, Cambridge University Library, Cambridge, Eng. The second minister was Boston's Andrew Eliot; Lucius Manlius Sargent, *Dealings with the Dead, By a Sexton of the Old School* (Boston: Dutton and Wentworth, 1856), I, 91–92. For another minister who passed on a tankard of rings to his heirs see, Lura Woodside Watkins, "Middleton Buries its Dead," *Essex Institute Historical Collections*, 98 (January 1962): 28.

100. Anita Schorsch, *Mourning Becomes America: Mourning Art in the New Nation* (Clinton, N.J.: Main Street Press, 1976).

trality in the region's culture, followed the example of Anglicans and Evangelicals by including church services in their funeral ceremonies. At the same time, the procession lost its central role, as both the body and attendees went to the grave in carriages. But even these changes were not as dramatic as those affecting gifts, the most characteristic element of the large funeral. By the end of the Revolution, families had simply stopped giving presents on a large scale. Although some localities continued to offer gloves to ministers, the gifts that remained tended to be small, designed as personal mementos rather than sumptuous public displays.

The rise of the "keepsake" (a term first used in 1790) marked an end to both the large funeral and the Puritan ceremony on which it was based. Although the large funeral had dramatically increased the extent (and the expense) of goods in its ceremonies, in many ways they were simply the old forms dressed in fancier and showier clothing. As such it redoubled the Puritan effort to create a ceremony based on communal interaction. The burial practices established by the first generation of New Englanders helped work toward the goal of Wait Still Winthrop's grandfather, the first governor of Massachusetts, who told people embarking on their mission that they "must rejoice together, mourn together . . . always having before our eyes our commission and community in the work, as members of the same body." But these ceremonies, even as they were expanded in the age of Sewall, were ill suited to the post-Revolutionary world where emotional and religious expressiveness were celebrated— and where people's "community in the work" of communal engagement was no longer as clearly visible, even in the "grand and showy" form of the large funeral.[101]

101. John Winthrop, "A Modell of Christian Charity," in *Winthrop Papers*, 6 vols. (Boston: Massachusetts Historical Society, 1929–1992), II, 294. Quotation from modernized text at http://www.lewishyde.com/pmwiki/pmwiki.php?n=Main.ModernText; *Boston Evening Post*, October 18, 1736.

Envisioning New England

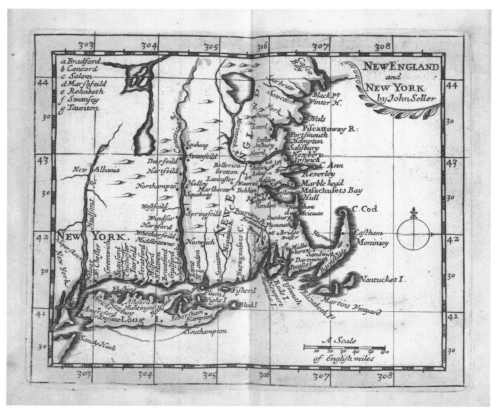

Fig. 1. John Seller, *New England & New York*. London, 1703. Rare Books Division, The New York Public Library, Astor, Lenox and Tilden Foundations, New York, N.Y.

The "New England" Cartouche: Tablets, Tableaux, and Theatricality in Eighteenth-Century Cartography

MARTIN BRÜCKNER

Introduction

WHAT MAKES A MAP a "New England" map at the turn of the eighteenth century? Looking at maps such as John Seller's *New England & New York* (1703; fig. 1), the answer seems to be threefold. A map was a New England map when it showed the territorial outline of British possessions between what are today the states of Maine to the north and New York to the south, with the Connecticut River (some would argue the Hudson River) providing a natural boundary to the west and the Atlantic Ocean to the east. Such a map distinguished itself further from other maps by depicting a specific set of topographic features, in particular the distinctly shaped coastline of Cape Cod. And last but not least, a map became a New England map because it was given the name "New England."

For maps to represent exclusively the geographic setting of New England was a relatively recent phenomenon in circa 1700.[1] The area that we know as New England today had appeared in printed maps in "embryonic form" as early as 1506. But it was not until the early seventeenth century when European mapmakers including John Smith, Willem Blaeu, Jan Janszon, and Nico-

---

1. For an introduction to the history of New England maps see Barbara McCorkle, *New England in Early Printed Maps, 1513 to 1800* (Providence, R.I.: John Carter Brown Library, 2001) and her "The Mapping of New England before 1800," in *Mapping Boston*, eds. Alex Krieger and David Cobb with Amy Turner (Cambridge, Mass.: MIT Press, 1999), 23–35; Peter Benes, *New England Prospect: A Loan Exhibition of Maps at the Currier Gallery of Art* (Boston: Dublin Seminar, 1981); the Osher Map Library exhibit, "The Cartographic Creation of New England," posted at http://www.usm.maine.edu/~maps/exhibit2/; and David Bosse, "'To Promote Useful Knowledge': *An Accurate Map of the Four New England States* by John Norman and John Coles," *Imago Mundi* 52 (2000): 138–154. See also the brief entry in Robert C. D. Baldwin, "Colonial Cartography under the Tudor and Early Stuart Monarchies, ca. 1480– ca. 1640," in *The History of Cartography. Cartography in the European Renaissance*, Vol. 3, Part 2, ed. David Woodward (Chicago: University of Chicago Press, 2007), 1774–1779.

las Visscher started designing maps explicitly geared towards showing British, French, and Dutch colonial possessions, which were respectively entitled:
"New England," "Nouvelle France," "Nieu Nederland." The "birth" of New
England in cartographic terms was more or less completed during the 1670s
and 1680s when British-made inexpensive atlas maps, showing New England
in its most rudimentary form, entered the marketplace in large numbers. Basic
"New England" maps were a staple component in works such as John Speed's
atlas *A Prospect of the Most Famous Parts of the World* (1675), John Seller's *Atlas
Maritimus* (1675), and Robert Morden's textbook, *Geography Rectified* (1680).[2]
Through the dissemination in print the cartographic form of New England
not only became popularized but a graphic fixture for representing as well as
discussing New England in courts, schools, and even private conversation. In
a letter from 1676, Nathaniel Mather writes to his brother, Increase: "I much
rejoyce in God's great mercy begun in your son Cotton. I heartily thank him
for his map of New England. It helps mee much in understanding your &
other narratives."[3]

But print culture alone did not make New England maps uniform and
instantly recognizable in 1700. Rather, the maps' basic visual and verbal differentiation reflected recent and profound changes in cartographic design.
Much of the maps' uniformity was the product of a historical process that Leo
Bagrow has called the "cartographic reformation." Roughly between 1670 and
1770, "maps ceased to be works of art, the products of individual minds, and
craftsmanship was finally superseded by specialized science and the machine."[4]
Theoretical geographers like David Harvey make a similar assessment, noting
that eighteenth-century maps were gradually "stripped of all elements of fantasy and religious belief, as well as any sign of the experiences involved in their

2. Similar map designs can be found in most small-scale maps that supplemented geography books and atlases published by Patrick Gordon, Herman Moll, or Robert Wells. See also
the anonymous "An Exact Mapp of New England and New York" (1702) inserted into Cotton
Mather's opus, *Magnalia Christi Americana* (1702). In many examples the maps' cartographic
rendering of "New England" does not always reflect the territorial dimensions dictated by royal
charters. On charters and New England in geopolitics see Philip S. Haffenden, *New England in
the English Nation 1689–1713* (Oxford, Eng.: Clarendon, 1974).

3. Nathaniel Mather to Increase Mather, Dublin, 26. Feb. 1676/77 in "The Mather Papers,"
Collections of the Massachusetts Historical Society, 4th ser., 8 (1868): 9.

4. Leo Bagrow, *The History of Cartography* (Cambridge, Mass.: Harvard University Press,
1985), 22.

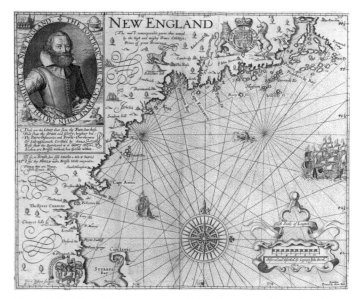

Fig. 2. John Smith, *New England.* London, 1727. Rare Books Division, The New York Public Library, Astor, Lenox and Tilden Foundations.

Fig. 3. John Speed, *A Map of New England and New York.* Engraved by Francis Lamb. London, 1676. The Lionel Pincus and Princess Firyal Map Division, The New York Public Library, Astor, Lenox and Tilden Foundations.

production," and instead became "abstract and strictly functional systems for the factual ordering of phenomena in space."[5]

This analysis seems to hold true when looking back in time and across the cartographic archive of the seventeenth century. For example, when comparing Seller's map to Captain John Smith's map of *New England* (1612; fig. 2) or John Speed's *A Map of New England and New York* (1676; fig. 3), we witness a general stripping of New England maps. Mapmakers purged the pictorial inventory, removing images of animals and Indians from the surface of the cartographic space. These concrete picture inserts were replaced by abstract map symbols, place names, and a lot of blank spaces when information about the area's physical and human geography was unavailable. Elaborate picture insets that used to cover large portions of the map, such as the portrait of John Smith or detailed sketches of ships and city views, were omitted. What was left to see on a growing number of late seventeenth-century maps was very similar to what we are used to seeing on modern maps henceforth: an abstract representation of spatial phenomena, delineated in varying graphic density but contained within the invariable contours of the geographic grid.

Looking forward into the eighteenth century, New England maps seemingly adhered to this anti-pictorial trend. For example, Thomas Jefferys' *Map of the most Inhabited part of NEW ENGLAND* (1755; fig. 4) documents many of the changes wrought by the cartographic reformation.[6] Inside the cartographic space of New England we can no longer find pictorial elements; there are neither iconographic depictions of wild Indians or beasts, nor are there realistically sketched city- or landscapes. However, by the same token that we find the main body of the map to be now devoid of pictures we are also quick to realize that a residue of pictorial energy has survived. It is now relocated in the map's lower right corner. There we find an enormous picture inset sketching with great detail a foundational scene of British colonial history: here the image shows how the Puritans, after making landfall at Cape Cod and aided

5. David Harvey, *The Condition of Postmodernity: An Enquiry into the Origins of Cultural Change* (Oxford, Eng.: Basil Blackwell, 1989), 249. On the cartographic reformation see also Matthew H. Edney, "Reconsidering Enlightenment Geography and Map Making," in *Geography and Enlightenment*, eds. David N. Livingstone and Charles W. J. Withers (Chicago: University of Chicago Press, 1999): 165–198.

6. For similar patterns among prominent maps of America see the work by John Mitchell, Thomas Kitchin, Emmanuel Bowen, Malachy Postlewayt.

Fig. 4. Thomas Jefferys, *Map of the most Inhabited part of NEW ENGLAND.* London, 1755. Courtesy of the Library of Congress, Washington, D.C.

by a female figure, made contact with a Native of New England. The picture we are looking at is, of course, part of the map's cartouche, the widely-used formal device used for publicizing the map's content in word and image.[7]

7. It's not absolutely clear that Jefferys—an engraver by training—created the cartouche himself since it is by now assumed that the map itself was co-authored by his employee, John Green. See the excellent discussion in "The 'Percy Map.' The Cartographic Image of New England and Strategic Planning during the American Revolution," Osher Map Collection (http://www.usm.maine.edu/~maps/percy/). On the difficulty of attributing primary authorship to the map or cartouche see J. B. Harley, "The Bankruptcy of Thomas Jefferys: An Episode in the Eco-

It is the presence of a cartouche like Jefferys' that complicates the narrative of the cartographic reformation and thus also the narrative of what makes a map a New England map. If it was the intention of reformers to be iconoclastic and banish pictures from maps, then the actual reform efforts were applied rather selectively. First, pictorial cartouches, ranging from the elaborate to the plain (depending on map size and price), were a ubiquitous element of mapmaking throughout the long eighteenth century. Second, considering Jefferys' cartouche—with its attention to print fonts and pictorial detail, not to mention its gesture at baroque picture frames—more than suggests that its design is all about being a work of art, craftsmanship, and individual minds. Even the most cursory glance must admit that the Jefferys cartouche is in equal measure about fantasy and belief, as it is about the practice and experience involved in their production. Indeed, this cartouche invites us to rephrase the opening question: instead of asking what makes a map a New England map, his cartouche is asking us what makes a cartouche a New England cartouche?

Because cartouche designs are spectacularly deviant from the modern abstract map they have received a lot of attention in recent years. There are a number of working definitions describing its form and function, ranging from the theoretical (as in Jacques Derrida's *The Truth in Painting*) to the etymological (see the *Oxford English Dictionary*). For map historians, the standard (and perhaps most neutral) definition is encyclopedic, describing the cartouche as a "feature of a map or chart, often a decorative inset, containing the title, legend, or scale, or all of these items."[8] All others incorporate a version of it but to very different ends. Definitions tend to turn the cartouche into a contested feature for making arguments about the nature of cartography, critical methodologies, and the various critics' disciplinary allegiances. For example, in the 1950s, when attention focused on the map as a product of empirical science, the cartouche's affinity with the decorative arts caused its hasty dismissal from analytical discussion. "Fancy borders, ornamental cartouches [and] curvaceous lettering," are considered to be a "source of pleasure" but as a formal device were not

---

nomic History of Eighteenth Century Map-Making," *Imago Mundi* 20 (1966): 27–48; and Joan Winearls, "Thomas Jefferys' Map of Canada and the Mapping of the Western Part of North America, 1750–1768," in *Images and Icons of the New World: Essays on American Cartography*, ed. Karen Severud Cook (London: The British Library, 1996), 27–54.

8. Norman J. W. Thrower, *Maps and Man* (Englewood Cliffs, N.J.: Prentice Hall, 1972), 168.

expected to "add to the functional quality of a map."[9] Conversely, during the 1980s and 1990s, when attention had shifted towards discourse analysis and the representation of power, the function of the cartouche became a highly productive source of map analysis. It was now considered to be a "cultural text" whose signs, symbols, and rhetoric not only evoked the "subtle relationship between the scientific and the decorative" but resolved this relationship. By providing "a series of interrelated indexes which bind the map within a series of ideological assumptions as to the way the land is viewed," the cartouche was now understood as the hermeneutic key to map interpretation.[10]

In keeping with the "literary turn" of the 1980s, the key to meaningful interpretation turned on the cartouche's legibility.[11] At the same time when the cartouche came under greater scrutiny for being the "visual register in which a map's cultural meaning is suggested," maps in general were increasingly assessed for their "*visual calligraphy* (the lettering, colour, thickness of lines, symbols)."[12] On the other hand, as Eileen Reeves has reminded us, thinking of a cartouche as being legible in the first place was a fairly new concept. It was only during the eighteenth century that map viewers made the distinction between the cartouche's pictorial and verbal features; subsequently, the cartouche became defined as the map's legend in accordance with the term's original Latin meaning, as the "*legenda*" or the "things to be read."[13] Seeking to decipher the cartouche as a readable construct, many studies have now demonstrated how the cartouche functions as a textual device which, when examined in relation to the actual map, can provide stunning insights into any given map's discursive and ideological agendas, including the way in which, for example, New England maps propagated political disinformation, territorial aggression, and genocidal violence.[14]

9. A. H. Robinson, *The Look of Maps* (Madison, Wisc.: University of Wisconsin Press, 1952), 17.

10. G. N. G. Clarke, "Taking Possession: the cartouche as cultural text in eighteenth-century American maps," *Word & Image* 4, 2 (1988): 471, 455.

11. See also J. B. Harley, "Text and Contexts in the Interpretation of Early Maps," in *The New Nature of Maps*, ed. Paul Laxton (Baltimore: Johns Hopkins University Press, 2001), 33–49; and William Boelhower, "Inventing America: A Model of Cartographic Semiosis," *Word & Image* 4, 2 (1988): 475–97; and debates published in *Cartographica* and *Imago Mundi* during the 1990s.

12. Clarke, 455.

13. Eileen Reeves, "Reading Maps," *Word & Image*, Vol. 9, No. 1, (January-March 1993): 51 [51–65].

14. See Stephanie Pratt, "From the Margins: the Native American personage in the cartouche and decorative borders of maps," *Word & Image* 12, 4 (October-December 1996): 349–65.

Invaluable and persuasive as these approaches are, they are somewhat tempered by letting the cartouche's discursive function trump its material form. In the literary approach the meaning of the cartouche tends to be established from within the map. Moreover, the cartouche's iconography is not only viewed as a map element but its form is often understood to be at once related and subordinate to the map's unique notational system, indeed to the very *telos* of cartography: the representation of space and spatial relations. Yet, most cartouches have by design very little in common with a map's spatial representation, be it in terms of structure (the curvilinear shape of Jefferys' cartouche frame is not a mimetic redrawing of New England's coastline) or in terms of iconography (there is no obvious correlation between the landscape and the actual land or the Indian figure's costume and the clothing worn by indigenous peoples living in New England in 1755).

If the discourse-school's argument is true that "far from being marginal the cartouche constitutes the map,"[15] then the design of and iconography embedded inside the Jefferys cartouche calls for us to engage more concretely with the formal and material constitution of the cartouche *per se*. In what follows I will reconstruct the morphology of New England cartouches by examining maps made predominantly in England and British America in general, with the goal to explain the meaning of the cartouche in Jefferys' *Map of the most Inhabited part of NEW ENGLAND* in specific.[16] In particular, I seek

For studies discussing New England maps in relation to the dispossession of Native Americans, see J. B. Harley, "New England Cartography and the Native Americans," in *American Beginnings: Exploration, Culture, and Cartography in the Land of Norumbega*, eds. Emerson W. Baker et al. (Lincoln, Neb.: University of Nebraska Press, 1994), 287–313; or, Margaret Wickens Pearce, "Native Mapping in Southern New England Indian Deeds," in *Cartographic Encounters: Perspectives on Native American Mapmaking and Uses*, ed. G. Malcolm Lewis (Chicago: University of Chicago Press, 1998), 157–186.

15. See Pratt, 362; also Clarke, 474.

16. My choice of New England maps for explaining the morphology of the cartouche is motivated in part by the genre's unique cartographic archive. Maps of "New England" continued to be defined consistently throughout the eighteenth century and as a result of this stable definition is today a well-documented thematic map genre within which it becomes possible to trace formal developments of the cartouche over an extended period of time.

Most of the maps consulted for this essay are now available in digital archives offered by the Library of Congress; the New York Public Library; the Osher Map Library at the University of Southern Maine; and the David Rumsey collection. Maps consulted but that cannot be found online are in William P. Cumming, *The Southeast in Early Maps* (Chicago: University of Chicago Press, 1974); Margaret Beck Pritchard and Henry G. Taliaferro, *Degrees of Latitude: Map-*

to revive the prematurely dismissed "ornamental" understanding of the cartouche. In this approach I take my cues from cartographic handbooks that
by calling a cartouche a "decorative inset" implicitly offer two lines of inquiry
for framing this essay. The first line of inquiry is to recover the "decorative
vocabulary" that informed and shaped New England maps. The second line is
to explore the cartouche as an entity that is at least on the surface formally and
functionally separate from the map. Ultimately, by considering recent scholarship on the visual and material culture surrounding eighteenth-century British
mapping projects, including the understanding of maps as "consumer" goods,
this essay seeks to examine the spatial work of the cartouche in both graphic
and cartographic media.

Towards a Morphology of the "New England" Cartouche

In order to understand the significance of Jefferys' cartouche separately from
the map we need to identify the basic cartouche forms that were decorating
New England maps during the eighteenth century. Two elements stand out:
the tablet and the frame. Taking John Speed's cartouche as a representative
example, we can see that the tablet is the cartouche's largest element (fig. 3).
Providing the primary space for either verbal or pictorial inscription it contains
here the map's title line, "A Map of New England and New York" and its commercial by-line, "Sold by Tho. Basset in Fleetstreet and Richard Chiswell in
St. Pauls Church Yard." The frame surrounding the tablet serves as the visual
and conceptual border separating the cartouche's content from its surroundings, that is, the frame separates the cartouche from the map's cartographic
inscriptions (including the map frame bearing the geographic grid numbers,
the rhumb lines emanating from the compass rose, and the cartographic image
of the land).

   In their totality, cartouches like the one by Speed simultaneously imitate
and conflate three design traditions taken from architecture, the decorative
arts, and early modern communication technologies. First, the curvilinear
symmetrical shape of Speed's tablet closely resembles the architectural feature
of the modillion, an ornamental bracket in the form of a scroll used, often in

ping Colonial America (New York: Abrams, 2002); Seymour T. Schwartz and Ralph E. Ehren-
berg, *The Mapping of America* (New York: Abrams, 1980); and Barbara McCorkle, *New England
in Early Printed Maps, 1513 to 1800* (Providence, R.I.: John Carter Brown Library, 2001).

series, under cornices or capitals in Renaissance and Baroque building designs. Second, the cartouche corresponds with decorative devices, ranging from heraldic insignia to pictures. In the case of Speed's cartouche the insertion of the royal crest into the cartouche's frame establishes the formal similarity between heraldry and material design of picture frames. Third, when viewed together, tablet and frame frequently resemble writing materials; using various *trompe l'oeil* effects, map engravers have cartouches create the illusion that they are hard or soft writing surfaces of various degrees of durability, including metal- and stonework, vellum and skins, and a host of paper products.

In this general overview of basic forms, John Speed's late seventeenth-century example simulates the iconic device of the genealogical seal indicating social rank and political status in Europe's feudal societies. Its heraldic or emblematic design is here imprinted on the paper of the map instead of being impressed on a piece of wax. In this form, the New England cartouche functions as both a legal and military device: on the one hand, it authenticates the map title and, similar to tokens or symbols appending legal documents, it serves to confirm and secure "New England" for the owner of the seal, here the British Crown. On the other hand, its symbolic effect not only demarcates territorial claims but works similar to a flag and show of colors by which military units marked their presence as a territorial power on the ground.

Indeed, by the end of the seventeenth century it is customary for cartouches in New England maps to operate like the imperial seals that divided North and South America between the various European powers one century before.[17] A different map by John Seller, *A Chart of the Sea-Coasts of New England* (1680; fig. 5), illustrates how a cartouche drawn in the British heraldic tradition makes its proprietary land claims by using a visual model of metonymic substitution. The map's cartouche in the lower right is drawn to resemble a seal. But it is only the shell of a seal, missing its symbolic content. Instead, the mapmaker transferred the armorial signs of England's royal household and feudal allies from the cartouche to the mapped space where multiple insignia are now displayed like miniaturized cartouches up and down the Atlantic coast and in

17. For critical discussions see David Woodward, ed. *The History of Cartography. Vol. 3. Cartography in the European Renaissance. Part 1* (Chicago: University of Chicago Press, 2007). For visual examples, see Pierluigi Portinaro and Franco Knirsch, *The Cartography of North America 1500–1800* (New York: Crescent Books, 1987), 57, 73, 79, 83, 102.

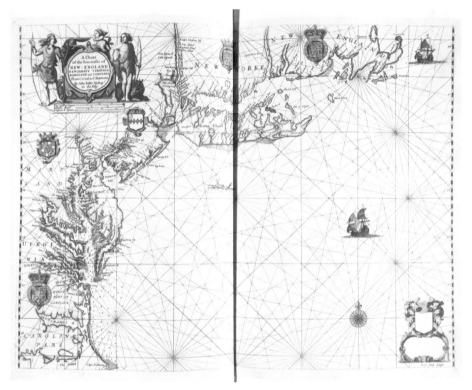

Fig. 5. John Seller, *A Chart of the Sea-Coasts of New England.* London, 1680. Law-rence H. Slaughter Collection, The Lionel Pincus and Princess Firyal Map Division, The New York Public Library, Astor, Lenox and Tilden Foundations.

series like so many escutcheons in a genealogical handbook or at a medieval jousting tournament. The overall visual effect is similar to the one generated by the Speed cartouche; while each armorial emblem is placed inside specific regional territories, together they provide a visual record documenting British authority over New England and its neighboring territories.

But a second look at Seller's map reveals that the basic morphology of the New England cartouche is undergoing dramatic changes by the end of the seventeenth century. Seller's heraldic cartouche on the lower right is counter-balanced and even upstaged by the map's eye-catching title cartouche in the upper left corner. While the heraldic cartouche projects the residual traces of an older pictorial tradition, the title cartouche signals an array of emergent designs. Influenced by continental and especially Dutch artists and engravers,

English mapmakers introduced new and more nuanced decorative devices, at once expanding the cartouche's decorative vocabulary while developing an increasingly baroque style that relied heavily on emblematic designs and symbolic figures.[18]

Important for the purpose of this discussion is the fact that one of the more prominent features differentiating new from old cartouche designs was the relatively sudden and pervasive addition of the figure of the "Indian" to New England cartouches.[19] The territorializing function inherent to the seal continued to inform the general cartouche design. However, with the inclusion of Indian figures the former message of feudal proprietary power morphed into a new message that had less to do with the political representation of New England but more with the representation of maps as such. A survey of New England maps published between the late seventeenth century and the middle of the eighteenth century reveals how two "Indian" designs, the "Indian frieze" and the "Indian tableau," changed the form of the New England cartouche and thus redefined the relationship of cartouche and map.

The Indian Frieze

As suggested by John Seller's cartouche in *A Chart of the Sea-Coasts of New England*, the elementary cartouche is expanded to incorporate discrete Indian bodies next to the shape of animals (beaver, elk) and the map's scale (the English, French, Dutch, and Spanish measures of distance). Each body is highly articulated, emphasizing posture, costume, and weaponry. A closer look reveals they are copies of existing book illustrations; both cartouches show the influence of Renaissance drawings made by John White and Theodor de Bry.[20] In carto-historical terms what they copy is a tradition of Indian representation, which, as Stephanie Pratt has shown, entailed a general shift of Indian figures from the map center to the margins where they became "extra-cartographic material in the decorative borders." More significantly, whereas early seven-

18. Clarke, 464; Svetlana Alpers, *The Art of Describing* (Chicago: The University of Chicago Press, 1983).

19. Throughout the essay I use the term "Indian" rather than "Native American" because the essay addresses artifacts and images coming out of a European lexicon of representation; conversely, this kind of address should therefore not to be mistaken for past or present representatives of American peoples.

20. On the mapmakers' use of White and de Bry in New England maps see McCorkle.

teenth-century maps displayed Indian figures to signify regional and ethnic identities in the form of picture galleries, late seventeenth-century maps included merely a "composite image of the American Indian." As composites their visualized bodies ceased to specify regional or ethnic differences but were instead abstracted into allegorical representations signifying the generic "Indian" as a mere type.[21] In the case of Seller's cartouche the figures are shown to be precisely such composites: each figure is a mixture of inherited forms whose visual frame of reference has been removed from that of particular local originals. In fact, the figures are copies of composites; they are borrowed from cartouches illustrating maps of regional entities like the West Indies or the American continent.[22] Being thus unspecific to New England maps (or the region), Seller's figures practically serve only one purpose: to assert the cartouche's "Indianness" and thus classify the map inside a Euro-centric reference system in which Indian figures are metaphors indexing the geographic space of America.[23]

That said, however, the cartouche was selected for a New England map, and since there is nothing about the Indians' figural form that could establish a link between the cartouche and specific New England tribes, their graphic function is less about locating New England as a territory on the map but more about locating the Indian within the cartouche design itself. Appearing in groups or couples, Seller's carefully etched bodies push, lean, and lounge with the effect that they seem to be caught in a permanent stasis. By drawing the Indian figures as if it were their purpose to better convey the cartouche's content by physically supporting its structural form, they recall a well-established tradition of graphic design that depicted Indian figures as neoclassical bodies,

21. Pratt, 352–56.

22. See John Seller, *A Chart of the West Indies* (1675); John Senex, *North America* (1710); Henry Popple, *A Map of the British Empire* (1733); Johann Homann, *Americae* (1746).

23. On the Indian as allegory of America see Hugh Honour, *The New Golden Land: European Images of America from the Discoveries to the Present* (New York: Pantheon, 1975), 84–117. Also see Clare Le Corbeiller, "Miss America and Her Sisters: Personification of the Four Parts of the World," *Metropolitan Museum of Art Bulletin* 19, 8 (April 1961): 209–21; E. McClung Fleming, "The American Image as Indian Princess, 1765–1783," *Winterthur Portfolio* 2 (1965): 65–81; John Higham, "Indian princess and Roman goddess: the first female symbols of America," *Proceedings of the American Antiquarian Society* 100, 1 (1990): 45–79. See also J. B. Harley, "Maps, Knowledge, Power," in *The New Nature of Maps*, 51–81; Barbara Mundy, *The Mapping of New Spain: Indigenous Cartography and the Maps of the Relaciones Geograficas* (Chicago: University of Chicago Press, 1996).

THEATRVM
ORBIS TERRARVM,
Sive
ATLAS NOVVS:
in quo
TABVLÆ
et
DESCRIPTIONES
omnium Regionum,
Editæ
a Guiljel. et Ioanne Blaeu.

AMSTERDAMI,
Apud Iohannem
et Cornelium Blaeu.
ANNO cIↃ IↃC XXXX.

Fig. 6. Johannes Blaeu, *Theatrum Orbis
Terrarum.* 1635. Beinecke Rare Book and
Manuscript Library, Yale University, New
Haven, Conn.

proportionate in form and symmetrical in function. Famous examples are book frontispieces, such as the one prefacing travel accounts like Thomas Hariot's *A Briefe and True Report of the New-Found Land Virginia* (1590) or geography books and atlases like Johannes Blaeu's *Theatrum Orbis Terrarum* (1635; fig. 6). In frontispieces like these the decorative body of the Indian operates both as a narrative and mnemonic device; while the figure provided access to the structure of the material book (or codex) it also reminds the reader about the book's contents, here that the book is about geographic knowledge that includes America.

If we apply the convention of the frontispiece to the Seller cartouche, it is only a short step to associate the figure of the Indian with design patterns taken from the decorative arsenal of architectural handbooks. By the same token that the cartouche operates like a frontispiece that seeks to introduce the text of the map, its sculpted Indian bodies stand out, frieze-like, from the title cartouche like the classical shapes of statues and statuesque ornaments that embellished public and private buildings. The Indian cartouche thus redefines the map as both a material object and architectural space whose meaning hinges perhaps as much on the cartographic representation of American geography as on the way in which Euro-American relations are defined by the structural stability of spatial representation.[24]

24. Pratt observes that the relationship between figure and architecture serves to "to produce a balanced design." Pratt, 356.

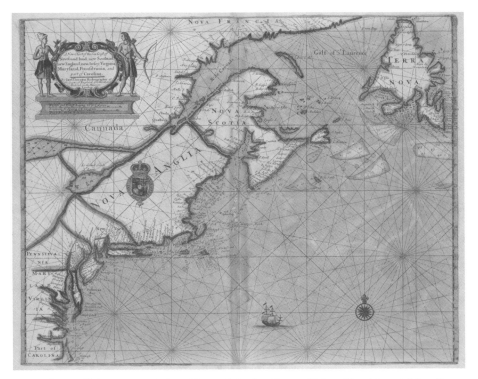

Fig. 7. Samuel Thornton, *A New Chart of the Sea Coast of New-Fund Land, New Scotland, New England.* 1702. The Lionel Pincus and Princess Firyal Map Division, The New York Public Library, Astor, Lenox and Tilden Foundations.

Yet, the Indian frieze design is never presented as an edifice or structure designed to actually house, that is, provide roof, walls, or for that matter a sheltering framework, for either the cartouche or the map. Instead, architectural elements appear limited to the cartouche's base, providing a stable foundation for grounding Indian figures. In that sense the Indian frieze patterns resemble at once neoclassical artwork and architectural décor. The link between public architecture and popular sculpture is most visible in cartouches such as Samuel Thornton's *A New Chart of the Sea Coast of New-Fund Land, New Scotland, New England* (1702; fig. 7).[25] Its core design—consisting of the stone-carved title tablet, the frame's material heft, and the corporeal solidity of the Indian figures—emphasizes the cartouche's material substance. Yet, its lack of a broader physical context presents the Indian frieze cartouche as decorative design imi-

25. See also cartouches such as Seller's cartouche of *A Chart of the West Indies* (London 1675); Lea's *A New Map of America* (1690).

tating not architecture but decorative design objects. Indeed, if architecture beckoned initially to provide a referential framework for explaining the Indian cartouche design, its freestanding appearance situates the Indian cartouche inside the broader culture of Restoration masonry and production of sculpture. The Seller cartouche's overall form—consisting of a horizontal base propping up the vertically attached Indian figures—points to an aesthetic derived from public monuments that were erected in city squares or cathedrals. At the same time, the cartouche's monumental design also invokes the miniature, the more inexpensive figures sold by masons and image peddlers. Appearing in print instead being made of marble, porcelain, or clay, the image of the cartouche projects a three-dimensional corporeality similar to the seal (or the modern paper weight). But whereas the seal is the official appendix accompanying a document, the Indian frieze design becomes the easily overdetermined object generating visual narratives about the New England map that are informed as much by ekphrastic stasis as by cultural fantasies of the docile Indian body.

The Indian Tableau

A similar visual narrative suggesting corporeal stability informs the second most frequent cartouche design, the "Indian tableau," found in early New England maps. Whereas the frieze style showed discrete Indian bodies in semiautonomous postures similar to fully-formed sculptures, the alternative pattern depicted Indian figures alone or in groups in situational contexts. It did so by reproducing picturesque or allegorical effects that were conceptually styled in the tradition of the literary and graphic arts (as opposed to masonry and sculpture). As shown in the cartouche for *A Map of New England* (1676; fig. 8) by Robert Morden and William Berry, we are still confronted by stock types, but get to envision them now in their material setting. This setting consists of a landscape vaguely marked as "American" by palmetto-shaped trees. The cartouche develops a contextual style that postcolonial theory has recently termed "*ethnoscapes*—landscapes of persons who constitute the shifting world in which modern subjects live and through which they represent one another and to themselves their relationships of identity and difference."[26] The identity and

26. Joseph Roach, "The Global Parasol: Accessorizing the Four Corners of the World," in *The Global Eighteenth Century*, ed. Felicity A. Nussbaum (Baltimore: Johns Hopkins Press, 2003), 94. He applies the concept developed by Arjun Appadurai, "Disjunction and Difference in the Global Cultural Economy," *Public Culture* 2, 2 (1990): 1–24.

Fig. 8. Robert Morden and William Berry, *A Map of New England*, 1676. Courtesy of the John Carter Brown Library at Brown University, Providence, R.I.

difference evoked by the Morden/Berry cartouche revolves around European fantasies of colonial economic production, here the diligent preparation of animal skins and other natural goods into bulky bundles by an Indian workforce that is steadily going about their daily business of being hunters and gatherers.

The image of commerce is central to later New England cartouches that apply the "Indian tableau" pattern, and can be found in cartouches introducing maps as different as the Homann Erben map, entitled *Nova Anglia* (1750; fig. 9) or William Douglass' *Plan of the British Dominions of New England* (1753; fig. 10). In both cartouches, Indian bodies appear in relation to European symbols of Atlantic commercial exchange (ships, fishing net) while at the same time representing their value as economic partners. In the case of the Homann cartouche the tableau revolves around the aesthetic principle of balanced symmetry: the Indian figure (still drawn in the de Bry mold) is equal

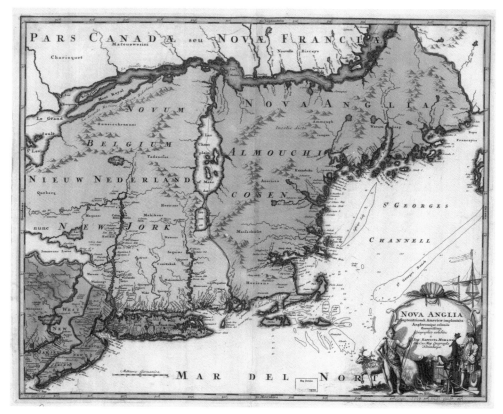

Fig. 9. Homann Erben, *Nova Anglia.* 1750. Courtesy of the Library of Congress.

to the European figure in size and pictorial detail; both figures are surrounded by goods that signify economic exchange between Indians (animal furs) and Europeans (rifles, textiles, etc). In contrast, the Douglass cartouche seems to upset this balance: it obliquely references the fur trade by depicting a gallery of animals at the top, but emphasizes New England's famous fishing harvests in the foreground (including a whale). Significantly, the Douglass cartouche omits the figure of the European trader while rendering the Indian figure ambiguously childlike and of racially indeterminate origins (the color black has replaced Native costumes).[27]

27. On the rationale of depicting Native Americans in a black color see Ellwood Parry, *The Image of the Indian and the Black Man in American Art, 1590–1900* (New York: Braziller, 1974); Alden T. Vaughan, "From White Man to Redskin: Changing Anglo-American Perceptions of the American Indian," *American Historical Review* 87, 4 (October 1982): 917–53; Nicholas

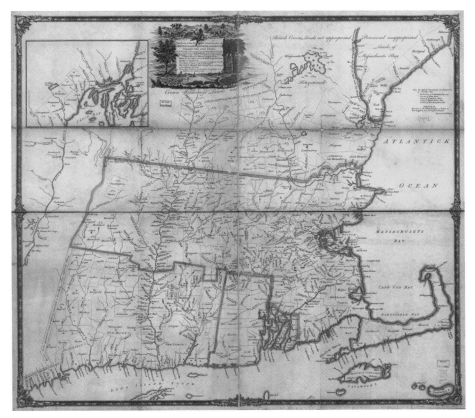

Fig. 10. William Douglass, *Plan of the British Dominions of New England.* 1753.
Courtesy of the Library of Congress.

Both tableaux create images of contained fragmentation: each figure is
shown to be part of a larger economic system; even though they seem to represent action—bow and arrow suggest the work of the warrior-hunter which
in turn is controlled by the emasculated appearance of the puttee-like hybrid
between African slave and Native American in Douglass's cartouche—they
are shown not *in situ* in a realistic New England space (or time) but as composite elements or personifications of the picture itself. Indeed, cartouches
drawn in both the vein of the Indian frieze and the Indian tableau internal-

Hudson, "From 'Nation' to 'Race': The Origins of Racial Classification in Eighteenth-Century
Thought," *Eighteenth-Century Studies* 29 (1996): 247–64; Nancy Shoemaker, *A Strange Likeness:
Becoming Red and White in Eighteenth-Century North America* (New York: Oxford University
Press, 2004).

Fig. 11. Jan Van Kessel. *America*. 1666. Bildarchiv Preussischer Kulturbesitz/Art Resource, NY.

ized the material logic of the early modern "Indian" curiosity cabinet perhaps best illustrated by Jan Van Kessel's allegorical painting *America* (1666; fig. 11). There we see multiple Indian sculptures situated inside the architectural space of a museum-like gallery that is devoted solely to the display of objects representing the people and animals found in the New World. The figures seated in the foreground correspond harmoniously with their stony counterparts who are decorously integrated into the architectural space, be it as classical sculptures or abstract masks looking down from the modillions that adorn the arched window frames. The living occupants of this *Wunderkammer*—ranging from the supinely reposed to the joyous band of returning hunters—are here hypostatized figures whose meaning hinges as much on projecting a composite

Fig. 12. Detail from Thomas Jefferys, *Map of the most Inhabited part of New England.* London, 1755. Courtesy of the Library of Congress.

American identity as on the assumption that such figures are discretely crafted art objects, even collectibles, and thus commodities intended equally for display and trade in the world of circum-Atlantic aesthetic exchange.[28]

Jefferys's "Indian Theater"

When addressed in the terms of decorative formalism as delineated above, Jefferys's 1755 cartouche in the *Map of the most Inhabited part of NEW ENGLAND* builds on the "Indian frieze" and "Indian tableau" tradition. But with a new twist: it adds the element of theater performance and the material culture of stagecraft to the pictorial content defining eighteenth-century New England maps (fig. 12).[29] If we turn to residual patterns first, Jefferys's use of

28. Alpers, 163–64; see also Dorinda Outram, *Panorama of the Enlightenment* (Los Angeles: Thames & Hudson and The Getty Museum, 2006).

29. Jefferys's focus on the Indian is unique in more than one sense. Mapmakers were hesitant to allow Indian figures to enter the actual tablet or interior space of the cartouche; after viewing much of the cartographic archive pertaining to New England and North America, I found only two examples in which engravers placed Indian figures on the *inside* of the cartouche frame.

Fig. 13 (left). "Habits of a Flemish Gentleman in 1620," from Thomas Jefferys, *A Collection of Dresses*, 1757–1772, Vol. 2, 62. HEW 14.7.6, Harry Elkins Widener Collection, Harvard University, Cambridge, Mass.

Fig. 14 (right). "Habit of an Ottawa, an Indian Nation of North America," from Thomas Jefferys, *A Collection of Dresses*, 1757–1772, Vol. 4, 114. HEW 14.7.6, Harry Elkins Widener Collection, Harvard University.

composite figures squarely grounds his cartouche within frieze and tableau designs. Between the Indian and the English, each figure is a personified type: local characteristics are negated while more generalized attributes become affirmed as the visual character of the group.

But unlike past map engravers who modeled their Indian illustrations on Renaissance travel books and ethnographies, Jefferys seems to have developed his figures by tapping into a new visual archive: close-ups reveal that Jefferys's cartouche figures strongly resemble picture prints entitled "Habits of a Flemish Gentleman in 1620," "Habit of an Ottawa, an Indian Nation of North America," or "Liberty"—all of which were published shortly after the map by

Jefferys himself as *A Collection of the Dresses of Different Nations, Antient and Modern* (1757–72; figs. 13–15).[30] True to the tableau's formal logic Jefferys's figural ensemble becomes an ethnoscape, asserting difference by subordinating particularity to generality: individual differences between Native American tribes (say, the Ottawa versus the Narragansett) or differences between European citizens (the Dutch versus the English) become blurred in order to accentuate the more general differences between Native Americans and Europeans. Drawing this distinction, however, comes at a price. All human subjects become too generalized, and thus the cartouche singles out inanimate objects to impress the stamp of a local identity on this spectacle of difference: the idea that this cartouche is about

Fig. 15. "Liberty," from Thomas Jefferys, *A Collection of Dresses*, 1757–1772, Vol. 4, 156. HEW 14.7.6, Harry Elkins Widener Collection, Harvard University.

New England (and not about Surinam or New Amsterdam) is signaled by the strategic insertion of a rock bearing the inscription "Plymouth MDCXX" and the ubiquitous image of the full fishing net below the rock.

In treating the cartouche like a tableau, consisting of a stable picture frame and stock-type figures, we end up with a pictorial construct that generates a predictable narrative whose sum total begins, at the left, with rowboats and English sailors unloading a ship in preparation of a European economic future in America, and that ends, at the right, inside the unpopulated but presumably rich in natural resources (remember the fish) mainland. Much of this narrative

30. Thomas Jefferys, *A Collection of the Dresses of Different Nations, Antient and Modern . . . Vol. 1–4* (London, 1757–1772); the Dutch figure is from *Dresses*, Vol.2, 62; the Indian figure, Vol. 4, 114; and the figure of Liberty, Vol. 4, 156.

is engendered by the female figure representing Liberty; holding a staff on which perches the liberty cap, or the *pilleus libertatis*, she invitingly gestures at the landscape, addressing the assembly of recent immigrants while at the same time bypassing the half-naked subservient figure of the Indian. In its overall configuration, the cartouche is thus another allegory in which its constitutive elements—be they borrowed from the architectural frieze or the picture tableau tradition—represent the moment when English colonists took possession of New England, while the European personification of "Liberty" predicts the historical process of invasion and succession, in short, the act of colonization and the British dominion over New England.[31]

Yet, as much as we recognize elements of the frieze or tableau, Jefferys's cartouche signals a fundamental departure in both the cartouche's formal design and thus the function of its pictorial content. On the whole, the cartouche resembles a *tableau vivant* in which human figures are less encoded as static objects but more as active subjects. The modernized and realistically drawn figures invoke, on the one hand, the *tableau vivant*'s situational techniques, which, informed by eighteenth-century genre painting as well as literature, were devoted to the representation of historical or allegorical motifs. On the other hand, Jefferys's figural arrangement invokes the graphic representation of theatrical scenes and stage performances. In this context it is perhaps not a coincidence that the same book from which I suggested earlier that Jefferys copied his figural designs also devoted a whole section to allegorical figures in period costumes and "the habits of the principal characters on the English stage."[32]

Indeed, just as it could be argued that Jefferys copies from existing ethnographic fashion plates, his Indian figure's dress imitates the theatrical wardrobe used by stage actors playing "Indian" characters: the feather dress displayed by the cartouche invokes a history of theater costumes dating from Inigo Jones and the early seventeenth-century masques to the tragedies of John Dryden's *The Indian Queen* (1664), for which Aphra Behn provided original feather garments from Surinam, which would then reappear later in Dryden's *The Indian Emperour* (1667) and Aphra Behn's own play, *The Widow Ranter* (1689).[33]

31. Here I expand from the reading by Clarke, 459–60.

32. Jefferys, *Collection*, Vol. 3 and 4.

33. See T. W. Craik (ed.), *The Revels History of Drama in English, Vol. V, 1660–1750* (London: Methuen, 1976), 145 and Plate 27; and Honour, 88. Also see Steven Mullaney, "The New World on Display: European Pageantry and the Ritual of Incorporation of the Americas," in

Jefferys's cartouche elaborates the theater connection further by placing the Indian figure at exactly the axial center of the picture and thus also at the axiomatic center of the pictorial narrative. Do the experiment: when folding the cartouche in half we find that it is not the vertical line of the liberty staff but the line connecting the Indian's head, left hand, knee, and foot that creates the optical boundary line separating the Dutch-English characters from "Liberty" and the unpopulated American landscape (fig. 12). As we look at the vertical axis of the Indian from top to bottom, dramaturgical elements such as body posture and specific hand gestures imitate representations that could be found in oratory manuals and acting handbooks, not to mention popular studies specializing in the classification of hand gestures and facial expressions such as John Bulwer, *Chirologia; or, Naturall Language of the Hand* (1644) and Charles Le Brun *Conférences sur l'expression* (1698).[34]

Once considered as a dramaturgical configuration, Jefferys's Indian figure simulates a character type that was habitually populating the English (and European) theater stage by the mid-eighteenth century.[35] The cartouche Indian resonates with a new generation of composite characters developed by what could be called "Indian plays," ranging from John Dennis's *Liberty Asserted* (1704) to Robert Rogers's *Ponteach: or the Savages of America, A Tragedy* (1766).[36] At the same time, the cartouche Indian also recalls the puppet-like images of the "Four Indian Kings" which in 1710 were used to advertise a puppet show ("a New Opera performed by a Company of Artificial Actors"). Or, in a similar vein, Jefferys's Indian invokes figures from pantomime shows like

New World of Wonders: European Images of the Americas, 1492–1700, ed. Rachel Doggett (Seattle, Wash.: University of Washington Press, 1992), 105–113.

34. Alice Nash, "Antic Deportments and Indian Postures," in *A Centre of Wonders: The Body in Early America*, eds. Janet Moore Lindman and Michele Lise Tarter (Ithaca, N.Y.: Cornell University Press, 2001), 163–76. On actor training see Marion Jones, "Actors and repertory," in *The Revels*, 119–57.

35. Jefferys's cartouche is not the only one to activate or mobilize Indian figures along theatrical lines. Other mid-century cartouches, such as those prefacing John Mitchell's *A Map of the British and French Dominions in North America* (1755) and Emmanuel Bowen/Henry Gibson's *An Accurate Map of North America* (1755), show actor-like Indian figures engaged in some form of dramatic dialogue.

36. For studies addressing Indians in eighteenth-century plays see, for example, Eugene H. Jones, *Native Americans as Shown on the Stage, 1753–1916* (Metuchen, N.J.: Scarecrow Press, 1988) and Julie Ellison, *Cato's Tears and the Making of Anglo-American Emotion* (Chicago: University of Chicago Press, 1999).

Arlequin Sauvage (1721).[37] In performances like these the figure of the Indian is cast in terms that suggest quasi-mechanical actions made by quasi-mechanical actors. The form and function of the Indian then is that of a moveable puppet who dances, jumps, or simply moves on command by the hands of a puppeteer. It is also that of an automaton that will jump, laugh, or even sing like a machine that is soulless, not human, just an animated thing.[38]

If we move from actors and acting to the material terms of stagecraft, then Jefferys's cartouche resembles a "scenographic stage." Since the 1660s the central feature of such a stage was its moveable scenery, which, being painted in perspective, was famous for altering the means of representing—and quickly changing—geographical settings.[39] Framing this moveable scenery was the proscenium arch. Placed upright between the stage and the audience, the arch functioned similar to the frame of the cartouche: both arch and cartouche frame separate the contents of the staged setting from the world that surrounds it.[40] Not to become too technical, it is interesting to note that while pulley systems and other mechanical devices shaped special effects behind the stage, during the Georgian period moveable scenery was increasingly replaced by inexpensive giant transparencies which, like the vertical display of the cartouche tablet, was suspended like a screen in front of the stage in order to imitate set designs through elaborate lighting effects.[41]

37. On the context for this play see Eric Hinderaker, "The 'Four Indian Kings' and the Imaginative Construction of the First British Empire," *William Mary Quarterly* 53, 3 (July 1996): 487–526. The irony is that the Native American guests, while being presented as Indian puppets on the playbill, were supposed to see a show in the Punch-and-Judy tradition, and thus would have not seen themselves presented as puppets.

38. My interpretation of Indians as puppets, marionettes, and automatons is shaped by Victoria Nelson, *The Secret Life of Puppets* (Cambridge, Mass.: Harvard University Press, 2001).

39. Roach 93, 94; he cites Katherine S. Van Eerde, *John Ogilby and the Taste of His Times* (Folkestone, Kent: Dawson, 1976). For studies on the history of moveable scenery see Richard Southern, *Changeable Scenery. Its Origin and Development in the British Theatre* (London: Faber and Faber, 1952) and his "Theatres and Scenery," in *The Revels History of Drama in English*, Vol. V, 1660–1750, ed. T. W. Craik (London: Methuen, 1976) 83–118; Richard Leacroft, *The Development of the English Playhouse* (Ithaca: Cornell University Press, 1973); and Roy Strong, ed., *Festival Designs by Inigo Jones* (London: International Exhibitions Foundation, 1969).

40. In A. M. Nagler, *A Source Book in Theatrical* History (New York: Dover, 1952), 205. Richard Southern, *Changeable Scenery* and his earlier *Proscenium and Sight-Lines* (1939; London: Faber, 1964); and Allardyce Nicoll, *The Development of the Theatre* (New York: Harcourt, 1927).

41. Southern, *Changeable Scenery*, 206. See also Louise Pelletier, *Architecture in Words: Theatre, Language and the Sensuous Space of Architecture* (London: Routledge, 2006), 80.

If we follow through the comparison of Jefferys's cartouche and the theater stage, his Indian figure now occupies a position that changes the meaning of space inside the cartouche. On the one hand, he inhabits the strategic place that on stage would be reserved for solo performances by actors or for stage announcers addressing the audience directly. But because the Indian addresses not us, the viewers, but his fellow actors he not only directs the flow of dialogue sideways but also assumes the figurative place of the proscenium arch, becoming at once the frame and medium for viewing the content of the stage. Thus, on the other hand, the Indian figure's body becomes the boundary that reorients and subdivides the *tableau vivant* into both a dramatic representation and a blueprint of an English theater: at the same time as the Indian resembles a cast member of a dramatic performance, it also is the figure addressing the implied theater's auditorium on the left (the English pilgrims) and the projected stage set on the right (the American landscape). With this adjustment of perspective, Jefferys alters the cartouche's pictorial narrative. We assume that colonial intent was implicit in the various elements of the tableau design. But in the old reading this intent tends to be interpreted as a historical fact. In contrast, Jefferys's cartouche changes the horizon of expectation: there still is colonial intent but through its theatrical configuration it becomes a social action; colonization is presented as a dialogic practice using human actors, not as a historical event producing faceless facts and historical dates carved into geological formations.

Conclusions

But since we are discussing decorative arts and not theater plays, cartouches and not Indian figures get to have the final word. I started this essay by observing how the cartographic representation of New England was unambiguous and constant in eighteenth-century maps. Looking over the various cartouches discussed above, only two aspects are constant: the words "New England" and the allegorical narrative celebrating British colonial history. Aside from that, when viewing the New England cartouches separately from the maps' contents it becomes evident that, in contrast to cartographic representation, the cartouches were anything but unambiguous when defining New England. Cartouches were switching formal and visual codes in what appears to be in rapid succession. This begs the question, did the frequent changes in design patterns change the meaning of New England maps and if so how?

If we look at internal designs first, "New England" is defined by a set iconography that is surprisingly variable. In fact, cartouches seem to struggle in determining a single attribute representative of New England. They tap generic images ranging from fish and fur to trade ships and European-styled figures, but in this they marshal a visual shorthand that is as regionally unspecific as it is universal in its application in cartouches introducing most of the maps about North America. Formal confusion upends the cartouches' symbolic function further: between the late seventeenth century and the mid-eighteenth century, New England cartouches make their territorial demands by using a multitude of graphic displays instead of one uniform design, invoking shapes from royal insignia to costumed actors, or from architectural monument to natural landscape. Even the Indian figures, though a constant as a composite type, do not generate a stable referent for defining "New Englandness." They mutate—like movable scenery—from passive object to active hunter, from adult to child, from classical sculpture to modern stage actor. This kind of iconographic flux affected not only the cartouches' internal but external macro designs. Between the 1670s and the 1750s the cartouches' basic shapes shifted from resembling escutcheons and architectural structures to pictures and picture frames.

The graphic permutations used for representing roughly the same allegorical theme (namely, that New England belongs to and is a part of the British empire), then, suggest that the changes in cartouche designs have less to do with the maps' actual content. Rather, as graphic inserts ancillary to maps but not necessary to their meaning (after all, New England is recognizable without the cartouche) they provide an iconographical index that allows us to gauge changing attitudes towards the maps as a material artifact. First, the cartouche's frame creates a visual faultline effectively isolating the cartouche from the map by segregating its overdetermined pictorial mode of signification from the map's mode of cartographic writing. Second, the cartouches' emphasis on material shapes, such as the frieze or the picture frame, aligns the map with a broader material culture of display objects. Subsequently, and third, by aligning the map with material culture objects the cartouche registers different modes of map reception. One mode of reception, and perhaps the central mode, is the map viewing habit; it makes for a very different viewing (or reading) experience if the planar projection of the map's cartographic image is suddenly thrown into relief by a non-cartographic image such as an asymmetrical cartouche frame, asking us to approach the two-dimensional paper map as if it were a three-dimensional construct made of plaster or marble. With these changing micro and/or macro-shapes comes a fundamental change in how we are to imagine the relationship between cartouche and map: is the cartouche a stamping device, leaving its imprimatur on the map and thus calling attention to the map's printed state? Is it to be seen as a discrete object that can be placed all over the map, like movable type? Or is it a display object, calling attention to its sheer visuality, from the specific pictorial to the general spectacle?

If we address these findings in the terms of cartography's material history, the Indian figures inside the New England cartouche transform the map into a spectacular commodity intended for circulation in the marketplace of picture prints and other visual art objects. While internal evidence suggests a visual narrative of Indian containment, once we locate this narrative inside the serial production of flexible cartouche designs, the Indian cartouches become symptomatic of the commercialization of map production. The recurring motif of the static Indian figure can be considered as a print label for classifying map genres (New England cartouches categorize themselves as maps about America) and for determining a map's market value (maps with elaborate cartouches cost more money). The less static theatricalized Indian of the tableau pattern continues in this vein, presenting the map as a crossover product in which a historical picture print could be viewed as a presentist commentary on a looming political conflict (here the soon to erupt British-French conflict in which New England would figure as a contested battleground). But in the end, the cartouches that are being circulated in New England maps are not neatly styled designs reflecting specific political or commercial attitudes towards New England, be they considered an English repository of natural resources or a staging ground of British history. Rather, what the New England cartouches show—and maps cannot—are competing notions of space, spatial representation, and spatial relations. This is the spatial work of the New England cartouche.

New England's Ends

WENDY BELLION

PROGNOSTICATION is a notoriously tricky affair. Unlike fortune-tellers, scholars have no crystal balls into which to gaze. We cannot rely upon tarot cards to predict the next big idea; nor can we use our palms to map lines of future research. It is all the more lucky for us, then, that New England studies already show discernible signs of new developments. One important shift involves an expansion of scope and methodologies: embracing the possibilities of Atlantic world scholarship, historians of visual and material culture are exploring the global as well as local implications of objects produced and consumed within the geographical territory of early New England. This work is sharpening our understanding of the means by which portraitists and their sitters, to take just one example, fashioned identities out of paint in places as diverse as urban art studios and backcountry cabins, thereby participating—whether consciously or unwittingly—in the broad circulation of people and ideas and goods that constituted the British empire. At the same time, specialists in visual and material culture are increasingly engaging in cross-disciplinary dialogues, with literary scholars initiating studies of visual images and art historians interrogating the functions of words within printed images (not to mention words upon gravestones, textiles, and other objects). In the process, disciplinary notions of "visual culture" and "material culture" are proving noticeably elastic.

With this evidence of such changes already underway, where do we go from here? How might we begin to remap New England's ends (in the double sense of New England's geographical and cultural boundaries as well as the sorts of objectives we define for ourselves as scholars)? This essay offers some preliminary thoughts in response to these questions. It considers how inter-disciplinary discourse, together with the evidentiary nature of early American objects, presents opportunities for reexamining the utility of the categorical descriptors "visual culture" and "material culture" for New England studies. In addition, it suggests that transnational (or rather, transcolonial) approaches to New England culture can be as conceptually productive as transatlantic methodologies. To elaborate upon these points, I offer some lessons learned from my own research on early New England: first, the interpretive challenges posed by an illusionistic spectacle called the "Invisible Lady"; second, the case study of a picture painted by the visiting Briton Joseph Blackburn; and third, the experience of designing and teaching a university seminar on colonial art across North America. For the purposes of this short essay, the latter example may be especially instructive, for in any predictions about the future of visual and material culture studies, the next generation of scholars must figure prominently.

By way of looking forward, it helps to begin by invoking an ocular figure from the past: the "Invisible Lady," a multisensory entertainment that enjoyed extraordinary popularity in the United States during the earliest decades of the nineteenth century. A broadside from an 1804 exhibition in Wilmington, Delaware, helps elucidate the peculiar functions of this contraption (fig. 1). According to the lengthy text, the instrument housed an invisible woman, one who could laugh, sing, whisper, and breathe. Indeed, this spectral presence could even view and converse with the people in attendance, describing their appearance and actions. Because the agent of these interactions remained indiscernible, the exhibition purported to "so completely deceive the senses as to appear the effect of magic." But if the Invisible Lady was an "inexplicable auricular and optical illusion," it was also a device for undeceiving: the broadside tempted observers to discover how the deception worked, promising that, in the process, they would learn to detect the artifice of would-be imposters and discredit claims of supernatural activity.[1] Contemporary illustrations of the Invisible Lady, which exposed the mechanics of the deception to view, help demonstrate precisely how this instrument functioned (fig. 2).[2] Spec-

1. "Astonishing Invisible Lady" (Wilmington, Del., [1804]), broadside, American Antiquarian Society. I explore the North American history of the Invisible Lady and its cultural functions at greater length in *Citizen Spectator: Art, Illusion, and Visual Perception in Early National America* (Chapel Hill, N.C.: University of North Carolina Press for the Omohundro Institute of Early American History and Culture, 2011).

2. This engraving, accompanied by an explanation of the illusion, was published in William Nicholson's *Journal of Natural Philosophy* (London, 1807), 69–71. Nicholson's exposé (but not his picture) was quickly reproduced in several American publications; see "British and Foreign Intelligence, Chiefly Scientific," *The American Register; Or, General Repository of History, Politics, and Science,* vol. 1 (Jan. 1, 1807), 67; "Literary and Philosophical Intelligence ... Great Britain," *The Christian Observer* (Boston) vol. 6. no. 2 (Feb. 1807), 127.

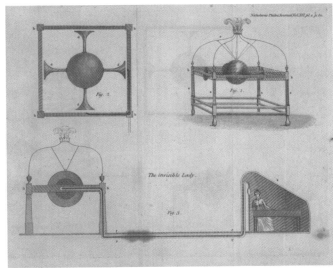

Fig. 1 (left). "Astonishing Invisible Lady," (Wilmington, De., 1804), broadside. Courtesy, American Antiquarian Society, Worcester, Mass.

Fig. 2 (right). *The Invisible Lady.* 1807. Engraving from the *Journal of Natural Philosophy, Chemistry, and the Arts,* XVI (1907), Plate 2, opposite 80. Courtesy, The Library Company of Philadelphia.

tators encountered a decidedly odd-looking contraption upon entering the exhibition spaces of the Invisible Lady. In its most familiar form, the device was comprised of a glass ball surrounded by four trumpets. It was surrounded by a square railing about waist-high and surmounted by a network of wires culminating in a form evocative of a plumed crown.[3] The cross-section view at the base of this engraving reveals how the machine was able to communicate vision and sound: a series of speaking tubes ran from the posts of the railing underneath the floor to a woman sequestered in a nearby closet. Seated behind a pianoforte (occasionally the exhibitions featured music), the woman leans to one side to peer through a hole in the wall. This, then, was how the Invisible Lady could see and chat with her visitors while remaining out of sight. Far from manifesting an actual immaterial presence, the spectacle drew upon the exhibitor's old-fashioned cunning and mechanical know-how. The key to solv-

3. Less frequently, the exhibition took the form of a rectangular glass box suspended from the ceiling by chains at each corner. On this construction, which was originally exhibited in Paris, see Jann Matlock, "The Invisible Woman and her Secrets Unveiled," *Yale Journal of Criticism* 9:2 (Fall 1996): 175–221.

ing the puzzle of this clever illusion resided in seeing through the tactics of concealment that disguised a simple architecture of pipes and peepholes.

This proved to be both a stupefying and highly amusing challenge for the majority of the Invisible Lady's visitors. According to advertisements documented in the America's Historical Newspapers database, the Invisible Lady was displayed up and down the eastern seaboard dozens of times between 1800 and 1820, with a concentration of exhibitions occurring in 1804–05. During the fall of 1804, New Englanders got their chance to spot a glimpse of the elusive lady. Massachusetts hosted no less than four competing shows: one in Boston, another in Newburyport, and two in Salem. One of the latter shows prompted the publication of an exuberant woodcut in the *Salem Gazette* (fig. 3), an image that suggests a machine nearly alive with implied movement.[4] Just a few months later, a Boston impresario named William Frederick Pinchbeck carefully detailed the operations of the instrument (fig. 4).[5] In a lengthy discussion of the Invisible Lady, Pinchbeck proposed that the exhibition would work even better if two agents collaborated to perform the deception. One individual could observe the assembled spectators through a latticework hidden by a girandole, eavesdropping upon conversations and conveying information to his partner; the other would play the part of the Invisible Lady's voice, returning answers to the spectators' questions via the speaking tubes that snaked through the room. For the proprietor of the illusion, the use of two people would result in a better deception, for the speaking agent could be located at a greater distance from the exhibition room, thereby forestalling easy detection of the illusion's mechanics. For the audience, on the other hand, this coordinated manipulation amounted to something potentially ominous: a conspiracy of sensory distraction as disconcerting as any of the ventriloquial

4. "Last Week of Exhibition," *Salem Gazette*, Dec. 11, 1804. Previously, the woodcut had been featured in an advertisement for the Newburyport exhibition; see "The Astonishing Invisible Lady," *Newburyport Herald*, Nov. 9, 1804. For exhibitions elsewhere in New England, see "Astonishing Invisible Lady," *Salem Gazette* (Salem, Mass.), Oct. 5, 1804; "An Extraordinary Aerial Phenomenon," *Columbian Centinel* (Boston), Sept. 1, 1804; and "The Exhibition of the Invisible Lady," *Eastern Argus* (Portland, Me.), Oct. 4, 1804.

5. William Frederick Pinchbeck, *The Expositor; or Many Mysteries Unravelled, Delivered in a Series of Letters, between a Friend and a Correspondent* (Boston, 1805), esp. 27–37, 85–87. For a discussion of Pinchbeck's exposé of the Invisible Lady in relation to contemporary discourses of acoustical deception, see Leigh Eric Schmidt, *Hearing Things: Religion, Illusion, and the American Enlightenment* (Cambridge, Mass.: Harvard University Press, 2000).

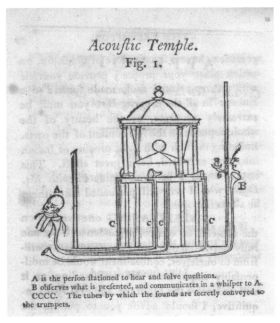

Fig. 3 (left). "The Philosophical and Mechanical Museum, Is Now Opened . . . ,"
Salem Gazette, Dec. 7, 1804, page 3, column 4. Courtesy of the Massachusetts
Historical Society, Boston, Mass.

Fig. 4 (right). "Acoustic Temple" and "Magnetic Penetrating Spy-Glass." Relief print
from William Pinchbeck, *The Expositor; or, Many Mysteries Unravelled* (Boston, 1805).
Courtesy, American Antiquarian Society.

deceptions imagined by the era's leading author of Gothic narratives, Charles
Brockden Brown.[6]

There is much more to say about the history of the Invisible Lady: about
it how it became a trope of political deception during Jefferson's administration; about how it modeled a female gaze only to invite the female viewer's
exposure; about how it posed an epistemological challenge to a republican
society schooled in the Scottish philosophy of Common Sense. With regard
to the specific issue of New England studies, though, the Invisible Lady helps

6. See, for example, the terrors visited by the ventriloquist Carwin upon a Pennsylvania community in Brown's 1798 novel *Wieland*, ed. and intro. by Jay Fliegelman (New York: Penguin
Classics, 1991). It may be no coincidence that the Invisible Lady enjoyed its greatest popularity
during 1804–05—the very years in which Brown's sequel to *Wieland*, the unfinished *Memoirs of
Carwin the Biloquist*, was serialized in *The Literary Magazine*.

raise questions about how we study New England's past. Importantly, it tests familiar academic constructions of visual culture and material culture. As both a material object and an object of historical analysis, the Invisible Lady confounds any distinction we might attempt to draw between these fields of study. Its appeal was predicated upon the operations of what we would today call a Foucauldian "gaze," the term that describes cultural systems wherein looking structures power, authority, and resistance. Yet the Invisible Lady realized these operations through its resolutely material form, a maze of trumpets and tubing that tempted people to run their hands along the square railing and take up the floorboards in exhibition rooms in an effort to learn how the deception functioned. Is this then an object of visual culture or an object of material culture? Or, if it belongs at once to both fields, how does it invite us to reckon with our understanding of these terms?

The answers to these questions are complicated by the fact that the disciplinary lines between visual culture, material culture, and related fields of study are not always firm or well-defined. Historically, visual culture has been aligned with the disciplines of art history and film studies. Whereas for some (such as historians of United States art) a primary value of this term resides in its challenge to the formation and content of disciplinary canons (a challenge which, in the case of American art history, posits that popular media as varied as lithographs, photographs, and advertisements shaped culture as much as fine paintings and sculptures), for others "visual culture" connotes broader ideas. "Visual culture" can describe a condition of western life—one defined by a global circulation of images and a modern episteme in which the visual organizes communication and experience. It can refer to the work of critical theory, in particular theory that explores the ways in which practices and ideologies of vision structure knowledge, representation, and subjectivity.[7] The term "material culture" often implies something more eclectic, more expansive and object-driven. As practiced in anthropology, archeology, folklore, and cultural studies (material culture studies, as Victor Buchli has remarked, is less a singu-

7. The scholarly literature on visual culture has grown to proportions too vast to cite adequately here. On the points briefly discussed in this essay, see Angela Miller, "Breaking Down the Preserves of Visual Production," *American Art* 11:2 (Summer 1997): 11–13; Nicholas Mirzoeff, "What is Visual Culture?" in *The Visual Culture Reader* (New York, 1998), 3–13; James D. Herbert, "Visual Culture/Visual Studies," in *Critical Terms for Art History*, 2d ed. (Chicago, 2003), 452–64.

lar discipline than "an intervention within and between disciplines") material culture describes a mode of critical and historical analysis that gives equal due to theories of space and the forms of vernacular buildings, to the everyday stuff of consumer culture as well as the rarified texture of silk.[8] Material culture examines the materiality of things, attending closely to issues of matter, shape, and style. At the same time, it concerns social practices and processes, asking how objects produce cultures, embody ideas, resist explication, and register loss.[9] Operative within both visual and material culture studies is the understanding that different sorts of objects do different kinds of cultural work: that a piece of fabric, for example, raises questions distinct from those posed by a building or painting, and therefore requires a specific set of analytical tools. Such interests and concerns have served to help draw distinctions between the scholarly purviews of visual culture and material culture.

Yet as the example of the Invisible Lady suggests, visual culture implicates objects, and material culture involves vision. Moreover, the Invisible Lady is hardly the only object from New England's past that evokes the fluid intersections of visual and material culture. As the essays gathered in this book demonstrate, scholarly research often defies easy categorization as "visual studies" or "material studies." Indeed, the volume's subtitle (*Studies in Material and Visual Culture*) implies a dialogue, or at least a complementary relation, between the two fields of study. Surely this enthusiasm for cross-disciplinary inquiry owes something to the influence of Margaretta Lovell's recent

8. Victor Buchli, "Introduction," *The Material Culture Reader* (Oxford and New York: Berg, 2002), 13.

9. For a sampling of recent approaches to material culture studies in different fields, see Sophie White, "'Wearing three or four handkerchiefs around his collar, and elsewhere about him': Slaves' Constructions of Masculinity and Ethnicity in French Colonial New Orleans," *Gender & History* 15:3 (Nov. 2003): 528–49; Elizabeth DeMarrias, Chris Gosden, and Colin Renfrew, eds., *Rethinking Materiality: The Engagement of Mind with the Material World* (Cambridge, Eng.: McDonald Institute for Archaeological Research, 2004); Susan Stabile, *Memory's Daughters: The Material Culture of Remembrance in Eighteenth-Century America* (Ithaca, N.Y.: Cornell University Press, 2004); Bernard L. Herman, *Townhouse: Architecture and Material Life in the Early American City, 1780–1830* (Chapel Hill, N.C.: The University of North Carolina Press for the Omohundro Institute of Early American History and Culture, 2005), esp. 1–32; Kariann Yokota, "Postcolonialism and Material Culture in the Early United States," *William and Mary Quarterly* 3d series, 64:2 (Apr. 2007): 264–74; Shirley Wajda and Helen Shoemaker, eds. *Material Culture in America: Understanding Everyday Life* (Santa Barbara, Calif.: ABC-Clio, 2008); Ann Smart Martin, *Buying into the World of Goods: Early Consumers in Backcountry Virginia* (Baltimore: The Johns Hopkins University Press, 2008).

book, *Art in a Season of Revolution: Painters, Artisans, and Patrons in Early America* (2004). Lovell's expansive study deftly maps a creole Anglo culture in which objects as dissimilar as paintings, tables, and dresses formed part of an integrated world of goods, a world in which cultural meaning was produced through peoples' encounters with both ordinary and extraordinary artifacts. Part of Lovell's mission is to contest art-historical constructions of colonial aesthetic hierarchies (questioning, for instance, the semantic distinctions often drawn between "artist" and "artisan") and to redirect our attention to the centrality of communities, families, and houses as the spheres in which a great majority of colonial objects were produced and consumed. The book achieves these objectives, notably, by drawing upon the methodologies of visual and material culture studies while refusing to explicitly align itself with only one or the other approach. Shifting the frame of analysis from disciplinary-specific interests to the "organic" nature of colonial "cultural life" enables Lovell to give equal due to the visual and tactile experiences of objects, to suggest how the same object (or a set of similar objects) can at once reveal cultural investments in "the value of optical . . . experience" and economic investments in a culture of finely-worked things.[10] With this scholarly model at hand, no doubt the future will bring more efforts to integrate visual and material culture studies. Or, to put it differently, it will bring more efforts to understand how and why many early New England objects—by dint of their form or manufacture or use—signified visually *and* materially, thereby begging a nuanced approach from interpreters.

In interrogating the bounds of visual and material culture, we may also ask how these fields of study overlap with that of print culture. Here the Invisible Lady is once again instructive. Significantly, the only material traces of the exhibition survive in the form of printed artifacts: in broadsides, book illustrations, engravings, and newspapers. Moreover, the printed images of the instrument call attention to the fact that readers experienced this spectacle in ways fundamentally different than individuals at the actual show. In direct contrast to readers looking at printed illustrations of the illusion (see especially figs. 2 and 4), those present in the exhibition rooms employed senses other than, or in addition to, that of vision—including touch, hearing, and even smell—

---

10. Margaretta Lovell, *Art in a Season of Revolution: Painters, Artisans, and Patrons in Early America* (Philadelphia: University of Pennsylvania, 2004), esp. 1–7.

in their attempts to undeceive themselves of the deception of an Invisible Lady. Unlike readers, they were never privileged with the optical access and visual knowledge afforded by the printed cross-section view. Further, the many advertisements and exposés that circulated through early national newspapers suggest that the exhibition occasioned a widespread discourse about illusion. Print expanded the audience for the Invisible Lady, producing a viewership that was national in scope if wholly virtual in form.

What we have here is a historical instance of interdependent systems of knowledge production—but again, not a unique one. Many of the New England objects examined within this volume pose similar opportunities for exploring the endlessly fascinating relation of pictures and texts. By setting words and images side by side as historical evidence—by probing their inter-relations instead of prioritizing one over the other—cultural historians not only engage in cross-disciplinary scholarship. They also come to terms with the mutuality of visuality and textuality. Puzzling through the codependency of images, texts, and objects equips us to better understand how print itself can function as a material artifact and space of looking.[11]

The geographical reach of print in early America, which literary historians have explored at length, raises a related question about the cohesion of New England as a discrete region of study. By the time the *Salem Gazette* print had appeared, the Invisible Lady had been exhibited in Philadelphia and New York. It was a sensation abroad in London and Paris, where it had originated in 1800. In the years to come it would appear in a host of small cities and towns, including Portland, Newport, Hartford, and New London in the northeast; Baltimore, Richmond, and Charleston in the south; and even as far west as

---

11. Like visual culture and material culture, the image/word relation has been the subject of long and extensive scholarly treatment. Print culture studies have a more recent genesis. For recent scholarship that usefully models an integrated approach to visual and/or material culture and print culture, see Jay Fliegelman, *Declaring Independence: Jefferson, Natural Language, and the Culture of Performance* (Stanford, Calif.: Stanford University, 1993); David Shields, *Civil Tongues and Polite Letters in British America* (Chapel Hill, N.C.: University of North Carolina Press for the Institute of Early American History and Culture, 1997); Lisa Gitelman, *Scripts, Grooves, and Writing Machines: Representing Technology in the Edison Era* (Stanford, Calif.: Stanford University Press, 1997); Laura Rigal, *The American Manufactory: Art, Labor, and the World of Things in the Early Republic* (Princeton, N.J.: Princeton University Press, 1998); Martin Brückner, *The Geographic Revolution in Early America: Maps, Literacy, and National Identity* (Chapel Hill, N.C.: University of North Carolina Press for the Omohundro Institute of Early American History and Culture, 2006).

Cincinnati and Lexington, Kentucky. At least two showmen speculated about the profits to be had in the West Indies, where the exhibition had not yet appeared as of 1805.[12]

The interstate and international peregrinations of the Invisible Lady invite us to reckon with the circum-Atlantic dimensions of New England culture during the colonial and early national periods. This Atlantic scope has already been the focus of much excellent scholarship in early American studies; the future will certainly bring more such Atlantic inquiries. How will this enlarged geographical frame challenge the way we study New England? The example of the Invisible Lady is helpful for two reasons. On the one hand, it demonstrates that we need to continue thinking very carefully about local or regional cultures: to raise the specter of magical or invisible forces in Salem, for instance, surely meant something different than mounting the show in a city that had not endured the sensational witchcraft trials of the 1690s. On the other hand, the Salem exhibition compels us to reckon with the ways in which this venue defined itself in relation to other Massachusetts cities as well as places much more distant. The proprietor of an exhibition in nearby Boston went so far as to reach for an overseas referent in attempting to prove that his Invisible Lady was the most authentic of all the versions on display in New England; he claimed that his device was superior because it best resembled the original instrument shown in Paris.[13]

To rephrase these observations as a question, we might ask the following: if we can discern when New England *begins*, then when, or where, does it *end*?[14] A number of the papers collected in this volume vividly convey the geographical porosity of New England, showing how its boundaries extended, both actually and imaginatively, across the ocean or into the woods of the rural interior. In these colonial borderlands, the English encountered other settlements of Europeans—namely, the French and the Dutch—as well as vast communities of native Americans, including the Iroquois, the Wampanoag, the Wabanaki, and the Narragansett. These New England borderlands are ripe for greater investi-

---

12. "For Sale or To Let," *The New-York Evening Post*, May 3, 1806; John Mix, see "Left with the Subscriber," *Connecticut Herald* (New Haven), Dec. 30, 1806.

13. "An Extraordinary Aerial Phenomenon," *Columbian Centinel* (Boston), Sept. 1, 1804.

14. Here I mean to recognize the enduring influence of the exhibition and exhibition catalogue *New England Begins: The Seventeenth Century* (Boston: Museum of Fine Arts, 1984), which remains an indispensable source for research about early New England material culture.

gation by cultural historians. For points of entrée into the material dimensions of intercolonial and native-colonial interactions, we can look to well-known histories of the region. Social and political historians remind us that the British and French competed for fishing grounds off Acadia; that colonists of both nationalities participated with native Americans in a smuggling trade routed across colonial borders; and that English captives from New England settlements, such as Deerfield, made new lives for themselves in Indian villages in New France. When, after a long history of occasional military skirmishes, the British and their Indian allies took Quebec in 1759 (an imperial transition so significant that modern Canadians call it "the Conquest"), a new chapter in colonial relations began. England newly doubled its colonial extent, laying claim to the vast expanse of the North American continent north of Mexico. Twenty years later, British Loyalists fleeing war in the newly-formed United States took refuge in New Brunswick—the place that the French had called Acadia, and from which they had been expunged by the British.[15]

To reiterate, then: when and where does New England end—or rather, when and where does it reinvent itself all over again? Exploring such questions might encourage scholars to revisit periods too often neglected in visual and material culture studies—in particular, the seventeenth and early eighteenth centuries. Such investigations would ideally also yield more scholarship on the material interrelations of settler colonies and native communities.

In the meantime, the case of a New Hampshire portrait, and the travels of its maker and client, help suggest the rewards of following people and objects beyond the familiar borders of New England—in this instance, west to the "middle ground" of the Great Lakes region, south to the Caribbean, and east to England itself.[16] In 1761, the immigrant British portraitist Joseph Blackburn painted a picture of Elizabeth Browne Rogers, a twenty-year-old resident of Portsmouth, New Hampshire (fig. 5). About Blackburn, scholars know little (he is celebrated largely as an influence upon the young John Singleton Copley); about his sitter, they know even less. Like so many colonial women,

15. For an excellent introduction to the history of colonial Canada, see Allan Greer, *The People of New France* (Toronto: University of Toronto Press, 1997).

16. On the concept of the "middle ground," see Richard White, *The Middle Ground: Indians, Empires, and Republics in the Great Lakes Region, 1650–1815* (Cambridge, Eng.: Cambridge University Press, 1991), and "Forum: The Middle Ground Revisited," *The William and Mary Quarterly* 63:1 (Jan. 2006): 3–96.

Fig. 5. Joseph Blackburn, *Elizabeth Browne Rogers.* 1761. Oil
on canvas. Courtesy, Reynolda House Museum of American Art, Winston-Salem, North Carolina.

Elizabeth's biography is tied to the powerful men in her life. Her father, Arthur Browne, was rector of Portsmouth's Queen's Chapel. Her husband, Robert Rogers, was one of the most colorful figures of the Revolutionary period and a man whose adventures as a military leader and British Loyalist help illustrate the complexity of connections between the colonial worlds of British setters, French traders, and native Americans. Rogers made a reputation for himself during the Seven Years War as the young commander of six hundred troops called "Rogers's Rangers," an army that executed devastating raids on Indian settlements and saw action from Montreal to Detroit. In 1761 he married Elizabeth ("Betsey") Browne in Portsmouth. To commemorate the occasion, Blackburn painted the young woman wearing a costume that might have been her wedding dress.[17] Standing tall against the low horizon of a natural landscape, Elizabeth is a choreography of feminine grace. Her lips are fixed in a smile, and her eyes meet the spectator's gaze. With the fingers of one hand, she delicately grasps the edge of her shawl, a gesture that calls attention to the sartorial details of a bow, lace, and pearling; with the other hand, she directs observation to the swell of her skirt, a vast expanse of shiny and costly fabric. Posed against the rosy glow of a sky at dawn or dusk, with her shawl billowing exuberantly (if impossibly) behind her, Elizabeth appears the picture of a hopeful, happy bride.[18]

In reality, her future quickly soured. Shortly after the portrait was completed, Rogers left his wife to join a campaign against the Cherokees in South Carolina. Elizabeth remained in New Hampshire with her parents for the next five years, during which time rumors circulated of Rogers's drinking and philandering.[19] By 1763 Rogers was back in the contested theater of the Great Lakes region, fighting in Pontiac's War. Then, in 1766—having sailed to England with Elizabeth in a vain attempt to persuade King George III to sponsor an expedition in search of a northwest passage—he obtained the command of Fort Michilimackinac, a former French trading post located on a strait between Lake Michigan and Lake Huron. Elizabeth, reared in the genteel surroundings of Portsmouth, joined her husband there. But not for long: Roberts was arrested on charges of treason and sent north to Montreal—now part of the British empire—for trial. He was found innocent, but he was disgraced and unemployable, and so he fled, alone, back to England, where he was thrown into debtor's prison. Bonded out by a sibling, Rogers salvaged his reputation by publishing two narratives of military life in America and a lurid play about Pontiac entitled *The Savages of America*.[20] He returned to the colonies in 1775, where, in the thick of mounting anti-British tensions, he aroused the suspi-

17. Mary Cochrane Rogers, *Glimpses of an Old Social Capital (Portsmouth, New Hampshire)* (Privately printed, 1923), 72. See pp. 72–81 for an account of the Rogers's marriage and biographical data about Elizabeth.

18. On the painting, and Blackburn's possible use of a print source for the composition, see "Elizabeth Browne Rogers, 1761," in Barbara Millhouse, *American Originals: Selections from Reynolda House, Museum of American Art* (New York: Abbeville Press, 1990), 23.

19. On these points, see ibid., 22.

20. Robert Rogers, *A Concise Account of North America* (London, 1765); idem, *Journals of Major Robert Rogers* (London, 1765); idem, *Ponteach: The Savages of America; A Tragedy* (London, 1766).

cion of George Washington. Discerning Rogers to be a spy for the crown, Washington returned him to jail. But the ever resourceful Rogers escaped, and soon he was commanding a Loyalist regiment called the Queen's American Rangers which engaged in combat and finally met defeat near White Plains in New York.[21]

How did Elizabeth Rogers respond to her husband's exploits? Much as any long-suffering wife might: in 1778, she divorced him. It thus seems woefully ironic that the only known image of her should be a marriage portrait. Painted by Blackburn, who came to Boston from England in 1755, the portrait represents Elizabeth as a proper Englishwoman. Blackburn's ability to fashion colonial sitters in this manner was precisely what made him attractive to his provincial audience. Blackburn was no master of psychological introspection (indeed, his subjects' facial features look very similar from one canvas to another). Rather, his emphasis was on the outward display of the polite body, on the appearances of the luxury goods that elite Anglo creoles donned to make themselves look more British. Recognized for introducing Rococo style and the English pictorial convention of the "conversation piece" to the British colonies, Blackburn excelled in the mimetic imitation of material stuff: the lustre of silk, the gleam of gold buttons, and the delicate intricacy of expensive lace.[22] Thus when families such as Elizabeth Browne's commissioned Blackburn to paint family portraits, they weren't just employing the latest painter from England. They were deliberately cultivating an association with a distant place across the Atlantic, staking—through costume, pose, and pigments—their place within the British empire.

This is not an especially original observation. Historians of art and material culture have long observed that British colonists imported English goods and imitated English fashions in an effort to retain (or outright invent) a

---

21. Rogers's military exploits have attracted the attention of a range of scholarly and popular writers, including Burt Garfield Loescher, *The History of Rogers Rangers, Vol. 1: The Beginnings, Jan. 1755–April 6, 1758* (San Francisco, 1946); James Cuneo, *Robert Rogers of the Rangers* (New York, 1959); Stephen Brumwell, *White Devil: A True Story of War, Savagery, and Vengeance in Colonial America* (Cambridge, Mass.: Da Capo Press, 2005); Walter Borneman, *The French and Indian War: Deciding the Fate of North America* (New York: Harper Collins, 2006). In 1937, Kenneth Rogers published a fictionalized novel about Rogers—*Northwest Passage* (New York: Doubleday, 1937)—that MGM made into a movie of the same title.

22. On this point see Wayne Craven, *American Art* (Madison, Wisc.: Brown and Benchmark, 1994), 97.

cultural relation to the imperial metropole. If Blackburn's portrait helps support this understanding of a transatlantic connection, however, it also possesses the potential to trouble this linear equation. For the picture not only refers us across the Atlantic Ocean to London: it also invites us to consider New England's relation to other places. One of those places is the Caribbean. Before Blackburn arrived in the Boston area, he spent two years painting royal appointees and plantation owners in the British colony of Bermuda. Many European artists passed through the Caribbean on their way to the northern colonies, in part because they had booked passage on ships that followed the trade routes. But the significance of Blackburn's presence in Bermuda has been overlooked—or more accurately, grossly under-appreciated—in scholarship about eighteenth-century American painting. Blackburn's Caribbean sojourn compels us to reevaluate the pictorial evidence that suggests New Englanders wanted to cultivate associations with England. What if Blackburn's Bermuda work was just as important to them? What if the cultural world in which they framed their sense of selfhood included the powerful planters of the Caribbean colonies?[23] Historians and literary scholars have done much within recent years to recognize the centrality of the Caribbean within the development of North America. Scholars of visual culture may likewise discern new significance in New England objects—like Blackburn's portrait of Elizabeth Browne Rogers—by triangulating immigrant artists and their sitters within a system of empire that included Bermuda and other Caribbean islands.

And what of the fate of the portrait itself? Did it accompany Elizabeth when she went to live at Fort Michilimackinac, some thirteen hundred miles from Portsmouth? If so, what did the varied populations of people there—British officers, French traders, and Indian visitors—make of it? Michilimackinac was both a military and commercial post; it controlled the lucrative fur trade of the entire region, connecting the Great Lakes to Montreal and points east and overseas. However removed, then, from the busy seaports of eastern colonies or the counting houses of London, this inland fort was nonetheless integral to the operations of the British empire, as vital to the control of commerce and land as the Caribbean plantations that exported slaves, sugar, and rum.

23. On the tendency to overlook the significance of the southern colonies in art-historical scholarship, see Maurie McInnis, "Little of Artistic Merit? The Promise and Perils of Southern Art History," *American Art* 19:2 (Summer 2005): 11–18.

Whether or not Blackburn's portrait made the trip from Portsmouth to Michilimackinac, the picture implicitly references a network of far-flung people and places through its painterly facture and imagery. It helps demonstrate how material culture could link the disparate regions of the British Atlantic world.

In closing, I turn from object lessons to lessons learned in the classroom. In 2007 and 2011, I collaborated with a University of Delaware colleague—Professor Monica Dominguez Torres, a specialist in colonial Spanish art—on the design and implementation of seminars on art across colonial North America. The courses took a wide and comparative view of early North America, exploring issues of cultural hybridity and material exchange in New Spain, New France, and British America. From the outset, the students were tasked with exploring how objects produced New World cultures: how trade brought diverse cultures into contact with one another; how objects linked places as diverse as New Orleans and New Amsterdam; and how the material evidence of objects posed challenges to familiar histories of colonial conquest and settlement. One class assignment involved conceptualizing a mock exhibition that illustrated the dynamism of early North American material culture through the study of places that were significant as colonial cultural entrepôts. Working in groups, the students focused upon four examples: California missions; late-eighteenth-century New Orleans; Cuba, Barbados, and Curaçao in the West Indies; and Salem, Massachusetts. To exemplify the material culture of the latter city, the Salem group selected a diverse range of artifacts, including a decorative sugar box made of silver mined in Mexico; a figurehead from one of Salem's fleet of merchant vessels; and a Federal armchair from the Winterthur Museum that reads like an index of international trade. According to Sarah Jones, the student who studied this chair, the design is English, from George Hepplewhite's *Cabinet-Maker and Upholster's Guide* (London, 1788), yet also resembles chairs being produced in Portsmouth, New Hampshire, and Baltimore, Maryland. It was made by an unknown Salem craftsman who combined local secondary woods with mahogany from the West Indies. And it features a shellac-based finish composed of ingredients from Asia and the Mediterranean. As Ms. Jones rightly concluded then, this chair is much more than an example of regional furniture production: it embodies the expansion of global trade in the United States about 1800, in terms of materials as well as the dissemination of design sources. In this New England chair, there is a bit of Old Europe, a lot of the Caribbean, and even parts of the distant Pacific.

As scholars and educators, we have the opportunity to convey the excitement of studying visual and material culture to those whom we mentor and teach—to encourage our students, interns, and advisees to put original questions to the stuff of history. The Salem armchair suggests the rewards of following new approaches. Like Blackburn's portrait and the Invisible Lady, the chair points at once toward the past and toward the future. As it manifests the formation of an Atlantic culture in wood and varnish, it also compels us to look beyond the borders of New England in order to understand the nature and consequences of that formation. That's a lot for a chair to do. The rest is up to us.

List of Contributors

EMERSON W. BAKER is a professor of history at Salem State University. His most recent book is *The Devil of Great Island: Witchcraft and Conflict in Early New England* (2007). He is currently writing a history of the Salem witch trials for Oxford University Press.

GEORGIA B. BARNHILL is director of the Center for Historic American Visual Culture at the American Antiquarian Society where she was curator of the graphic arts collection for over forty years.

WENDY BELLION is an associate professor of American art history at the University of Delaware. She is the author of *Citizen Spectator: Art, Illusion, and Visual Perception in Early National America* (2011) and essays about Charles Willson Peale, William Birch, and Patience Wright, among other subjects. Her current project explores sculpture and iconoclasm in American history.

MARTIN BRÜCKNER is an associate professor in English and Material Culture Studies at the University of Delaware. He is the author of *The Geographic Revolution in Early America: Maps, Literacy, and National Identity* (2006) and the editor of *Early American Cartographies* (2011). He has published widely on the relationship between cartography, literature, visual culture, and social history in America between 1700 and 1900.

STEVEN C. BULLOCK is a professor of history at Worcester Polytechnic Institute. He is the author of *Revolutionary Brotherhood: Freemasonry and the Transformation of the American Social Order, 1730-1840* (1996) and *The American Revolution: A History in Documents* (2003). He is completing a project on "The Politics of Politeness: Gentility, Government, and Power in the American Provinces, 1688-1776."

PATRICIA JOHNSTON recently joined the faculty of the College of Holy Cross as the Rev. J. Gerard Mears, S. J., Chair in Fine Arts; previously she was a professor of art history at Salem State University, author of *Real Fantasies: Edward Steichen's Advertising Photography* (1997), and editor of *Seeing High and*

Low: Representing Social Conflict in American Visual Culture (2006). Her current research examines the influence of global trade on visual arts during the Early Republic.

CATHERINE E. KELLY teaches history at the University of Oklahoma. She is the author of the prize-winning *In the New England Fashion: Reshaping Women's Lives in the Nineteenth Century* (1999) and co-editor of *Reading Women: Literacy, Authorship, and Culture in the Atlantic World, 1500-1800* (2008). Her essay in this volume is part of a forthcoming study on visual culture in the early American republic.

KATHERINE STEBBINS MCCAFFREY is an Assistant Dean at Hult International Business School, where she teaches communications. She is at work revising her dissertation, *Reading Glasses: Consuming Spectacles in the Age of Franklin*.

KEVIN MULLER's research focuses on themes of identity and representations of cultural exchange in American art. His essays have appeared in *American Art* and *Winterthur Portfolio*. He currently teaches and curates in the San Francisco Bay area.

MARTHA J. MCNAMARA is Director of the New England Arts and Architecture Program in the Department of Art at Wellesley College and the Corresponding Secretary of the Colonial Society of Massachusetts. She is the author of *From Tavern to Courthouse: Architecture and Ritual in American Law, 1658-1860* (2004) as well as a number of essays in scholarly journals. Her current project is a study of the New England landscape in the late eighteenth and early nineteenth centuries.

KEVIN D. MURPHY is John Rewald Professor and Executive Officer in the Ph.D. Program in Art History at the CUNY Graduate Center. He is the author of articles in scholarly and popular journals, as well as of the book, *Jonathan Fisher of Blue Hill, Maine: Commerce, Culture and Community on the Eastern Frontier* (2010).

KATHERINE RIEDER received her Ph.D. from Harvard's History of American Civilization program in 2009. She focuses on American art and material culture, the eighteenth century in particular, and has held fellowships from the Henry Luce Foundation, the Smithsonian American Art Museum, and Winterthur. Katherine is currently working on her book manuscript *Possession: People and Things during the American Revolution,* which examines the multiple meanings and movements of objects, particularly those belonging to loyalists, during the war.

Index

New Views of New England

HAS BEEN TYPESET IN CASLON TYPES
PRINTED AT KIRKWOOD PRINTING, WILMINGTON, MASSACHUSETTS
BOUND AT ACME BOOKBINDING, CHARLESTOWN, MASSACHUSETTS

DESIGN BY PAUL HOFFMANN
LANCASTER, NEW HAMPSHIRE